Evil Paradise

Evil Paradise

By

Jane Schwalger-Wyatt

Strategic Book Publishing and Rights Co.

Strategic Book Publishing & Rights Co. LLC
USA | Singapore
www.sbpra.com

For information about special discounts for bulk purchases, please contact Strategic Book Publishing and Rights Co. Special Sales, at bookorder@sbpra.net.

ISBN: 978-1-63135-766-4

To my children Zelma, Daniel and Dayne

I was blessed when you were chosen to be part of my life. I love the three of you unconditionally.
Mum xxx

To my wonderful husband, Boyd Wyatt

without your love, support and helping me with this book, my story would never be told. I love you immensely.

Hope gives us a reason to keep going
Faith can move mountains
Love conquers all!

Table of Contents

Author's Note

This book results from a forty-year journey of slowly facing up to and dealing with memories I had suppressed. I have written my story as I experienced and witnessed it, leaving nothing out. I have told the truth as I lived and perceived it. To a child the world is new, mysterious and terrifying. I regarded as normal much of what I saw and suffered. The knowledge that my experience was not normal came with passing years and my insatiable desire to know my place and identity in this world.

I know my story will displease some members of my extended family, but I felt compelled to write it and I make no apology for telling the truth. A major force in facing and confronting memories that I would rather forget is a relentless voice deep within me, driving me on to finally bring this into the light.

In order to protect the privacy and dignity of others, I have disguised the names of all my siblings, their spouses and their children. My parents and other names are real, and so are all the events written in this book.

I am deeply grateful for the support and encouragement I have received. Fortunately, I was able to speak to many people who also witnessed the events of which I write. Often they confirmed my recollections and added first-hand accounts of events that I had forgotten or driven from my memory. I fear that if I had further delayed the telling of my story, many witnesses would no longer have been alive to confirm what I recount. I am also aware that in such an enlightened and modern world the occult and spiritual elements I describe may seem fanciful or pure fiction. Nonetheless, I have written about these events exactly as I saw and experienced them. The memory of them is as vivid as if I saw them yesterday.

This is the story of a little girl who escaped the clutches of evil and ultimately triumphed through the devotion and support of those who truly loved her.

Foreword - Historical Context

For you to better understand my story I must ask you to read a brief description about the Samoan culture into which I was born. As with all human cultures, it shares a great many similarities to others, yet at the same time has facets that are markedly different. These differences can be subtle or at times jarringly opposite to another cultures' sensibilities. These differences can have profound effects when cultures merge. With the onset of Westernisation, it is a world that is changing rapidly, not always for the better. The noble Samoan traditions are being discarded, while the best aspects of Western democracy are shunned. What remains can sometimes combine the least attractive aspects of the two traditions.

Samoa, formerly known as Western Samoa, lies in the central South Pacific, 2,613 miles south-west of Hawaii and 1,800 miles north-east of New Zealand. The islands of Samoa were created by volcanic eruptions. Huge plugs of magma thrust out of the boiling sea then slowly cooled and hardened, forming jagged black peaks amid the bright blue of the Pacific Ocean. Over eons, lush tropical rainforest covered the peaks, attracting the migratory birds and animals of the Pacific regions. Other creatures thrived and multiplied until all of the islands hosted varied and abundant life. So it remained for millennia until the last of the ocean wanderers reached the islands 2,800 years ago. They are now known as the Polynesians.

The two main islands in Samoa are Upolu and Savaii. Upolu, where I was born, is about 1,115 square kilometres and Apia, the capital city of Samoa, is located on the central north coast. Upolu is the main administrative island of independent Samoa. There are 362 villages in Samoa and it is divided into eleven political districts known as *Itumalo*.

A fringing reef about 100 metres from the shore rings most of Upolu and provides a barrier against the fierce storms blowing in from the Pacific. The shallow, coral-filled lagoons the reef creates are safe fishing grounds for the villages nestled along the shoreline. In early times before the clash of cultures, an abundance of fruit, coconuts, fish, birds and animals resulted in a relaxed and plentiful life. The basic staples of existence came with little effort. The resulting leisure time fostered a cultural heritage rich in music, song, complex rituals and stories. In almost complete isolation, the Samoans developed unique skills and sophisticated medical practises that many other cultures might envy.

Island legend predicted that a light-skinned people from across the sea would arrive on white clouds of thunder. The impression made by the early European ships, with their billowing sails and invincible cannons, was that these strangers could only be the people of legend. Samoans, in contrast to other nations, embraced the new arrivals, expecting them to herald the dawn of a great new age prophesied since ancient times. Samoans called the European people *Palagi*, which translates as "thunder cloud."

Contact with Europeans began in the early 18th century, but did not intensify until the arrival of the British. By the 19th century, missionaries had settled on the islands, and in the latter part of the 19th century, the United Kingdom, Germany and the United States all claimed parts of the Samoan Islands. A treaty made Germany the colonial power on the western island of Samoa, while the US controlled the eastern island, now American

Samoa. By the second half of the 19th century, Germany's influence in Samoa dominated, expanding with flourishing and highly profitable coconut and cocoa plantations. Later, with the outbreak of the First World War, New Zealand occupied the German sector. Samoa became independent from New Zealand in 1962.

The German administration, four years into their reign over Samoa, shipped in Chinese and Melanesian labourers. The workers frequently and bitterly complained about the tough working conditions and brutal physical punishment by the Germans, but during the uncertainty and political chaos in Samoa their plight was largely ignored. Germany's relatively late imposition of effective colonial government prolonged the experience of the frontier ethic. As a consequence, interracial liaisons were more or less accepted and this accelerated the development of a mixed-race community. There were no prohibitions to children of mixed heritage inheriting family properties and businesses. Many of them had been educated as Europeans but retained strong ties to the Samoan kinship system, the *Aiga*, which gave them many considerable advantages in life.

The Samoan kings and chiefs, with the wisdom and pragmatism that made them powerful rulers, adapted to these cultural changes with ease. A collision of cultures is seldom without hardship, especially when each culture formed in isolation from the other. Nevertheless, Samoan pragmatism certainly appeared to ease the process. Having said that, laws and customs that served one system well often clashed violently when a merger was forced. To an outside observer, it might have seemed obvious that neither system could function successfully with the conflicts that arose in modernising a feudal system of chiefs and kings into a western democracy. It would probably also not be unfair to say that the kings and chiefs didn't take kindly to losing some of their privilege and power in this brave new world. The political and economic systems established by the Germans were maintained but not strictly enforced if dealing with traditional matters. This ultimately resulted in Samoans returning to their communal way of life based on *Fa'a Samoa* (the way of Samoa), customs and traditions the Germans had vigorously tried to suppress if they were seen as contrary to German interests.

Ancestral links to family identity are the focus of ritual obligations in Samoan culture. The *Fa'a Samoa* custom, in most cases, takes priority over an individual's immediate needs. This level of tight social integration and responsibility is the reason there are no homeless people on the island. A tight family and village network guarantees no one goes hungry and no one is forced to deal with a trial or hardship alone.

Family (*Aiga*)

The vital foundation of Samoan society is the extended family unit or kinship group called the *aiga*. The Samoan family, in contrast to the Western version, includes everyone descended from the family line of both parents. With brothers, sisters, aunties and uncles and all of their children, first, second and third cousins and all of their children, at times the extended family can seem a confusing and convoluted alliance bound by blood ties. But families take pride and gather strength from banding together; this system is the core of Samoan society.

Chief (*Matai*)

In Samoan tradition, a chief makes all the important decisions, and all of his children and their families must comply. Every *aiga* has a *matai*, usually the head of the family. A *matai* plays an important role in daily life and represents the family at village council meetings. The *matai* settles family disputes and makes decisions in what he regards as the best interests of the entire clan. He dictates to his children and their spouses and corrects them if needed. His decision is law and must be obeyed without question. The Samoans believe that 'the way to authority is through service', and so the cycle continues. The *matais* have a right to impose fines or punishments depending on the gravity of the offences, and hence unity and obedience have developed into revered tradition in Samoan life.

Samoan Way (*Fa'a Samoa*)

Traditional dress, customs and complicated rituals reflect the strong family and tribal allegiances that remain to this day. The culture and custom known as *Fa'a Samoa* remains a potent regulator of people's lives, often causing hardship when mixed with the demands of modern life. This is partly due to the fact that Samoan culture is divided into many aspects. Religion, traditional ceremonies, funerals and weddings are all events that Samoan people support as a central part of their lives. Unfortunately, some have abused and used the custom for their own benefits.

Christianity

In general, Christianity is crucial to the lives of Samoan people. Nearly 100% of the Samoan population is Christian. The three main denominations are the Roman Catholic Church, the Congregational Christian Church of Samoa and the Methodist Church. Around the mid-20th century, other groups such as the Church of Jesus Christ of Latter Day Saints (Mormon), the Seventh Day Adventists, and the Assembly of God started to spread throughout Samoa, and have continued to grow in influence. Consequently, Sunday remains a day of worship and rest in Samoa and must be respected by everyone.

Spirituality

Despite Samoans' enthusiastic adoption of Christianity, ancestral spiritual beliefs have not been forgotten. Samoans see no contradiction in blending beliefs of many kinds. It is common to believe in ghosts (*aitu*), demons, and in the reality of the dead moving among the living; such apparitions are mostly ignored unless they conflict with the living. Even today, both uneducated and highly educated Samoan's belief in *aitu* is common and viewed as nothing unusual. Samoans also believe strongly that the spirits of deceased relatives will harass or even possess a living ancestor if some traditional social convention has been violated.

The *Taulasea* (spiritual healer or traditional healer) was as important in the old medical system as were the herbal and physiological practitioners. They have a long history of highly regarded service in Samoa. All displayed high levels of effectiveness in their respective disciplines. These spiritual healers were called in when the dead caused problems for the living.

Discipline and Violence

Beating held particular meaning for a child in traditional Samoa. Once a child's behaviour offended an adult, whether at home, in the village, in church or at school, punishment was swift. The adults showed no mercy; they did not talk of compromise or warnings, only consequences. Even if the child had been hit or strapped at school or Sunday school, a message would be sent home and the child would receive more punishment. Rules and harsh discipline are the norm in Samoan families. The adult's words were never to be debated or challenged. Children were not to make mistakes but to strive to be respectful and to please, showing good manners at all times.

I was born into this turbulent and confusing time in Samoa, a living example of the merge of two cultures who never truly belonged to either.

Prologue

24 September 2013

I am now in my fifties and am rushing to see my sick mother whom I vowed ten years ago I would have nothing to do with ever again.

Our flight to Pago Pago, American Samoa, was scheduled for 10am. My brother Jonathan knocked at my bedroom door teasing that we were going to miss our plane. I knew he only wanted us to talk some more before I left. I was apprehensive about my trip and talking more would not help. My brother and I had always enjoyed a tremendous relationship even though we only shared one biological parent. I am the only child of my mother and father's relationship, but between them they supplied me with nineteen siblings in total. Jonathan was the second eldest child of my father and stepmother. I didn't need to check the time when he rapped on the door, I was already wide-awake. My thirteen-year-old son Dayne and I had arrived in Samoa from Brisbane, Australia a few days earlier. I had been unable to get a good night's rest since my arrival. Extreme conflicts of emotion and tumultuous thoughts swirled through my mind allowing me no peace. They were my constant companions.

The day before, while we were in Apia sorting out our tickets in front of a shabby shop next to the travel agent, we'd spotted a maltreated, malnourished, homeless dog. He was a pitiful sight with his rib cage prominent through his mangy brown coat. His sagging testicles looked raw, as though they would drop off if the wind picked up. My heart ached for this loathsome mongrel who in many ways reminded me of my younger self. It was impossible for me to ignore his pitiful suffering, so I rushed into the store looking for some meat to feed him.

"Sorry, we are more of a craft shop. We do have sandwiches though," the shopkeeper told me.

"It's for a dog. Do you have any with meat?" I asked in a panic, as though the dog had only a few seconds to live and I had to be the one to save him.

"We only have two ham, cheese and tomato sandwiches left. The rest are tuna," he informed me with a quizzical expression.

I paid for the lot and raced back out to feed the dog, much to the amazement of local folk standing outside the shop. The dog's sad, dull eyes were watery, as if he had been crying his entire life just for someone to give a damn. Weakly, he wagged his tail to show me his appreciation.

"That dog is not used to eating like that, it might kill him with the sudden shock of so much rich food," one man called out.

"At least he would die knowing that someone showed him kindness," I snapped back. From my reaction to that incident, I felt my decision to go to my mother was right.

Glancing at my watch, I saw it was 7am. I needed to check in half an hour before the flight, leaving me quite a chunk of time on my hands. I dreaded the empty time, knowing all the past hurts and terrors would come flooding back. There were so many things I wished I could erase from memory; perhaps that was why I had to return. I needed closure, as well as answers, while my mother still had the breath to give them to me. When I was first told that my mother was deteriorating, slowly losing her faculties from dementia, I nearly paid my fare the next day to rush to be by her side. I was thwarted from taking that step immediately as a tidal wave of bad memories washed over me like a tsunami. They twisted and turned in my psyche to the point where they caused me physical pain.

I had been planning the trip for six months by the time I left Australia. Nevertheless, as I lay on a single bed in the downstairs room of my brother's home, I found myself gasping for air to placate the raging anxiety that once again roared with deafening ferocity. Thank goodness for the chaos at Jonathan's farm, it was sufficient to distract me from the negative thoughts that started to overwhelm me. I actually sensed a smile spreading across my lips, subduing the roaring rage of uneasiness when I heard my son chatting and laughing with his cousins outside, or my brother barking out orders to his children. In fact, I discovered I was giggling to myself at the delightful dysfunctional normality of it all. Jonathan, his wife and their nine children lived on their farm at Aleisa. It was pleasantly cooler where they lived in the mountains just below the rainforest, a welcome refuge from the constant heat and humidity on the coast. Their parcel of land was previously part of the Schwalger family estates and very well known in the area.

Gazing around my green-walled and curtain less room that first glowed orange with an amazing morning sunrise, I was now almost blinded by the bright Samoan sun, which now blasted dazzling light into my temporary dorm. Jonathan's rooster began to crow close to the room, which in turn appeared to alert the cows that it was time to moo (or perhaps they were telling the cock to shut the hell up, I couldn't be sure). My attention drifted to the mirrored wardrobe next to my bed. The vision prompted an instant recall of my Auntie Tilie and Uncle Bentzen. That same piece of furniture was once situated in the bedroom of my Auntie's estate. It was imposing and solid like any quality antique should be. Seeing it also brought back terrifying memories of the dread apparitions I had seen in that very same mirror. I quickly shifted my gaze, not wishing to recall or reconnect with whatever those things were. Instead, I glanced over to my son's empty single bed with dusty old suitcases underneath it. Faded and age worn family photo albums lay precariously stacked on a table in the corner.

I had a few hours before departing so I sat on the grimy, cold concrete floor and browsed through piles of photo albums. Photographs of my Auntie Tilie and Uncle Bentzen fluttered out from between some of the albums. Seeing them spread out on the floor brought tears of extreme sadness to my eyes, so much so that they flooded unabated down my cheeks and landed on my sweaty legs. In turn, more bitter memories were provoked into tumbling out. I shook my head in disgust at my own weakness as a pathetic human being. Deciding to take swift and affirmative action, I quickly took out only the pictures I wanted to keep and placed those safely in my suitcase. I had plans for the day ahead and the reality was I needed to get on with it. It was at least comforting to know that Jonathan's wife Abbie and her daughter were travelling with us.

As Jonathan drove us to the domestic airfield at Fagalii, I glanced at my son sitting in the back seat of Jonathan's blue van happily playing with his cousins. It made me feel proud. Dayne had told me what a beautiful country Samoa was and that I was lucky to be born and brought up there. He also thanked me for bringing him to Samoa. Like me, my son preferred the outdoors, freedom, breathing in fresh air and being surrounded by animals, children and people. We didn't care where we slept, and simply being around my brother and his close-knit loving family filled me with a sense of belonging.

Although the flight to American Samoa was brief, the vistas were endless and spectacular. American Samoa had high mountains surrounded by a sapphire sea, but it was not as majestically beautiful as Upolu. Landing was almost a disappointment, although perhaps that emotion wasn't shared by the other passengers as they all disembarked quickly, most with family cars waiting for them. As though disappearing in a puff of smoke, suddenly they were all gone. The four of us were the last passengers left at an airport almost bereft of any trace of humanity as we waited for someone collect us. Right on time, my niece Jenny pulled up in a taxi. Abbie and her daughter could go off shopping while we visited my mother.

"We won't be long," I shouted to them as we sped off.

By the time the taxi pulled into my mother's driveway, my damn anxiety started asserting itself again. My palms were sweating so badly I had to constantly wipe them on my bright summer dress. Fortunately for me, years of too many traumatic experiences had taught me to be a great actress when it came to hiding my real feelings. I had been doing it all my life. As my tension mounted, the happier I pretended to be and the louder I became in conversations. I guess somewhere in my muddled brain I figured if I spoke loudly enough I wouldn't be able to hear my inner thoughts at all. The truth is, I lived in fear of uncertainties and was terrified of my own overwhelming emotions.

My sister Kina, my mother's youngest daughter, screamed with joy and ran from her house next door to greet us the moment we pulled up. It had been over twenty years since we'd last seen each other face-to-face. Although my sister was born and brought up in New Zealand, she moved to American Samoa with the folks when she was a teenager. We hugged, we cried, we touched each other's faces – it was such a beautiful feeling to soak in that genuine love full of happiness.

At last the time I both longed for and dreaded was finally here. I was led into the main living area near the kitchen, which due to her infirmity had become my mother's room. The first thing I noticed was the big wooden queen size bed, a few chairs, a table, and a plasma TV sitting on the table by the window. It was all clean and orderly. Just then, the toilet door three meters away from the bed creaked slowly open. Framed in the doorway was a very frail and feeble old woman shakily grasping a walking frame as she struggled back towards her bed. She was only wearing a *lavalava* (sarong) tied loosely around her chest. The gulf of years between us instantly slipped away as quickly as a morning mist in the hot sun. With no warning and against my will, tears welled up in my eyes. I tilted my head back and tried with difficulty to suppress a sob. I had promised myself, I had sworn solemnly on everything I held sacred, that I would not cry. I turned away to compose myself and dab my eyes. The last thing I wanted was to lose it in front of my mother. I didn't want her to see that she still held such power over my emotions.

"*Sieni, si au tama,*" she stuttered out as she tried to talk through her pain.

What? Had she just said "Sieni, my daughter"? All my life I longed for this woman's recognitions . . . but not like this. "What was she playing at?" I asked myself.

"Mum, what happened to you?" I changed the subject as I stepped forward to help her to a chair.

In that moment, the feeling of her now needing me and me helping her filled me with a sense of self satisfaction, and that was even more confusing. My mother was slurring, struggling to both talk and walk; she had lost a staggering amount of weight.

Her once raven black hair was now a listless grey, her smile faint and edged with sorrow. She spoke like a little girl trying to recall happy past events. This was definitely not the woman I used to know, a woman who was once dominating and vibrant with a fun personality. I recalled a distant memory, a vignette of the past flickered through my mind that took me back to a time when she used to laugh a lot. It had been a loud and contagious laugh. When she told a joke she would have her family and friends in stitches. Such was the irreverent sense of humour I recalled. When she ate, she really ate with gusto, to the point of stuffing her mouth until both cheeks looked like they were about to explode. No matter what it was, she ate like it was the most delicious food she'd ever tasted. Now she could barely eat enough to sustain herself.

In decades long gone, my mother had been a very vain and beautiful woman. She was five feet and eight inches tall with long, sexy legs and a lovely figure crowned with exotic looks. In her younger days she looked like an Asian model that you might see on glossy calendars. Her long straight jet-black hair was always a striking feature no matter how she styled it. I believe she had the best genes from both her parents. Even in her wizened state I could glimpse the faded beauty of her past. That jaded past was now eclipsed by the fear, hopelessness and apathy in her eyes. It seemed as she was barely with us.

While I tried to glean more about her condition from her husband, mother kept eyeing me with a strange and unsettling childish grin on her face. Feeling uncomfortable, I abruptly asked her why she stared at me so.

"*O lena lava ete aulelei. Ete aulelei i lau fanau uma*," she haltingly and weakly uttered. It meant that I was the prettiest of all her children. I do believe my heart skipped a beat, because I could swear I heard sincerity in her words, even though they stung me to my very core. I was close to being outraged that she would dare to say such a frivolous thing after the putrid past she'd condemned me to.

I quickly glanced over at my sister Kina hugging my son, attempting to ignore what our mother was saying. Then it dawned on me, slowly but very deliberately I looked back towards my mother. Our eyes met and locked, and I realised she had never said anything like that to me before. She may have thought it, maybe, but those words had never been uttered from her lips. I had heard her praising her other daughters with pride but never me. I found myself wondering if my mother really meant what she just said. Or did she just say those things to me because she was now totally dependent on others for her survival?

That briefest of reunions was all I could stomach in the first sitting. I would return the next day and assess what could and should be said once I'd processed what had just transpired.

"Why are you going back so soon? Can't you stay the night with me?" mother begged.

"I can't. My husband Boyd is arriving from Australia tomorrow to join us. He will be expecting me to pick him up from Faleolo airport," I explained without a great deal of conviction and felt proud of myself for saying no to her.

Back at the hotel, I couldn't sleep a wink. Our flight back to Samoa was booked for 12 noon the following day. We all awoke early, packed our things and then waited for my stepfather to pick us up to say our last goodbye to the woman I grudgingly called my mother. On the way over, I asked stepfather to stop at a local food store so I could buy my mother some freshly cooked Samoan food. Part of the previous night's processing manifested some measure of real empathy, compassion and forgiveness in me for this woman. For the first time I looked at the situation in front of me and felt the need to do what was right. No matter what had transpired in the past, I believed it was only proper to afford my mother some understanding and dignity. There was no need to talk about the past or relive horrible memories. Perhaps karma had intervened to save me the pain.

Having reached that cathartic decision, I felt a sense of relief, as though past hurt was slowly eradicating itself from being so entrenched as part of my every day being. Slowly a leaden burden was finally being lifted from my shoulders. All I had to do was channel my energy for the next few minutes in a positive fashion towards the woman who had given birth to me, to make her feel loved even if she did not deserve it. I wanted to focus on her rather than my own needs. From the bottom of my heart, I wished my mother no suffering, but peace.

We said our goodbyes, gave her husband some money to help with her medications and I assured her that if I could I would return one day soon. As I walked towards the front passenger seat of my stepfather's car, I looked back. Mother was determinedly forcing herself to stand, shakily holding onto her walking frame looking out through the window. In a desperate and desolate tone that pierced my soul, she called to me, "I love you, Sieni."

For over fifty years I had so desperately yearned for my mother to say those words to me. Every ounce of my being wanted to rush back into the house, break down the door and wrap my arms around her, squeezing her. I wanted to give her all the years of longing to love her in one fell swoop, yet in that same instant I was completely incapable of independent movement. While my heart felt as though it might pound clear out of my chest, the rest of my body couldn't or wouldn't respond. I quickly slammed the car door shut then broke down sobbing like a pathetic little girl as my stepfather slowly drove away without saying a word.

"Why are you crying, Mum?" Dayne asked.

I was unable to answer him. How could I explain to my son that I was crying because today was the first day that my own mother ever told me that she loved me? How could I tell him that all my life she sneered at my existence as an embarrassment for her? Or that I had been abandoned, ignored when her brother sexually abused me and that she had encouraged and watched people inflict unimaginable pain and suffering on me? Or that this was the last I would ever see of my mother?

So, for you to understand my bizarre life and how any of this came to be, it is necessary to take you back to the very beginning.

Chapter 1

A Magical Estate

My father's Auntie Ottilie had a destiny that would impact hundreds of Samoans from all over the island. As sole female heir to a vast property, it was Ottilie's privilege to be blessed with a substantial income and status when her father died. She developed her inherited estate into one of the best-known and most productive enterprises in Samoa. Such was the impact on hundreds of Samoans who were employed on this property for many years to come.

At first glance, the estate was aesthetically an idyllic paradise. Over a hundred lush, fertile acres supported a private and secluded haven in the rear section of the boundary between Salepouae and Lotosoa villages in the district of Saleimoa. Recent archaeological finds date the village as one of the earliest settled and historically most important parts of the island of Upolu. Beneath the surface however, lay dark and deadly secrets I would not discover for many, many years.

Wilhelm Schwalger, who came to the island as an overseer for a German agricultural company, originally owned the land, which he settled in 1890. Wilhelm was an industrious worker who established himself as one of the main farming producers. For many years he nurtured the estate, the epicentre of his farming operations, developing it into a unique and remarkable place, employing Chinese as well as people from the Melanesian Islands. Like many Germans, Wilhelm saw opportunities in Samoa to make money, but found the Samoan people lazy and unproductive.

Wilhelm was forty-six when he married his first wife Silafaga, a twenty-seven-year-old *Taupou*, a ceremonial queen of her extended family. A woman known as a Taupou is highly respected and a significant part of a Samoan high chief of king's ruling system. They lived on the estate with their five children: Fritz, August, Ottilie (the only girl), Hans and Martin. The marriage did not last. Silafaga left the property, taking the two eldest boys with her. The remaining children stayed with their father. Later, Wilhelm formed a relationship with Silafaga's niece Mafa, a liaison that added two more sons to the Schwalger clan.

Ottilie inherited the estate without any dispute from her elder brothers. She was the third eldest child of the family and without doubt "daddy's girl." As such, she was groomed to run the property. So fierce was her sense of belonging and so powerful was her pride in her birth right, that after Wilhelm passed, Ottilie had no compunction whatsoever in unceremoniously removing her stepmother from what had become solely Ottilie's land.

Intermarriage between Samoans and non-Samoans became commonplace once the indigenous people witnessed the power and money foreigners brought to this Pacific nation. Samoan parents encouraged their daughters to marry white men, hoping the union would bring good luck and prosperity for the future of their families. The arrival of the famous author Robert Louis Stevenson and his love for the Samoan people embedded this belief, many Samoans assuming that all white men were like him.

When Samoan girls could not catch a European man, they settled for Chinese men as second best.

Ottilie's property was surrounded by a thriving plantation of coconut trees, cocoa and banana plants. In neat rows across the property, yam and taro plants flourished alongside the tropical fruit trees of breadfruit and pawpaw (papaya). The aroma of overripe mango, guava and banana was pungent, creating a heady, sweet perfume that permeated the whole estate. This attracted hordes of hungry fruit bats and a profusion of colourful native birds singing and fighting noisily over the luscious fruits hanging off the tree branches or rotting on the ground. The plantation was a sanctuary for the native animals; in other areas they would have been killed as welcome food.

The entire estate was encircled by a barbed-wire fence almost four metres high. The only way in or out was through the high-security gates topped with barbed-wire rolls and secured by heavy chains and locks. The first gate lined up with the outer perimeter fence, the second was about twenty metres down the driveway from the main living compound, providing selective entry and exit.

A small, well-built hut on the right-hand side between the gates was home to a trusted crusty old local man, who guarded the gates. There was a pleasant, fully self-contained two-storey house on the left-hand side, which was a guesthouse for visiting family and dignitaries. When it was first built, the guesthouse was occupied by a family member with young children. The sound of laughter filled what my innocent childish eyes once saw as a magnificent sanctuary with happy sounds. There was a melodic joy that resonated, as if heralding this to be heaven on earth. Directly ahead and founded on a rise, stood a grand and majestic white two-storey mansion. This manor had a profusion of windows to allow light to flood in and invite breezes to cool the hot, humid Samoan days. The mansion, built in the early 20th century, stood regally overlooking the whole landscape. Far from being imposing, it seemed to beckon everyone entering this wondrous paradise.

From the second gate, towards the stately home, family members and visitors were surrounded by a strikingly beautiful garden crowded with exotic flowers that thrived in the tropical climate. This carefully landscaped garden was thronged by multi-coloured butterflies that danced in the air as if entertaining the trees. Child and adult alike would be mesmerised watching this spectacle of nature. Hidden among the flowers and fruit trees not far from the outer gate and few meters away from the main house lay three graves.

During the working week, the powerful aroma of cooking copra and roasting cocoa beans filled the air, tantalising the olfactory senses. The fragrant wafts drifted through loud and distinctive noises from the workers as they bustled about their daily duties in the copra house. The sound of men labouring and machines whirring was so intense during harvest time it created an atmosphere of purpose, excitement and good cheer. This was a place of majesty and magic, of magnificence and bounty.

On the other side of the compound fence, in the main field, women, men and some children tended the soil, humming and singing in rhythm. Their voices blended with the birds' chirping and the swamp of bees lazy buzzing. The snuffling of happy pigs from a nearby sty seemed to add a rhythm to the agreeable cacophony. Chickens roamed around the yard showing off their beautiful plumage while fighting noisily with the native birds over the ripe fruit that had fallen to the ground. Added to this menagerie were ten playful farm dogs of various breeds and sizes. They were always on guard, protecting the property's boundaries. They must have been the best-fed and most-loved dogs in all of Samoa. Wafting seductively from inside the house was the mouth-watering aroma of the meals prepared by the housemaids; this could at times confound the fresh but fecund smell of the rain forest and bushland wafting in on the island breezes.

The farm had three vehicles. A large truck parked near the homestead picked up and dropped off the workers and transported the farm's harvest to market or for export. Hiding in one of the securely locked garages was a priceless old Mercedes Benz, a stately saloon awaiting the next opportunity to grace the light of day. The other sedan was a working car for daily tasks.

To me this was a purely magical place, a symphony for the senses. It was a place you could look forward to visiting and never want to leave. The beauty, energising aromas and vibrant sounds beckoned and enveloped mind, body and soul. Never did I want to depart from all the bounty it had to offer.

In that paradise of a plantation, once worked a pretty, petite maid in her twenties whose headstrong character of Samoan and Chinese heritage made her a standout among the staff. Her name was Melekihna Ah Sam, from the village of Tuanai and she was considered lucky and privileged to have found work at the Schwalger estate. As her name was too long for most, it was shortened to Mele. Mele was an excellent cook, specialising in the island's now diverse cuisine. Exhibiting high morals, she became a trusted employee and it was not long before Ottilie promoted her to manager of the household. These two women became such good friends that Mele's life started to completely revolve around Ottilie's desires. When she was not on duty, the madam of the estate missed her so much she would make any excuse just to have Mele at her side. Ottilie was heard to say, "I have many family and friends but none I could trust like Mele."

They were an odd couple to be sure: a rich matron and an illiterate maid from an impoverished family who did not even own shoes, the friendship was based on trust, mutual admiration and perhaps a small measure of fear.

Mele was fascinated by Ottilie's adventurous life, her beauty, her sense of style, her many fine shoes, clothes, jewellery and belongings, but most of all she was intrigued by her influential friends. Ottilie was well educated, worldly, and fluent in Samoan, English and German. She was sophisticated and a no-nonsense, ruthless businesswoman who also enjoyed entertaining and partying a little too much. Mele became well accustomed to seeing her mistress become intoxicated and aggressive. At other times Ottilie could be profoundly generous, giving away money and belongings from drunken exuberance, only to sheepishly request the gifts be returned the next day.

The two women's relationship came to an abrupt end when Mele fell in love and eloped from the estate with Ta'ateo, a local man from Salepouae village. Ta'ateo was one of Ottilie's most reliable copra workers. In the harvest season, Ta'ateo and the other men spent weeks at the plantation, tending the furnace around the clock so that the copra was baked at the correct temperature and did not burn. Due to the volume of money at stake for the Schwalger enterprise, there were only a few select workers trusted with the task. Exercising both prudence and foresight, those trusted workers were all fed from the main house to guarantee they didn't stray, thereby ensuring the operation ran without hindrance. It was this prudence and foresight that paved the way for Mele and Ta'ateo's affair to begin. Ottilie never suspected a thing until the couple had eloped. To say her departure came as a shock would be to damn with faint praise the impact losing Mele had. Ottilie had lost her most honest and trusted friend, not to mention one of her best workers. Ottilie was convinced that Mele was too young to marry and too good for Ta'ateo. She was both furious and deeply hurt by what she saw as a betrayal of her trust and friendship. Her fury and rage were so fierce she attempted to have Ta'ateo thrown in jail on some trumped-up charge, accusing him of stealing coconuts and goods from the farm when he left. She relented and dropped the charges when she discovered that Mele was pregnant.

Many years would pass before Ottilie finally forgave Mele. When she returned, begging for a job in the fields to help feed her now family of ten, Ottilie could not refuse her. By then the mistress of the manor had just married her second husband, Bentzen, and the plantation was booming. Over the years that followed, most of Mele's children were offered work at the farm to help with their schooling. The environment was so abundant and welcoming that some of those children continued working there when they finished school. For extended family members to be employed under one roof was rare in Samoa.

Mele understood how fortunate she was. From the moment of her return she would demonstrate her gratitude with loyalty and diligence unsurpassed among Ottilie's staff. It wasn't until her daughter, Amilaina, gave birth to a baby girl and was unable to care for her child that Mele resigned. The year was 1961 and this time Ottilie, while again lamenting Mele's loss, was more than understanding and supportive.

Amilaina took the opportunity to be free of responsibility for her baby girl by leaving to find a new life in American Samoa, taking her older daughter Agnes (from a previous relationship) with her. In American Samoa, Amilaina married a Tokelauan man named Sinafoa. In those days, the Tokelau Island was under the umbrella and protection of New Zealand, which meant the people and their families could obtain residence visas easily, and that was a prospect Amilaina intended not to jeopardise.

Amilaina's girl child held a very special place in Ottilie's life and her heart, and not solely because she was Mele's granddaughter. The infant girl had been fathered by her favourite nephew Karl Schwalger, conceived during a torrid affair when Amilaina worked at the estate. Karl had been a constant visitor and was like a son to Ottilie. Although they were both single and in their early twenties, marriage was never on Karl's mind. This dashed Amilaina's dreams for a fairy-tale life, far removed from village toil and drudgery. She was forced to return to her village in a cloud of shame and hopelessness. While Ottilie supported Mele's decision to leave, she bound her with a verbal agreement: Mele would take good care of this little girl, and in return Ottilie would support the child financially. Ottilie's one demand was for the little girl to be delivered to Ottilie's estate on her tenth birthday, to be brought up where Ottilie felt the child rightly belonged.

I was that little girl.

I was named Sieni by my mother before she handed me to Mele, my grandmother. Sieni is Samoan for Jane, which is what Ottilie preferred to call me. For some reason Ottilie always favoured the Anglicised version of my name. I was instructed to refer to her as "Auntie Tilie." It would be many years before I found out the truth of my conception, my relationship to Ottilie and to the Schwalger family.

Through my childish eyes, my Auntie's estate was a magical paradise. It was a place where I could lie on the manicured green grass of the front garden watching rainbows and white clouds drift by though as if they were heading off somewhere majestic and mysterious. The air was filled with colourful butterflies, some landing on my toes if I kept still long enough. During those days of innocence it didn't occur to me to question the sense of not being alone, of thinking I saw something out of the corner of my eye only to turn and find nothing there, or of swearing that on occasion I'd seen something odd sweep past me.

The estate overflowed with the aroma of roses and other exotic flowers, a far sweeter scent than was found in my village. I had been visiting frequently since I was a toddler, and on every occasion I was spoiled with treats and candies. This was a place I went to receive gifts of shoes and nice dresses. Money and food were handed to me without having to work for them. I could have anything I wanted. From a young age I learned there was greener and sweeter life of abundance and plenty just over the rainbow, or at least through the walls surrounding Ottilie's property. This was in sharp contrast to the hardship of village life I had known since birth. I was tantalised and tempted with its sweet riches for fleeting moments, only to return to servitude and subsistence before the sun sank once more.

I now know it was also the reason why my grandmother had no option but to agree to Auntie Tilie's deal, though she knew the dark and sinister truths that lurked beneath the surface of this apparently idyllic estate. She knew Ottilie's true nature, and secretly my grandmother had no intention of fulfilling her part of the bargain. Our family was poor and I happened to be the golden goose, the little girl with the magic wand to help the family in an instance whenever they were desperate for food and money. My grandmother had vainly hoped that by the time I turned ten, her financial struggle might be over and none of us would need to deal with the money lady anymore. She also believed my mother would send for me to live with her and her family in New Zealand before Auntie Tilie came for me. It was a very dangerous game Mele was playing; she was well aware there would be a terrible price to pay if it all went wrong.

Chapter 2

My Grandparents

To the rest of the people in my world my grandmother was called Mele, but I called her Tina, which is Samoan for "mother." For the rest of this story, I prefer to use Tina (pronounced Tee-nah) for my grandmother and Tama (Ta-Ma) for my grandfather, instead of their given names.

I felt loved and protected by both my grandparents, especially my beloved Tina. I was her little shadow and she was the centre of my world. I had no recollection of my mother, and therefore grew up thinking Tina had brought me into this world. However, when I was four years old I came home from the minister's school and found my grandparents and two of my mother's sisters talking to a very attractive lady. Sitting next to her were three nicely dressed young girls, one looked bigger and older than I was. The family were whispering among themselves, which made me wary and suspicious. I noticed that Tina had been crying. I guessed whatever they were talking about was serious, especially as the moment I walked into the house, no one looked happy and everyone stopped talking. The atmosphere was so sombre I felt that I should remain silent as well, but for a four-year-old this was nigh on impossible. Finally, I could not bear it anymore.

"Why is everyone crying? What's wrong, Tina?" I blurted out.

In response, Tina started to sob loudly, which started everybody else up again. It was like someone had just died. I watched them with agitation until Tina managed to calm herself down and introduced me to our visitors.

"This is your mother and your sisters. Oh, and your mother is going to have another baby again, so you will have lots of sisters and brothers. They will be leaving for New Zealand next week."

Tina struggled to say more but could not find the words, and none of what she said made any sense to me. I was bored and untouched by this shocking revelation, so I merely asked my big sister Agnes to go outside and play with me. My other sisters, Ceal and Cinta the baby, were guarded by my mother who showed no interest in me. Her only focus was to get on the plane and leave to join her husband in New Zealand. Of course nothing was going to be that straightforward.

Time had little meaning in Samoa, so when a week blended into a month (and they were still with us) I hardly noticed. My biological mother was unhappy because there were problems with her travelling visa. Although she did not have much to do with me, she had been recorded as my mother and this is what had caused complications with the immigration office. I remember her returning home from Apia one day seething with rage.

"We can't leave because of her," she yelled at Tina, pointing at me. "You shouldn't have put my name on her birth certificate!"

Tina stopped weaving her mat and gave my mother an astonished look. She gazed over at me squatting in the corner trying to put things in order for her weaving, and then became angrier than I had ever seen her.

"How dare you say that? I didn't tell you to get pregnant. Sieni didn't ask to be born. How on earth do you expect her to attend school without a birth certificate? Or didn't you want her to go to school either? You are a mother. You can't ignore one and carry the rest."

I tried to pretend I was not the subject of the argument and asked Tina to be excused to go to play. Although I was very little then, the words that came out of my mother's mouth that afternoon somehow became etched in my memory. I sensed she didn't like me, and thereafter I kept close to my grandmother for protection. Things did seem to calm down the next day when Tina came up with the idea of having me adopted out in order for my mother to go to New Zealand. It was an adoption only in name, so to serve the purpose Tina selected my mother's older sister Salaki. Apparently everyone agreed and my mother was happy.

Finally the time came for her and my sisters to leave for New Zealand. This was a big occasion; a traditional farewell feast must be prepared. It would involve the minister and his wife and all the chiefs of the family and their wives. The whole neighbourhood took part in helping orchestrate this banquet. Our family's fattest pig was killed to honour my mother, as she was the first person from our village to leave the country in pursuit of a better and brighter future. She was greatly admired for this momentous achievement, and hence Tama and Tina were seen as the honoured proud parents. My elder sister, Agnes, had been legally adopted by our stepfather and was leaving with my mother and the two youngest sisters. I was left permanently in the care of Tina, which to my four-year-old way of thinking was just exactly how the world should have been. I was so wrapped up in my grandmother's complete adoration that little else mattered to me. We did everything together so I couldn't muster even a meagre sense of loss at losing a mother I didn't even know.

Most Samoans lived in villages, residing in traditional Samoan houses called *fales* (huts). Ours was oval, floored with coconut trunks a foot off the ground and thickly thatched with palm fronds strung together in mat form. There were no walls and it was supported on the sides by strong posts of tree trunks. Blinds were fashioned from coconut leaves and constructed in such a way that they could be folded down to exclude high winds or rain. Floor mats woven out of pandanus leaves were laid out for us to sit and sleep on. Those mats were the only thing separating our bodies from the uncomfortably hard and dirty floor. Growing up I shared a small *fale* with my grandparents and four of my single uncles, Faalua being the youngest. He was only ten years older than I. Gradually my other three uncles moved away.

Tina and Tama became the head of our family when Tama became one of the village *matais*. Even as a child it was impossible to mistake how much my grandparents adored each other. Being raised around so much love, I was a very happy kid, even though life in our village was harsh. My grandparents were inseparable and complemented one another with their polar-opposite personalities. Tina was loud and active, a diminutive cyclone that could not be ignored. She was also fearless. Before she married my grandfather and had her children, Tina decided to get a painful Samoan female traditional tattoo (*malu*) done to mark her place in a Samoa society, although she was not a Taupou. She said she did it because she got tired of people calling her half Chinese. At the age of fifty she started to pull out her own teeth using a string when they became rotten. Within a few years she was completely toothless. Tama, on the other hand, was a gentle and retiring soul who agreed happily with almost everything Tina suggested. For a Samoan *Matai* to allow his wife to do all the talking was frowned upon, but Tama saw things quite differently. They were a loving team struggling to bring up a large, hungry family. Tina was able to push and cajole to get things done. She had a canny mind full of ideas to achieve almost anything in the cheapest and most efficient manner. This was a woman who would not have been out of place in the hustle and bustle of Hong Kong as she ceaselessly wheeled and dealed to procure whatever was needed for her family.

After a hard day's work, Tama would relax and unwind by listening to a small radio my mother had bought for him. This little magical miracle from the modern world had become his pride and joy. The only time I witnessed Tama lose his temper was when one of his sons touched his radio. Until that moment, I couldn't have imagined there was such power and volume in this gentle man. It completely shocked me (even though I was silently full of admiration) when he swore at the top of his lungs and threatened hideous vengeance on anyone who damaged his precious radio. From that moment on, Tama took his radio everywhere with him – a good plan but with a minor flaw. They both went into the sea together when his canoe capsized; sadly, the radio didn't make it.

Tama and Tina worked hard for what little they had. There was virtually no money and the hours toiling on their plantation were long. Anything that could be consumed, woven or practically utilised in any fashion was planted, cultivated and harvested season after season. The surplus was sold at the markets for desperately needed cash. Everyone was expected to share in the work regardless of age, according to their abilities. By these means, our large family managed to have one substantial meal a day, dinner, which was routinely at 7pm after evening prayers. If any of us were hungry during the day, which we kids often were, we simply had to fend for ourselves. We would often turn to coconuts, mangoes or whatever fruit we could find to ease the ever-present hunger pangs. Waste was not tolerated in Tina's world; everything went into the pot, whether it was a fish's brain, a pig's intestines and offal or the chicken's head and eyes.

"Just eat it and let the stomach deal with it," she'd say with great earnest. "What doesn't taste quite to our liking is usually the best thing for our bodies."

It was not uncommon to see me and Tina sitting in the corner on the dirty concrete floor at the market in Apia. From there we would sell mats and vegetables, even if it took all day before all our wares were traded. Most, if not all, of the income from market days was to help Tina and Tama's church and village obligations. If there was any money left I was treated with something to eat before rice, flour and sugar were purchased for the whole family. Although Tina loved all of her grandchildren, we came to have a very close and special bond. Never did I feel quite as safe as when my grandmother was around. Although I was a scrawny kid, I was seldom bullied because Tina would always come to my rescue. This saved me from many harsh beatings, and when she couldn't stand up for me in person she taught me that if I showed fear I would be targeted.

"If you don't want to be a victim, don't be seen as one. If you must, fight back with your brain," she said. "You have a big one, Sieni."

Over time, my grandmother's wisdom paid dividends. We were a good team. She was my saviour and my ultimate protector. One incident I still remember with perfect clarity is when I started to feel dizzy at church one mid-morning, already tired after the rigours of Sunday school. I had sat through the hour-long service in oppressive humidity, unable to move, expected to focus on the minister waffling on without pause. My head was hurting, my stomach was agitated by hunger pangs and I felt faint. I was dehydrated by fever and desperate to go to the toilet. I asked the stern old lady armed with a whip who policed the children in church to let me go outside.

"Sit still and hold until the service is finished," she barked gruffly back at me. She could clearly see the pained expression on my face but chose to ignore it as part of her pious duty. Every minute, every creeping second I held on in my agony. Thankfully, the last hymn faded out and I was allowed to go. With the sudden motion of standing up, my bladder muscle decided it could no longer help me. No matter how hard I willed it, holding on was no longer an option. Outside on the concrete steps I sat and peed all over my white dress and legs.

The fear and shame I immediately experienced were palpable. As quick as a cricket, I ran behind the building to hide before the congregation started coming out. If other children found out I had wet myself I would be teased without mercy for the rest of my life. Whilst waiting for everyone to leave, a horse tethered to a tree caught my attention. He was calmly and happily doing his poos out in the open. I can't imagine what insanity possessed me to do it, but there in the midst of my shame, in my urine soaked dress, I started picking up the fresh, steaming green horse dung and throwing it at the pristine white walls of the church building. Each one I blasted on the wall stuck like an emerald splattered magnet. It felt gloriously good to see every handful I aimed strike just where I wanted them to go. It looked so wonderful I decided to make it into a pattern that spelled "Lying Minister." Every Sunday after church, my family would joke that our minister was a liar over our Sunday lunch because he talked about love and sacrifice, yet his family were the only people in our village who lived well.

My artistic creation stuck out like, well it stuck out like horse manure on whitewashed walls! I thought it looked pretty good and was quietly proud of my work of art. I continued to pelt these equine excretions until every single nugget had stuck like glue on the outside wall. It was only then that the initial elation subsided and I realised with dawning horror what I had done. The church was the pride and joy of our village. As though it was choking me, a cold fear suddenly swamped my being with the realisation of the sacrilege I had just committed. I tried to remove the few I was able to reach, noticing to my dismay that the remaining dark stain did not come off. Petrified, I quickly looked around for any witnesses before making a run for it. Standing slightly behind the horse tree was a girl my age staring wide-eyed and slack-jawed straight at me. Unfortunately she did not stay stunned long. She started calling out to her father loudly and fearfully, as though she had seen Satan himself. That was all the cue I needed to run as fast as my legs could carry me, with my still sodden dress slapping madly against my pumping legs.

An hour after I arrived home, cleaned myself up and had lunch, I began thinking I was in the clear. Then a messenger came with news the minister wanted to see me. My grandparents both glanced in my direction. I shrugged my shoulders, pretending I had no idea what he wanted. Ministers only sent for children when they were in trouble. I should have confessed to my grandmother, as without a doubt Tina would have come with me to sort it out as she always did. Instead, I wrongly decided that if I told her my crime it would warrant a double punishment. I preferred to have one big one instead of two.

On Sundays, it was a tradition for the minister to share a feast, provided by his flock of course, with some of his deacons. The deacons were mainly high chiefs of his congregation and were accompanied by their wives. This weekly tradition would see those of privilege gorge themselves over pleasant chatter and frivolity before they departed to ready themselves for the second service. They were all present when I came to face the minister.

"You have obviously invited Satan into your life," the minister began. I said nothing. "Do you realise what you did was very bad?" he asked.

"Yes, I am sorry," I offered sincerely.

"Why did you do it?" he asked.

"I don't know. But I was sick and angry, the lady wouldn't let me go to the toilet. I nearly wet the church seat," I replied.

With no further questions, the fat minister struggled to his feet. In front of his children and the assembled people, he took off his belt and ordered me to kneel as if I was praying. Crouched in supplication on my knees, the minister proceeded to lash me with all his considerable might across my back with his thick black belt. With every blow I released a scream so forceful it hurt my vocal cords. Dredging up some vocal ability between my screams, I would plead for him to forgive me and to have pity. The more he struck, the more I blurted out whatever came into my head, without considering what I was saying.

"I was bored. I wanted to pee. I wasn't feeling well. I was hungry. The church was boring."

This of course only served to heighten the minister's insane fury. He must have interpreted what I was yelling as extremely offensive. Even after he broke his belt on me, he ordered one of his children to get a green stick from outside. Sweating and gasping for air, the minister started again. His sweat beads actually started to spray on my face as I looked up at him, begging him to condemn this sinful child of God in some other way. Every inch of my body was bursting in pain. This was worse than the belt; it was like someone was stabbing my skin with a lot of hot needles at the same time. My screams for help became so deafening that they were heard by my grandmother at our home no short distance away.

She must have moved with lightning speed, because before I knew it Tina strode in with force and rage. It was impossible to miss what was happening. Her instinctive reaction was to wrap her body around mine to prevent any further blows. Only then did the minister stop.

"You are supposed to be a servant of God and you are about to kill this little girl," she bellowed at him. "That is enough!"

"Do you know what she did?" one of the deacons asked, trying to reason with Tina for talking to the minister without respect.

"I don't care what she did. No one should punish a seven-year-old girl like that. It is barbaric," Tina snapped back with a fierce glare.

Everyone could see I'd been beaten so badly I was in a pitiful state. I was completely incapable of standing, never mind walking. My uncle Faalua had to carry me home. Luckily, Tama had instructed him to follow Tina when she stormed out of our hut after hearing my yells for help.

No one else said a thing. They may have thought that Tina was brave to talk to the respected minister that way, but the fact was that my grandmother was not brave – she was murderously enraged.

For the next few days, Tama tried to calm her. She did not want our family to have anything to do with the church, and especially the minister, anymore.

"No more donations and no more feeding the fat swine," she fumed.

"You know we can't do that. We swore to serve our church and its minister," Tama tried to reason with her.

It did not take long for my scars to heal, but Tina's misgivings about the church would not lessen so easily.

"See, it is all about money to them," she told me. "Jesus did not get paid for preaching to people. How stupid are we?"

My grandmother was always my superhero. Regardless of my grades in school, she was always proud of me. She encouraged me to do my best and never expected anything more from me. She instilled confidence and self-worth in me, assuring me that no power on earth could ever destroy me. She was the love of my life, and because of this, I strove to do well – just for her.

Tina often cried at the thought of my mother being so far away. Something intuitively told her that she might never see her daughter again. Receipt of a letter from New Zealand would temporarily ease her anguish, even though each communiqué was previewed with squeals from the entire neighbourhood that Mele's daughter had sent her a letter containing money. As Tina and Tama were illiterate, as soon as I could read and write (by the age of five) I became their secretary, reading and replying with the only mode of communication available to us. Although my mother never wrote to me directly, we did open some dialogue through Tina and Tama's letters. It was of little consequence to me, but it made Tina happy so I obliged. Every day after primary school I would walk to the local post office to ask if there was mail for my grandparents, hoping this tiny shred of paper from afar would bring a smile to my beautiful grandmother's lips.

As far back as I can remember Tina would take me to visit Auntie Tilie. Although the property was an hour's walk away, it was something special for both of us and exciting because we always dressed in our best for these events. Never did we arrive empty handed. There was always an offering of either one of Tina's beautifully decorated mats or something home baked that she knew Auntie Tilie enjoyed. This was our token of respect and gratitude. In exchange, Auntie ordered boxes of food and big bags of rice and flour to be delivered to us with a respectable amount of cash after each visit.

During these visits, Tina would sit humbly on the floor in deference to Auntie Tilie's status. With unguarded adulation, she would watch me transform from a poor little girl into a spoiled, gleeful imp. I have such fond memories of sitting smugly on a comfortable chair with my Auntie as she lavished me with kisses and treats. I often dreaded going back home, knowing in few days I would be hungry again. Boxes of food supplied by Auntie didn't usually last. There were too many mouths to be fed. My visits were highlights for Auntie and I and there were no restrictions to my access to her estate. Auntie Tilie made it very clear she was thrilled and delighted to see me at any time.

Naturally enough, as I grew up the prospect of visiting Auntie Tilie's farm became more and more enticing. There I was treated differently. I was served by maids and ate beautiful food, the likes of which I had never experienced before. Everything was abundant and joyous. I was blissfully ignorant at that tender age. I could not know that, while these encounters were precious for both me and my Aunt, they were deeply troubling to my grandmother. Nevertheless, despite Tina's misgivings and her deepening concern about my growing attachment to the estate, whenever we were in dire need of money or food, I would be quickly dressed in my finest and rushed over for a quick visit. Auntie Tilie never denied us, and the cycle and her hold on us continued.

The older I became, the more I came to realise that secrets were being kept from me. My grandmother had groomed me to become the perfect little actress, always shining with a ready smile and plenty of kisses for my Auntie when we needed her help. Tina was happy enough for that charade to play out in Auntie Tilie's presence, yet as soon as we returned home her name was never even whispered, as though it was taboo. As any child would, I became curious and that curiosity grew with each passing day.

After one of our desperate dashes for aid, I could contain my questions no longer.

"Instead of you and Tama working hard and us sitting at the market all day selling things for very little money, why don't we go to Auntie Tilie every week?" I probed, thinking it was a reasonable and logical enough question. "She would give us more money in one day just by visiting her than what we get from the boring market in a whole year."

"Nothing is free in this world, Sieni, even if it appears so," Tina answered solemnly. "Don't ever depend on other people for anything."

I didn't understand the answer, but I did understand it was the end of the conversation and I would have to accept it as such.

Chapter 3

The Way it Was

My home village of Salepouae and the cultural life it contained were in stark contrast to my Auntie Tilie's Western-style plantation and the privileged lifestyle it offered. In the preceding sixty years, the Europeanization of most villages in Samoa has been relentless. The overall effect is homogenizing the villages into a facsimile of everywhere else in the world, a phenomenon sadly occurring in most cultures previously alien to the now all-encompassing Western influence. At that time, apart from the church and some school buildings (which were funded by foreign countries and missionaries), everything else was as it had been for the many centuries before colonization. Today, the relentless drive to homogenise indigenous cultures into a Western look with Western dress, Western values, Western food and Western sensibilities is marking even the most remote villages in Samoa. The status quo, which had typified the Samoan way for centuries prior to colonisation, is rapidly being relegated into the pages of history books.

Back when I was a child, woven clothing and leaves had already been abandoned in favour of cloth lava lavas. These were simple rectangular cloths that would cover a woman from above her breasts to just below the knee, and on a man would cover his lower torso. Men's chests were bare as they went about their daily tasks, their trim muscular frames glistening with sweat. Footwear didn't exist, and the only adornments were flowers placed behind an ear (left or right, depending on marital status of a female) and fragrant leis around the neck. Before the missionaries came women went bare breasted, the sight of a woman's breast considered no more stimulating than a person's nose.

Until we were eight years old, we girls went running around freely attired only in our crude, hand-sewn cotton underwear fashioned from the cloth no longer fit for adult use. All clothing was a scarce commodity and shared by the family. The only time we wore something clean was when we attended church or school. At that time, there were no cars in the village; only the wealthy could afford them and most travelled by foot, or if they had the money, by the few buses. As a small child I thrilled at the bustle of hard working men, creative women and children burdened under heavy loads of bananas, strings of brightly hued fish, or the ever-present green coconut frond woven baskets bursting with produce. With little money, the economic system of the village was based on barter of surplus wares. There were virtually no opportunities to earn actual money in our villages. Feeding the family was the result of hard toil supplemented from whatever the lagoon provided. That was the world I was raised in and I had accepted it as normal, a life a million miles from the affluent world of my father and his family.

Although we were poor and life was difficult, we were culturally, spiritually and socially rich. My young life was filled with laughter and fun. Not only did I have many cousins to play with, but our whole neighbourhood belonged to our extended family. Subsequently, all the children became playmates and friends to each other. From as early as I can remember we were taught to share everything we had with others. No matter how meagre our bounty, we kids would perform our own loaves-and-fishes magic so that everyone received their share of whatever we had. Even a few pennies in our pockets made us feel like royalty with the world at our command. One family in the village made coconut brittle to sell to locals with a sweet tooth and a few pennies to spare. When we were lucky enough to afford a piece, seven or more of us would sit around taking turns sucking the sweetness out of this lolly, knowing that when it was finished we could all share in it again just by talking about it. Those were the moments I treasured the most. The hardship we endured together fostered a deep bond of friendship, trust and love for each other.

We attended the local primary school in the morning. The girls wore starched blue skirts with white shirts and the boys wore blue lavalavas. Once we entered the school grounds, it was a very strict and disciplined environment. Fingernails were to be cut short and our hair had to be well groomed, even if it was nit infested, our teeth were not brushed and our underwear was dirty. From as young as two years old, or as soon as we could talk, we would attend the minister's school in the afternoon. There we were first introduced to our Samoan alphabet, which meant reading and writing skills were developed even before we started the government school. Naturally, the main topics of study centred on God and Jesus. It was therefore unsurprising that owning and reading a Bible was mandatory for every villager.

In between school times, we were all expected to pull our weight with the many daily chores. All village families have a small and separate *fale* for cooking their food on the ground using wood, charcoal and rocks. The copious smoke mingled with the aroma of the cooking food and wafted around the village. On Sundays, this was even more intensified with smoke pluming as if from scattered chimneys while all the villagers were dressed in dazzling white. We girls would help with the weeding and planting in the family garden and collected water from the stream to hand-wash clothes and dishes. Our dwellings and the surrounding yard were to be kept swept and clean at all times. The boys did most of the heavy and dangerous jobs.

Once our many labours were done, we had our treasured free time to play and explore. In those days of innocence, the biggest drama was wrestling over sweet mangoes that fell to the ground, even when they had been half-eaten by bats. If it wasn't mango wrestling, we might be climbing trees to swing from branch to branch like monkeys. We were never bored. Our creativity was constantly challenged, inventing new and exciting games to keep ourselves occupied.

The highlight of growing up in a traditional village was the ceremonial events. These occasions were frequent and they were the cement that bonded us to our cultural identity. When we had one of these occasions, which are called *fiafia*, they were usually held in our central village field. In those moments I would witness the noble and ancient part of my culture of which I am most proud. The village's young adults would perform traditional dances, girls in beautiful traditional costumes fashioned from flowers and leaves, the guy's in colourful and vibrant lavalavas. Their anointed bodies shone in the bright sun from the coconut oil as they danced energetically in the rituals. Some dances recounted ancient love stories, great battles or moral tales that harked back to ancient times and the legends of Samoan creation. The fire and the slap dance performed by adult males lit up the whole field; the noise resounded like thunder and recalled visions of our ancient warriors preparing to fight. Today these traditional dances are performed mainly for tourists, but in the old days they were a monthly event with deep importance and meaning.

Sport was greatly encouraged, and one of the most eagerly anticipated events was when the two sides of our village held a cricket match. The Samoan version of cricket looked more like a blending of cricket and baseball. The bat was virtually identical to a traditional war club and was often used as such when things became a bit heated. No matter how old or young, brave or terrified, fit or disabled, if you lived on your team's side of the village there was a role to play. If someone was unable to hold the bat or run, they could cheer or make raucous noise to support their team. These games were invariably a chaotic cacophony of dancing, laughter, teasing and yelling.

Although we may appear to have a free and easy going lifestyle, our villages were strictly regulated in many ways. *Sa*, meaning sacred, was used to create clearly defined times for spiritual observance. Each day at 6pm, all villagers were commanded to be quiet and remain in the *fale* praying. A loud gong or bell would herald the commencement and conclusion of this daily observance. Anyone caught breaking this tradition would be fined or punished with unpleasant chores.

Sunday was the day of worship and rest. Children attended an hour of Sunday school and everyone went to church. It was also the only day of the week we were able to dine well. On this special day each week we would be treated to meat or fish, instead of our starchy staples of taro, green bananas or breadfruit cooked with coconut cream. By Saturday we had suffered through six days of starch and more starch washed down with litres of water, so Sunday was always a welcome relief.

Our family and most of our village belonged to the Congregational Christian Church, now called EFKS. It was one of the most influential churches in Samoa and the most traditional. The attractive Salepouae cathedral remains perhaps one of the most imposing buildings in Samoa to this day. It towered over our village and was the centre of community spirit, also serving as a refuge from the devastating cyclones that frequently lashed the islands. The building was a huge brick edifice, its exterior rendered with stucco cement lime-washed a brilliant white. Set into the high walls were huge, beautifully coloured stained glass windows. Inside, grand chandeliers hung resplendently high above the varnished seat rows. Adorning the walls were pictures of Jesus and fresh assorted fragrant flowers. To fill the cavernous void with heavenly sound, a large pipe organ sat strategically on the left-hand side.

As soon as we entered the cathedral, we children were expected to be silent. Our eyes, ears, hearts and minds were required to be fixed on the minister for a full hour. In our village, the congregation supplied the appointed minister and his family with a nice house that the villagers had built for the purpose. As well as receiving free accommodation, the minister and his dependants were fed by families from the congregation in turn. Each family had an assigned day to send breakfast, lunch and dinner all fully prepared. Families also made donations on every second Sunday to the minister to educate his children, buy clothes for his family, and to fund whatever they wanted. The congregation, including my family, had this stupid idea that the more they donated to the minister the more blessings they would get. It didn't seem to be working, because all through my young life I witnessed my family struggle and we kids never had much to eat.

The most important event for us kids was White Sunday, held once a year in October. This was momentous for several reasons. This was the only day of the year when children took centre stage and made speeches during the service instead of the preacher. It was the only day of the year when we would be fed first, receiving the choicest morsels, and wore new clothes.

We girls were trained to be saintly, never to sully our names by talking to strange boys. We were only permitted to talk to close family males, and our hair was cut incredibly short or even shaved to make us as unattractive as possible as we blossomed into young women. Sex was a completely taboo subject and intimacy outside of marriage was severely frowned upon. After dark we were forbidden to walk around without the company of males from our family, and marriage wasn't to be contemplated until we'd reached our twenty-first birthdays. In the years leading up to finding a suitable mate, we were rigorously trained to become a desirable bride and wife. We were taught to plant, cook, wash, iron, weave, fish, prepare the catch for cooking, kill and de-feather chickens and clean slaughtered pig's organs. If we were useless, lazy or discovered not to be virgins before our wedding night, our names would be talked about in a very negative way among his family. Our husband might beat us up with impunity. This was the harsh reality of being a woman in Samoa – and the reason my grandmother insisted I marry a European. She would tell me that I, of all her grandchildren, should never settle for that sort of life.

Chapter 4

The Day My Life Changed

Until I was eight years old, I considered my life to be almost perfect. I was so loved by my grandparents, especially my Tina, that it was impossible to believe anywhere or anyone in the world could be cruel or that people could be evil. When our preacher gave me a sound beating, I believed it was my fault and deserved it. Inexplicably, despite the charmed and enchanting life I saw myself living, one night I woke startled and shaking from a most vivid and terrifying nightmare. I had seen Tina with only one leg and I was trying to carry her to safety. It was not long after that the unthinkable happened. Had it been a premonition or merely a coincidence? Even if it had been a premonition, could I have done anything to thwart the unerring and undeniable hand of fate?

We were fishing in the lagoon, which was entirely normal. As Tina waded around fossicking for whatever she could find on the bottom, she stood on a huge stingray lying hidden in the sand. The creature instantly responded by arching its powerful body and lashing its whip-like tail in fury. This drove its long, wickedly barbed, poison-coated spike deep into Tina's leg. The serenity of my world was shattered in that instant. Tina staggered around in the blood-streaked turbulence before collapsing below the surface, her wounded leg spewing a cloud of blood into the water.

"I am hurt!" she cried, breaking to surface briefly before sinking again.

Tama rushed to her side, scooping her swiftly out of the murky, blood-soaked depths. Placing her in the canoe, he paddled as hard as he could for the shore. My heart was pounding furiously as I put my hand on my Tina's face, assuring her we would soon be home. She looked pale and in great pain. I felt completely helpless and so utterly terrified for her that I almost lost the power of speech. Villagers fishing from the beach had seen the commotion and stood waving and shouting for us to hurry. The bottom of the canoe was a swirling broth of blood and seawater. The day's catch was flopping hopelessly in that bloody soup, gasping for breath. It was a scene of carnage, and it was to herald much worse times to come.

The moment we reached the shore, Tina was hurriedly hoisted out and rushed to our hut. There was no conventional medical care in the village but we used whatever resources and skills we had to treat her. In spite of their best efforts, it didn't take long to realise the traditional Samoan healers treatment of boiling leaves with seawater to try to stop the bleeding and prevent infection was not working. After two long months without proper medical care she was fading away. The leg first become infected, then gangrenous. Six agonising months after the accident, her left leg was amputated up to the knee, saving her life. While in body this kept her with us, her general health and vibrant spirit were already destroyed beyond repair or recognition. She was disabled, homebound and profoundly miserable. From that terrible time on nothing was the same.

Auntie Vaitogi's husband crafted wooden walking sticks for her. She made a valiant effort to recapture her mobility using them, but the deep sores she developed under her armpits soon put an end to that. It was clear the pain was unbearable, and the only way to ease her suffering was to administer medications that often rendered her unconscious for hours at a time. She would become almost comatose to the point where I would rest my ear on her heart just to hear if she was still alive. The grandmother I had known was gone.

One night, I was drifting off to the magical dreamlands of childhood, weary after a happy, active day. I lay on the mat next to Tina in one corner of our *fale* to sleep. I remember with perfect clarity that there was a full moon because I had to drop some of our coconut leaf blinds down to block out the brightness. I kissed my Tina goodnight, but she was already fast asleep. Tama was a heavy sleeper, and because he snored so loudly, he slept right at the other side of the hut, far away from where Tina and I slept. Once Tama lay down, he always started snoring in moments. Unless he was shaken from his slumber, he would remain in a catatonic sleep until morning. Uncle Faalua lived with us in our hut, although we rarely saw much of him after dark. He would often go out at night, returning home late and setting up his bed in a vacant spot to sleep, usually behind Tama or in the centre. This night was different. He slept behind me. It never occurred to me that this was odd, as I'd learned to feel safe surrounded by people who had always loved and protected me.

That night was the beginning of the end of innocence. Suddenly something hard and uncomfortable was being pressed into my back. I tried to move closer to Tina but it was too late. Uncle Faalua's hand clamped hard over my mouth and I heard his voice whispering, "It's all right."

Struggling frantically to escape what was coming my effort was in vain. He was far stronger than a scrawny eight year old and able to wrestle me onto my back with deft ease. As I gazed up with saucer-like terrified eyes, he clamped his leg on me and wrapped his arm over my shoulder. I was pinned and prostrate as he pushed his hand roughly into my cotton handmade underpants. His fingers were hard and callused from work, the nails long, thick and jagged. Tears stung my eyes as he worked his hand into my crotch, digging, gouging and forcing his way between my tightly closed legs. My mind reeled with terror as confusion, pain, shame and disbelief filled my head until it felt like it might burst. My heart was pounding furiously in my heaving chest, it seemed so loud to me I was sure Tina or Tama would hear it and come to my aid. But the only sound was Tama's loud snoring and my world falling around me.

I lay there, numbed and terrified, as his fingers finally tore into my *pipi* (vagina). While he was hurting me, he rubbed his private part on my leg. It was hard and hot. I felt his disgusting hot sweaty body undulating against mine. Repulsed by his foul breath, I could hear him moan as though he was in pain. While still hurting my pipi badly with his cruel hand, his big hard *poki* (penis) just about poked a whole into my tiny top left leg. Of course I had no idea what was going on, and when he suddenly became rigid I thought he might be having a seizure. Trying not to exhale a sound from his mouth, his *poki* grotesquely released hot sticky stuff all over my leg. I could only imagine he had just peed on me.

With his hand still clamped hard over my mouth, he again whispered, "You mention anything to Tina or anybody and I will tell them that you started the whole thing. No one will believe you. Now be my good girl and go to sleep."

After I nodded agreement that I would not say a word, he slowly took his hand off my mouth and then released me to go back to sleep. Out of sheer confusion, I instantly remembered when uncle Faalua used to look out for me when kids picked on me. It was not that long ago he had carried me home in his loving strong arms after the minister beat me. But now my every pore feared him. From the depths of my soul I didn't know existed I cried. While my uncle started to snore happily, the refuge of sleep eluded me. Something was terribly wrong and I did not know how to fix it.

The next morning, my uncle acted as though nothing had happened, but every so often his eyes glared at me to reinforce his warning. He was still all smiles to everyone else, but from then on I didn't trust his feigned pleasantness. Just being around him was a source of constant fear and uncertainty. I made a wish and prayed every night that my Tina would be better again so we could cuddle each other to sleep as we had always done before. With her arms around me at night as we shared our sheet, I was comforted and protected. I prayed and prayed so hard, but no matter how hard I talked to God, he did not seem to hear me.

That first rape occurred on the day of my eighth birthday. Earlier that day, Tina and I had been discussing how to best spend the money Auntie Tilie sent for me from New Zealand. She was there receiving treatment for a breast cancer. I had always wanted an ice cream in a cone. Out of the ten tala ($10), Tina gave me five and sent me to the local shop to buy myself the biggest ice-cream cone possible. She had told me to consume it away from my cousins so they would not see me stuffing myself. With the change, I would buy mutton for dinner for everyone to share as a celebration.

That was the plan, but instead I changed my mind and bought plenty of lollies to the value of my ice cream to share with my cousins. I can't help but smile at the memory of how proud Tina was at my decision. I can remember as though it was yesterday the elation of showing off to my cousins and other kids. My birthday card from Auntie Tilie and the lollies bought with the money she sent were a source of enormous pride for an eight-year-old

Samoan village girl. I had also saved a candy for Uncle Faalua for when he returned from the plantation. He had picked me up and swirled me around for thinking about him. I remember giggling like the little girl I was as he spun me around while my grandparents looked on with pride. My spirit was filled with nothing but love and happiness. He was sticky, smelly, dirty and sweaty, but I did not care.

"You are getting heavy and becoming a big girl," he exclaimed as he laughed with me.

Because I never spoke about that first incident, my uncle knew he was in control. As a confused eight-year-old girl, I really believed his threats. From that awful day on I became his toy, his play thing. Although I was scared and tried to avoid any contact with him, he was watching my every move like a ravening predator. He used every opportunity to come to me, especially when Tina was drugged up. The peace and happiness that had once accompanied my night-time hours were replaced with fear, dread and loathing. There were many, many times when I nearly blurted everything out to Tina, but on every occasion I would lose my voice and my courage along with my rapidly diminishing self-esteem.

To survive the ordeal, my mind created an alter ego. In my mind this other person would step into my body to endure the torment while the real Sieni watched helplessly from a distance – it was a hopeless emotional defence. That imaginary friend became my mask throughout the rest of my life, coming to my rescue whenever I was put into a position of extreme suffering and fear. Sadly, these experiences with my uncle were the first, but not the last, time I would need to deploy this technique.

My Uncle Faalua's nightly visits to touch me while he played with his *poki* became infrequent after we moved to our new hut next to Auntie Sia's house. Auntie Sia produced baby after baby, and for years she was often up at night tending to them. As a result, she almost caught Faalua in the act one night.

She became aware he was unconscionably close to me and screamed across the still, quiet night air, "Why are you sleeping so close to Sieni?"

Angrily, she shone her torch right in his eyes. He was like a rabbit caught in headlights. He feebly replied that he didn't realise, he was just cold and moved closer for warmth, but from then on he was very careful. The next day, Aunty Sia firmly ordered him to sleep on the other side of Tama, not near Tina and I. Being surrounded by so many people made it more difficult for him to molest me, but not impossible. Always he was waiting patiently for an opportunity when I would be alone.

The months following Tina's accident soon turned into a year, and at around that anniversary my beautiful grandmother suffered a minor stroke. As if what she'd suffered wasn't enough, the stroke left her paralysed down one side of her body. She depended on her family for everything. I was nine years old, she was bed-ridden and I became her main carer. Tama did the lifting, but I attended to all her personal care. In our quiet moments together, Tina and I made a pact, solemnly swearing we would always be together, taking care of each other no matter what. We were not allowed to leave each other under any circumstances until the other one was okay. I didn't know then she was more worried my Auntie Tilie would come for me on my next birthday and she may never see me again. On the other hand, she didn't know my world had already crumbled around me.

I walked around seemingly normal, but inside I felt dirty and deformed. For eight years, I was kept safe and happy in the cocoon of my grandmother's love, and now she was no longer able to take away my fear and pain. In the ultimate role reversal, it was I who had to care for Tina; it was not about me anymore. It was the first time in my life I had to defend myself and to learn about my position in other people's lives. I had to learn very quickly what I needed to do to survive.

Chapter 5

My Loyal Friend

While life continued with the strict and busy routine of our family, the village children were happily playing as always. It was my daily routine that had changed so traumatically. Due to the demands of caring for Tina, I often missed school and exam times. Other members of the family claimed they didn't have the stomach to clean Tina's soiled clothes or deal with the mess she made. One day I could be cleaning diarrhoea and the next, because Tina could not move around anymore, she suffered badly with agonising constipation. She would cry, begging me to help her. With no knowledge of how to ease her suffering, I used my fingers to gouge it out from her. The smell of faeces on my fingernails could not be removed for days no matter how hard I tried to scrub them. My relationship with Tina had morphed from a loving mother/daughter connection, one where I would rush home from school to be impatiently scooped into loving arms and covered with kisses, to one where Tina was the patient and I was a very young and inexperienced nurse. When I made it to school I usually fell asleep from being up all night tending to my grandmother. Socialising with other children became a distant memory. Even visits to Auntie Tilie became infrequent.

I missed the treats and distraction those visits provided, so when my Auntie turned up in her fancy car after my tenth birthday I was close to euphoric. Moreover, when I heard she'd appeared to take me with her into the bosom of her estate, my heart leapt with such joy I think it nearly jumped clean out of my chest. Not surprisingly, no one in my family appeared pleased – they would have to take over my chores. Given what I know now, what followed is rather surprising. Tina begged my Auntie to allow me to decide. In essence, I was advised that Auntie Tilie was offering to take over my care because Tina was too unwell to be my guardian, but the final decision was to be mine. This was a pivotal moment in my life, even on the face of it, but there was much more to it than I was being told.

"For how long will I be with Auntie Tilie?" I asked.

"For good," Auntie Tilie firmly replied.

I tried to appear composed, but my heart was pounding with excitement. There in front of me were the two women who meant more to me than anyone else on earth, asking me to make a choice between them. On the one hand, there was the rather mysterious but rich benefactor whom I called Auntie Tilie who promised to open up heaven for me. There would be no more hunger, fear or abuse. In its place would be everything a little girl desired. On the other hand, there was a very sick old woman whom I nursed and cared for. My Tina was no longer able to protect me and she could do little to further my life.

I looked over at my Tina as her eyes filled with tears of remorse and anguish. She gave me the most terrifying look I had ever seen; it was as though it came from deep within her, as if she was slowly dying and my leaving would end her there and then. I looked to my rich Auntie impatiently waiting for me to decide. As much as I wanted to live with Auntie Tilie for a better life, I could not possibly abandon my grandmother. I couldn't blink away that look she gave me from my mind. I had made a promise to my Tina that I would never leave her as long as she needed me.

I could not let her down. With a sad resignation, I knew there really was no choice.

Although Auntie Tilie was very disappointed, she understood my sacrifice and agreed I could remain until Tina "got better." After my Auntie left, I wanted so much for my grandmother to get well and be happy like before. I began to fantasise on how wonderful it would be if my grandparents moved with me to live at my rich Auntie's farm. But Tina never recovered. I felt so alone, and my grandmother's suffering became so confronting and heartbreaking that sometimes I silently lamented the decision I'd made. Perhaps the one benefit was the constant demands of caring for Tina kept Uncle Faalua away. Tina did not sleep well anymore and was always up at odd hours of the night complaining and crying in pain. Her wretched circumstances were compounded by the fact that her medications became too expensive for our family to purchase, and my poor grandmother suffered enormously without them.

One day when I was feeling particularly sorry for myself, my favourite uncle, Fai, turned up with a piglet for me. He thought I deserved a little friend to cheer me up. The piglet was grey with five black dots scattered all over his body. I thought he was the cutest thing I'd ever seen. My new friend was named Puka (Samoan for "fat") and he became the ideal distraction from my daily routine.

Little Puka grew up thinking I was his mother and I treated him accordingly. I would talk to him and share my food with him. He slept under our hut's rough wooden floor directly beneath where I slept so we could hear each other and be comforted. I would say good night and Puka would squeal back with excitement. He knew when I was up tending to Tina and he would accompany me in the dark during the wee hours of the night to empty Tina's potty in a nearby bush. His presence and his snuffling, grunting noises as he scurried around me gave me courage when I was frightened in the dark. That little piglet followed me around everywhere. I no longer felt I was missing the company of the other children I had no time to play with. Puka filled every void in my life. After Tina was cleaned and fed, he and I would go for our little walk around the house or I would read to him under a breadfruit tree while he listened intently, gazing up adoringly with his little piggy eyes. He thought he was human, frequently making me laugh with his little antics. We made each other happy and I truly loved him.

Two years passed quickly with the never-ending drudgery and routine. Puka was certainly no piglet any longer and Tina faded gradually but unerringly further into oblivion. On the fourth time she was admitted to hospital, her coffin had already been built by Auntie Vaitogi's husband; it hung like an ominous omen from the ceiling of our hut. The family suspected Tina didn't have much time left in this world.

My only escape to anything that resembled sanity was to focus on my pig rather than dwell on the unthinkable. I really missed Puka when I did end up going to school or stayed at the hospital with Tina. Tama always cared for him when I was not around, but we both missed each other horribly when separated. I couldn't wait to get home and tell him about my adventures or sorrows and he always seemed to understand. Perhaps it was the imagination of a child within me who was crying out for sympathy. Either way, Puka always grunted or looked surprised or happy in all the right places when I told him my stories. My family often teased me about this odd relationship I had with a pig but that didn't bother me in the slightest. In my darkest hours, at times of pure loneliness, resentment and frustration, Puka was the one I could turn to. He would put his wet, dirty snout on my lap, lavishing me with emotional comfort and unconditional love.

During one of my visits to Tina in hospital, I was lying beneath my grandmother's bed on the cool concrete floor listening to the sounds of the sick and dying around me. Needing to escape, at least in mind if not in body, I drifted into thoughts of my Puka. I wondered if he was missing me. I wondered if Tama had fed him. Thinking of him helped take away my fear and uncertainty. I do not know what time I dozed off, but I remember waking up feeling tired and exhausted. The noise and the banging of the patients' morning breakfast had stirred me from my slumber. Realising how late it was, I tried to creep out quietly so the nurses would not see me. I was not supposed to sleep in the hospital, but Tina was not doing well and had begged me to stay with her.

Most families of patients made beds under the nearby trees to be close to their loved ones. The hospital provided medical care plus basic foods, and the family supplied all other needs during the stay. I was only eleven, and it was not safe for girls to be sleeping outside alone, or in the hospital for that matter. The wards were all open, with no outside walls or windows. There were storm covers, but they were only put down when it was rainy or windy. When it was hot and humid, those covers always stayed up so that a breeze could trickle around the ward. This environment meant that anyone could see patients on their deathbeds, along with all the other activities in the hospital.

Stiffly standing to greet the dawning light, I realised that Tina was not on her bed and her breakfast was untouched. Panic stricken, I started searching for her. As I recall, the duty nurse was not helpful at all.

"She might have died last night and has been taken to the morgue. I will find out for you when I am free," she yelled in the most callous, matter-of-fact manner before nonchalantly carrying on with her duties.

"No," I gasped. Tina couldn't be dead. I knew she was sick, very sick, but it was impossible to think she had died while I was fast asleep under her bed. The shock of the insensitive manner in which the nurse had spoken to me struck me like a knife. I collapsed onto Tina's bed, sobbing so uncontrollably I had to bite into the pillow so my cries would not shake the hospital foundations. My heart was aching. I did not know what to do next. I wondered whether she had needed me during her last hour and I had not been able to hear her. My wailing alerted the staff, and mercifully this resulted in locating Tina.

"She had a stroke at three o'clock this morning," I was told. "So she was taken to intensive care."

"Is she still alive? Can I see her?" I asked impatiently.

The nurse told me that my grandmother was still alive but was not doing too well. She suggested that I rush home to inform my family.

"Children are barred from the intensive care unit," she snapped abruptly before simply walking off with no hint of concern for my sorrow.

Still shaking, I sat on Tina's hospital bed for a little while, trying to hold myself together and calm my racing thoughts. I dried my eyes and timidly looked around the hospital ward to see some of the patients watching me. I felt foolish, but that moment of intense grief was emotionally exhausting. The threat of losing someone so dear to me was so terrifying it had caused a complete meltdown.

Recalling the events of the night before, Tina was weak and fatigued. She held my hand and thanked me for everything, as though she was saying goodbye. I stroked her fine white hair, telling her she was going to be okay and that I would not know what to do if she was no longer around. She started to cry, but through her tears she managed to instruct me that no matter what happened I should go to New Zealand, where I would marry a *Palagi* and have a good life. At one point, she seemed to be trying to tell me something about Auntie Tilie and her farm, but apparently she changed her mind at the last moment. Nonetheless, her insistence for me to leave Samoa confused me.

"You must never ever go to live with your Auntie Tilie," she pleaded.

Our conversation had become deep and dark, making me uncomfortable and Tina upset. I eventually changed the subject to Puka.

"Tina, I am terrified that one day they will ask me to have my pig killed for a funeral or something. You and Puka are the most important things in my life," I told her. Tina assured me that Tama would never approve it so I should not worry.

Before I left the hospital that morning, I quickly gobbled Tina's untouched breakfast and took the slice of bread, hiding it in the pocket of my dress. It was for Puka. My two bus rides home were long and tedious, but I knew Puka would be waiting to comfort me and delighted to receive his treat.

Finally, I reached the path that led to the family's area and then the world stopped. I could hear a terrible screaming. It was horrible. I knew that sound; it was the unmistakable, grotesque, ear-piercing, soul-wrenching sound of a pig being slaughtered. I was nauseous, dizzy and terrified all in the same instant. Running as though my life depended on it, I came around the corner of the bush that obscured my view. There in front of me was Puka, on his back, his legs bound, lying and struggling for his life. Across his throat, crushing it, was a stout branch. Four children sat on each side attempting to strangle my friend to death. Their weight alone was not sufficient for the task at hand and Puka had no intention of giving up without a fight. With each of his valiant struggles, my beloved Puka managed to gulp fresh breath into his lungs.

"Get off him," I screamed. "That's my pet! He's my friend!"

The children found this funny. My heartfelt pleas only served to make them rock harder, taunting me and causing more distress to my Puka. I turned to Tama standing nearby, shouting at him to help, to have pity, to make them stop. Tama tried to comfort me by telling me that it was the family's turn to feed the minister and they did not have anything else to offer.

"I can go to Auntie Tilie and get some money and food for the offering. Please, please not my pet. He is my friend and I need him," I argued desperately.

I saw Puka's bulging eyes staring at me in desperation and pain, pleading with me to help him. Feeling absolutely hopeless and in a hysterical mess, I threw myself to the ground, drew out the piece of bread from my pocket and tried to show him that I had not left him, nor had I forgotten about him. This would be the last time we would look at each other and that look of horror in his eyes haunts me to this day.

Tama dragged me away, holding me so I could not see, and ordered Uncle Faalua to cut my pig's throat. I struggled to break free, but when he finally let go I turned around to see blood gushing from Puka's neck. His tongue lolled out to the side of his mouth with white foamy flecks covering it. His terrified and pained eyes were about to pop out of his head. It was the most ferocious and cruel way to die. I was overwhelmed with a pain and grief I could not imagine would be equalled had I just watched Tina die.

"I'm so sorry, Puka. I am so sorry I could not save you," I sobbed over my friend's limp but still twitching carcass. An awful emptiness filled me. It was a chilling, sickening emptiness that brought with it a pain from which I truly believed would be without end.

A big *umu* (a traditional hot rock oven in the ground) was prepared. Fire heated the lava rocks that would cook meat, vegetables and whatever else was available. Burning wood and embers were heaped onto the rocks until they were heated to temperature. The rocks were then spread out over the food to be cooked that was wrapped in banana fronds and placed in the middle. More hot rocks were subsequently placed over the food before more banana leaves were piled up everywhere to trap the heat in.

I fled into the bush nearby, sobbing my heart out, trying not to think of his internal organs being removed and his stomach filled with hot rocks. Witnessing the brutal murder of my Puka was more shocking and horrific than anything I'd experienced before or could even imagine. Those violent and vicious images incessantly loomed before my vision. Even if I closed my eyes tightly, there was no escaping them. Each time they loomed up in front of me it served to renew and intensify my pain. I vividly recalled that it was the same minister who nearly beat me to death when I was seven that was the reason my dearest Puka was murdered. In that moment, I learned to hate and I learned the meaning of despair.

Chapter 6

Tina's Death

A year had passed since Puka was murdered and I was six months away from my thirteenth birthday. We all marvelled at the fact that Tina was still with us. Even though her condition continued to deteriorate with each day, she had successfully managed to cheat death more times than I could count. Her coffin had been prepared for some time, and as the day was certainly drawing, her grave was prepared near our hut. Tina had requested to be buried close to us, to be close to us even in death.

Life became harder and lonelier for me. I missed my Puka terribly. I was bitter and resentful, and if not for my grandmother, I would have certainly run away long ago. There would be no forgiving myself if I had left Tina before the end; my wistful notions of escape were moot. Tina and I had made that pact not to leave until we knew that the other was going to be okay. I was far from okay and Tina was dying, but until there was an end one way or another I was going nowhere.

It was March 1974. Tina's extended family from all over the island were called together to say their last goodbyes. They would stand in solemn vigil, awaiting her last breath as prayers were chanted and preparations were made. No longer capable of eating, Tina was sustained by family member's gently spooning water into her mouth over her dry, cracked lips. She lay there motionless as the pupils of her eyes grew a little smaller each day. This formerly vibrant woman lay helpless as her life force slowly passed from this world to the next. She was barely breathing and for the most part not conscious of her surroundings. The end was near.

Mourners packed tightly around her, talking to her, sobbing, wailing and gripping her skeletal hand when it was their turn. I found the entire spectacle unbearable. Although I had been her primary carer, I had to slip away to look for Tama. My grandfather was being comforted by his nephew Pao Salu in his *fale*. Pao was the orator *matai* of our extended family, and grandfather had come to depend on him. He was the only child of Tama's favourite older brother, who had died at the age of fifty. Tama took his brother's son under his wing from then on. At a time like this, it was fitting that Pao was the person Tama would turn to. As I entered Pao's *fale*, Tama's eyes met mine with profound sadness.

"No matter what happens, we'll still have each other," he whispered sadly, his tears wetting my hair as he hugged me close.

We both knew we were about to lose someone precious to us both. Our worlds would never be the same again. As we clung to each other like frightened children lost in a dark wood, a shrill scream jarred me from his embrace. It was Tina screaming, calling out my name just once, "Sieni!"

Something in the frantic tone and power of her delivery chilled me. I ran back to our hut, pushing through throngs of mourners to kneel at my beloved Tina's side. The family all pulled back as one, shocked that someone who was unable to speak a single word for weeks had the strength to call out my name. They watched on, humbled by the power of the bond between us.

Softly clutching her hand, I stammered, "Tina, I am here."

She attempted to speak but no words would come. I looked into her eyes. They were unseeing and without focus, staring off into a distant place only the dying can see. A tear slid down one cheek. I felt she wanted to say goodbye. It was time for her to leave, but our pact could not be completed until she knew I would be all right. It was time to let her rest from all the pain and suffering she endured for the last four years.

I rested my cheek on hers and whispered, "You can go now, Tina. I'll be fine. Thank you for loving me."

Weakly she squeezed my hand in reply, struggled to draw in a final staggered breath, held it for a moment and exhaled for the last time. A surge of loss and loneliness swept through me like an arctic abyss. Flinging myself onto her, I grasped onto the final warmth of her body, unaware I was screaming hysterically. The pain was as intense as the shock, horror and devastation I'd experienced at witnessing Puka's brutal and unexpected murder, even though I'd known Tina's time was coming. My heart broke into million pieces as I wept by her bedside until my aunts finally wrenched me away. A great collective wail arose when the family realised that Tina had departed. A powerful but loving soul had left this life – and I felt I had lost my entire world.

Tina's funeral would be the next day; there was no time to waste. Most cultures that lived in or originated from hot climates have very swift burial traditions, for probably obvious reasons. Amid the wailing and the mourning there was the hurried bustle of organising the preparations. The large network of extended family had to be informed; money and fine mats needed to be gathered to pay for the feasting, as well as gifts for the many dignitaries who descended like vultures at these events. Mountains of food needed to be supplied; livestock would be slaughtered to feed our village residents, the *matais* representing villages from all over the island and representatives of the churches. Traditional

Samoan funerals could last for weeks after the body was interred. More would be spent on Tina after her death than was ever spent on her while she lived. It was a matter of family pride, the culture of *Fa'a Samoa*. To fail in this task would bring great dishonour to the entire *aiga*.

My grandmother's body was washed, perfumed and dressed in a beautiful white outfit my mother had sent from New Zealand especially for her funeral. It had been stored for a year for her to wear on this day. Her straight white hair had been trimmed to her shoulders and combed to nicely frame her face. Tina was placed on a cotton mattress and covered with new white lace sheets topped with the finest traditional mats. Prepared for her journey, she lay in state in one corner of Pao's *fale*, her varnished shiny brown coffin awaiting her in the opposite corner. Ministers and choirs from various congregations arrived to sing hymns and offer prayers as they paid their respects.

When I was ready, I crept next to Tina, wondering at how serene and striking she appeared. As the singer's voices rose and swelled powerfully in the *fale*, the resonance carried my spirit to a place of sheer melancholy as the finality of it all set in. In a few hours Tina's body would be buried. This would be the last time I would be close to my Tina. Guilt gushed over me like a massive tidal wave as I remembered that when Puka was killed I had momentarily wished that my grandmother was dead. If she had been dead, I would not have been away from Puka and could have saved his life. I also blamed Tina for all my consequent hurt and suffering, and hated her sometimes for not getting better so we could be happy again like we used to be. I wept inconsolably, quietly apologising, telling her that I did not mean to think those terrible thoughts and that I did love her until the end.

When the last choir and the multitudes of mourners finally departed, I was exhausted and bereft. My eyes could no longer open properly. I gave Tina a kiss on her cheek and curled up next to her cold, stiff corpse. I wanted to be close to her for as long as I could.

That night, safe in the sanctuary of a dream, Tina came to me. This was like no dream I had ever experienced before. It was so clear and vivid that I could see, touch and smell the dreamscape. It was as if I had travelled to another world. Everything seemed solid and real, colours and lights were vibrant, the air was brisk and invigorating. I stood in the middle of a field of flowers without end. I sensed someone was behind me and spun around. It was Tina. I knew it was her, though she looked much younger. She was glowingly beautiful, somehow lovelier than she had ever looked during her harsh life on earth. Her eyes held the diamond sparkle of the sea under glistening rays of sun. Her long black hair cascaded down her shoulders as she tossed her head back to laugh at the look of astonishment on my face. The air was full of butterflies, similar to the beauties I had seen at Auntie Tilie's farm. They fluttered colourfully in dazzling display, stopping only to alight on the multi-hued blooms and then dart back up again. Tina took my hand and we began to walk through the field, but I struggled to break free. I wanted to chase the butterflies. I wanted to explore this amazing place but Tina held me firmly.

"Sieni, the flowers need the butterflies to survive, just as the butterflies need the flowers to live. They come together and cannot live without each other; they are as one," she explained to me.

As we walked, Tina held my hand and I bounced up and down, frolicking happily until she abruptly stopped. She let go of my hand and held me firmly by both shoulders, looked straight into my eyes and her words penetrated my soul.

"Sieni, you can carry on walking. I can go no further," she said, smiling.

"Where are you going? Why can't I come with you?" I pleaded. "You promised you wouldn't leave me."

"I will always be with you, watching over you even if you can't see me. If you keep walking further on, you will come across some amazing things. Remember whatever happens, things aren't always what they may seem," Tina proclaimed prophetically.

"If I can't come with you, why can't you come back with me?"

"I promise I will be here when you return. I have something to do here and you over there. So keep walking, my darling, and be happy."

Once she'd uttered those words, Tina turned me around to face the direction I was meant to go. I looked back just to tell her I was going and that I loved her, but she had already gone. I could not possibly leave without saying goodbye, so I started calling her name frantically.

Tama shook me. "Sieni, Sieni, wake up, it's all right. You must have had a bad dream."

I rubbed my eyes briskly, trying to clear my mind. The light was still on and the first thing I saw was Tina's body. She had 20-cent coins on her eyes. Unexpectedly, a warm sensation washed over me. It was as though I knew without a doubt that my grandmother was happy and at peace. A relief enveloped me at the knowledge she was not suffering any longer. I felt she wanted me to forgive her for leaving, but I also felt she had remained until I was ready to let her go. I was indeed ready to start the next chapter of my life from the day she said goodbye.

Tina's service and burial were planned for 10am the following day. Her body was placed in her coffin, which was shouldered by the men of her family to the church cathedral. There it was placed on the altar a few feet away from the minister's pulpit, surrounded by flower arrangements prepared by the congregation. Apart from my mother and Uncle Siaega in New Zealand, all Tina's family were there. Her six other children and her many grandchildren sat on the front row seats. Other members of her extended family sat behind us. I didn't realise Tina had such a big family until she died. Some of these people never visited her when she was sick.

Once the service concluded, her casket was carried back to our home where Tina's body would be buried. We followed in sombre procession to the grave that had been patiently awaiting her internment. It was time for her body to be committed to the earth. In the instant the men started to scoop soil onto her coffin, the wail of mourners pierced the morning air. I wept quietly among the family, the whiff of Tina's body odour suddenly occupying my attention. These were the scents I had been breathing in every day for the last four years. Perhaps incongruously, a sense of pride took precedence over some of my grief. I knew I had done the very best I was capable of doing for my grandmother while she was alive. For that I was happy. As my Tina used to say, "Love and compassion are not just words; actions can go a long way – all the way to God's feet."

Auntie Tilie had come to pay her respects and donate money at the funeral. She also took the opportunity to remind me that she was still waiting for my arrival. I promised her I was coming to live with her before the end of the year, but I wanted to complete my last year at primary school. I explained I had missed so much schooling when Tina was ill that I needed to catch up with as few disturbances as possible. Auntie Tilie readily understood and accepted my explanation and even gave me the funds I needed for my expenses.

"I will wait for you eagerly," she said, smiling at me. Never could I have imagined what lay behind that smile.

Chapter 7

Time to Live

After Tina's passing, I moved in with Auntie Sia, her husband and their young children. Tama continued to sleep in our *fale* with Uncle Faalua. Not long after this arrangement was in place, my mother arrived unexpectedly from New Zealand with my elder sister Agnes. Although dressed in her fancy New Zealand school uniform, Agnes showed every sign of unhappiness on her face. Explaining the reason for their rushed and unexpected arrival, mother announced that Agnes was uncontrollable and rebelling against her.

"She needs to find out how hard life is in Samoa," she spat venomously. "She needs to appreciate her living standards and the benefits of being educated in New Zealand. I am leaving her here. Use her as your slave," my mother ordered Tama.

Although Agnes couldn't speak Samoan, she understood everything our mother was saying. She threw an angry and disapproving glance at her but held her tongue. Despite my misgivings about the sudden arrival of my mother, I was reminded of Tina's instructions. "When I am gone, I would like you to go to New Zealand to your mother without delay. I don't want you to go to Tilie's."

Waiting until there was an appropriate moment, I spoke with my mother about the possibility of returning to New Zealand with her. Moreover, I told her everything, including the nauseating detail of her youngest brother's constant physical abuse of me. Had the world opened up and swallowed me whole, I could not have been more shocked by her reaction. She flatly refused to hear any more, and she didn't want me to discuss it with anybody else. In her eyes, my role in life was to take care of Tama, nothing more and nothing less. Could these really be the words of my biological mother? Not only did she not want to know what had occurred, she made no attempt to stop the abuse. She simply shrugged it off and told me that it happened in families; it was not the end of the world.

I was in such shock that any human being, never mind a mother, could talk like that. She was brushing off my abuse and pain as if I had just told her I had nits in my hair. I did not know the woman that well, in fact not at all, but her comment brought back a few horrible memories. One was when she was outraged with my grandmother for recording her as my mother on my birth certificate so I could attend school. I knew what it was like to be in a loving relationship with a grandmother, but I had no idea what it felt like to be loved by my maternal mother. I knew all of my aunties loved their children and I believe they would die for any of them.

It was only when mother left a week later to go back home that my sister Agnes opened up to us. I found myself being further shocked, which I would have considered impossible, to hear the truth about my sister's abusive and miserable life with her parents. At least it partially explained my mother's reaction to me, not that the explanation helped much.

"I wish she didn't take me to New Zealand. I would have been better off if I stayed in Samoa," my sister blurted out to her aunties.

During the time Agnes stayed in Samoa we bonded well. I came to really love my sister during those months and wanted to be close to her, so when our mother calmed down and called her back to New Zealand six months later I was faced with another loss.

Feeling wounded, abandoned and unsure about my future, I was back to my initial plan. Why shouldn't I go to Auntie Tilie's and have the life I had always dreamed of? How could anyone expect me to refuse such an opportunity? How could my grandmother, who was supposed to love me so much, ever think that I did not deserve to be with my wealthy Auntie and live in her mansion? I saw no obvious reason for Tina's concerns. In all the years I was growing up, one of Tina's annual routines was to take me to Auntie Tilie's farm. She encouraged me to go even when I complained about the long, hot walk, saying, "Come on, Sieni. Your Auntie will have all those wonderful gifts for you. Think of the delicious food. She treats you like a princess."

Auntie Tilie had always showed us kindness, giving us much-needed money, food and a few of the luxuries of life we could never have afforded on our own. Without her constant help, I would have had no money for school fees or books. Each year, Auntie Tilie would arrive regally in her chauffeured car to bring my Christmas presents, or my expensive pretty dresses for White Sundays. I was the only little girl in the village to have dolls, balls, shoes and beautiful dresses from the shops. Children's birthdays were never celebrated in any way in the village, but Auntie Tilie always remembered mine. Children of my village were envious whenever she visited me. And who could blame them? Although my mother's sisters were kind to me, they had their own large families to care for. Understandably, I was not their responsibility, and providing for me took away from their own children. They were as good as they were able and I loved them all dearly, but none could offer me the future that would be laid out in Auntie Tilie's paradise estate. How often I would fantasize about a wonderful and happy life there. Frequently I found myself formulating a plan to run away without hurting my Tama, but even from beyond the grave, Tina's earnest protest would ring in my ears.

Uncle Faalua wasn't getting any better with the passage of time – if anything, he was becoming impatient with my calculated avoidance of him. Never had I imagined I wasn't the only member of the family he was abusing. I may have been forced to grow up fast, but in reality I was still a child and still innocent in many ways. On the day my Auntie Vaitogi strode into Auntie Sia's house with a thick green branch clutched like a sword in her shaking hands.

Without word of warning, as we all sat eating our dinner, she unexpectedly and savagely lashed out at my bad uncle with all her might. While she flailed and smashed the branch into his cringing form, she screamed out that he was interfering with her second eldest daughter. Auntie Vaitogi proceeded to thrash out a sound beating to her youngest brother, stopping only when the thick supple branch finally shattered into a fibrous tangle. Throughout the well-deserved punishment, the slithering snake of my nightmares denied the accusation. Tama did not believe him, commanding him not to move or he would help Auntie Vaitogi with the flogging.

Every fibre of my being wanted to yell out that Uncle Faalua had done exactly the same thing to me, yet I remained impotently mute. Stunned, perhaps by the ferocity of Auntie Vaitogi's rage, I suddenly felt sorry for him. I could not understand those feelings, because even as I experienced them I simultaneously wished each blow he received would kill him instantly.

After Aunty Vaitogi left, disgusted and exhausted, Tama scolded Faalua, warning him if anything like that happened again he would be disowned and exiled from the family and the village.

It was then I thought I was safe. I could not have been more wrong.

It was only a few nights later, as I walked home from visiting my cousins at Auntie Vaitogi's, that Uncle Faalua lay in ambush. He pounced on me with all the insane savagery of a starving carnivore who had just escaped from a prolonged and tormented incarceration. His hands clamped tightly over my mouth as he dragged me struggling, terrified and sobbing to a nearby bush at the back of our neighbour's pigsty.

"If you tell and Tama comes for me, I will pick up a machete and cut his head off," he warned me.

That statement sucked out any fight in me. The thought of my grandfather's head lying on the ground staring at me froze me in terror. I did not care what my uncle did to me. I would willingly give up my body to save my grandfather, not doubting for one moment that Faalua's threat was in earnest.

Up until this encounter, the penetration had been with his fingers, but this time he wasn't stopping there. As my uncle thrust inside me repeatedly, I felt as though I was lying there in a conscious coma. My body was being tortured but I was not present. This well-practiced technique notwithstanding, I couldn't deny the overwhelming feelings of hopelessness, hatred, fear, shame and disgust – until there was nothing. When he finished with me I was left with such a feeling of nothingness that I could no longer connect with the deeper inner me. Inside I was crying, but even my tears would not flow to release the pain. Bruised, bleeding, in agony, I slowly dragged myself up.

Once more Faalua reminded me of the consequences of exposing him. I was permitted to leave but my legs wouldn't move. I stood stunned, paralysed and alone for a good time before the power of movement returned to my body. Even then I wandered aimlessly, trying to gather my shattered thoughts.

When I finally made it home and Tama scolded me for being late. I was incapable of responding, much less of offering any reason or apology for my tardiness. I hated myself to my very core. There had been an opportunity to oust my bad uncle from our family home during his justly deserved beating, yet I had chosen not to. In the shame and confusion following the aftermath of my first full rape, incredibly I discovered I was asking myself if I secretly wanted it. Why else would I not have spoken up when I had the opportunity?

My disgrace overpowered me. I no longer believed I was a worthwhile girl with any hope at all. It was as though my spirit had left me, taking all my stamina and dignity with it. I felt betrayed by my grandmother. She had said she would watch me from a distance and protect me; she had lied to me. I felt obliged to protect Tama, not least of which was because if anything happened to him it would be a death sentence for me as well. To remain meant living under the constant threat of daily rape and torture. Leaving meant deserting my beloved Tama.

Samoa has been and remains a devout Christian country, filled with love, tempered with discipline. Marring this piety, the dark curse of incest was an evil infection in many families. When the worst happened, averting the tarnishing of the family name became more important than justice for the victim. Pride and family honour took priority over any other consideration. For this reason, incest was able to continue. This code of silence protected and emboldened the guilty as it punished innocent victims in a manner only those wronged could fully appreciate. I had seen many cases in my village alone of little girls being sent away to never been seen again when they fell pregnant by an immediate family member. After witnessing my own family mock and revile our neighbour's pregnant teenager, I had little faith that a good outcome would await me in a similar circumstance.

The next morning, without hesitation, remorse or thinking through any future plans I awoke, dressed in my school uniform and walked purposefully to Auntie Tilie's farm. I did not talk to Tina's grave as I had done every morning prior, neither did I pause to say goodbye to Tama, my friends or anyone else in my family. I did not even glance over my shoulder as I left. I was going to my new life; the past was dead.

Chapter 8

Arriving at My Dream Life

As I trudged to Auntie Tilie's estate, I fantasised I was escaping to the Garden of Eden, a place filled with perfection – all a young girl could wish for. I counted myself the luckiest girl in the whole country. I was happy to the point of euphoria and ecstasy. The weight of the world had just been lifted from my young shoulders. I felt avenged that the village part of my life no longer existed. I was positively convinced that once I entered paradise everything was going to be sublime for me. I was going to be protected and saved.

It was an overcast day and severe thunderstorms were predicted. By the time I arrived at the rough road to Auntie's farm it was raining. This was the first time I had walked to the property unaccompanied by an older member of my family. As I approached the first gate, an old woman headed towards me from the opposite direction, burdened with a heavy load of coconut leaves. She asked me where I was going. I had never met or seen this lady before, but as I was not from this area I thought little of it.

"To my Auntie Tilie's place," I answered politely.

Without stopping, she called to me to hurry because a big storm was coming and to be very cautious. "I wouldn't go there if I were you. That house is not what it seems. Be very careful," she warned with an expression of concern. I shrugged her caution away, just another crazy old lady.

It was a regular working day, so vehicles were coming and going, meaning the first gate was wide open. This was a good omen, I considered cheerfully. I did not have to holler out to the guard and wait to gain entry. As I'd done a hundred times before, I trotted through that gate with a song in my head and hope in my heart, when quite unexpectedly I felt apprehensive. I was suddenly scared of the unknown, worried about my family's reaction when they found out I was gone, fearful of what the old lady had warned me about. The profusion of conflicting emotions froze my progress. I could not go on. Pausing to rest and reflect, I noticed what I presumed to be Auntie's workers toiling nearby, waving to me as if they were welcoming me. I remember thinking it was very unusual that they were dressed in fine clothes, as if they were going to town rather than grubbing in the fields. With a smile and renewed courage I waved back, stood on recovered firm legs and proceeded onwards with confidence. When I noticed the guard unlocking the second gate and heading towards me I took this as a positive sign of recognition. I knew this old man well. He had been working for Auntie Tilie for years and felt more like a trusted member of the family. His name was Mase, a gentle, kindly old man from the local village.

"What happened to you?" he asked, looking at me in my school clothes.

"Nothing," I sheepishly replied. "By the way, why are the workers dressed up today? Why are they not wearing working clothes?"

He gave me a puzzled look, as if he did not really understand my question. "The people working down there on that side of the fence," I added, pointing at the direction I just came from.

"There are no people working there. They are all in the main compound field," Mase replied, closing the gate behind us. As he led me towards the main house, he threw a glance in my direction as though I had sunstroke and lost my senses.

"The mistress isn't in a very pleasant mood today," he warned me. "I should be wary and be on my best behaviour if I were you."

I had never seen Auntie Tilie in an unpleasant mood so I did not understand exactly what the warning was about. As I expected, she was thrilled to see me. In fact, she was ecstatic and proud that I had come to her without asking consent from my family. It didn't take long, in fact no time at all, for Auntie Tilie to start criticising them, frequently reminding me they were poor and that my grandmother had not kept her side of the bargain to bring me to her on my tenth birthday.

"I hope you know that Mele was only looking after you for money," she sneered.

Defending my grandmother, I told Auntie that I wanted to look after my Tina, explaining (as though she didn't know) that she had been terminally ill for a long time. Nevertheless, the past was the past and best left there. I promised my aunty that I was there forever from this day forth and I would repay her kindness in any way she needed. That gave our conversation a deeper meaning.

Her apparently happy mood made me feel welcome. In an instant any misgivings and anxiety about the uncertain future I faced vanished. I was still fragile and emotionally damaged by the abuse, but I used all the strength I could muster to try slowing my racing heart as we talked. The past was gone, I didn't want it clouding my new life. The last thing I wanted was for my benefactor and saviour to suspect there was something wrong with me; I was terrified of rejection. In my mind, I thought that if she found out I was not a clean girl, she might not want me and send me back to my family. I smiled when she smiled and laughed when she laughed, even though all I wanted to do was to flood the estate with my pathetic tears. Ultimately, I wanted so much for someone to wrap their arms around me to assure me that everything was going to be okay, that I was going to be safe and protected, and that no one was ever going to scare me or hurt me again. I would have done and said almost anything to please or appease her. I longed for Auntie to stand up and give me a hug, to suck out all the bad things that had happened, to reinvigorate my heart with beautiful new feelings. Instead, she gave me the rules of her palace. She ordered me not to talk to anybody there apart from her and Uncle Bentzen.

"The staff are here to work, not to be gossiped with," she told me.

She also warned me that I was forbidden to touch or go near the firearms in the house, as they would always be loaded and dangerous. After these and a few other important rules were given to me, she showed me to my nicely furnished bedroom downstairs and ordered one of the maids to fetch me something to eat. This, I hoped and believed, was the beginning of the perfect life I had longed for.

I had not visited Auntie's farm during Tina's last year or the year following her death. It was only after I moved in that I noticed how much had changed. The inside of the house was not how I remembered it. The massive open plan living area had become an office and bedrooms for Auntie and her husband, Bentzen. Auntie's single bed was near the windows on the side closest to the kitchen and the back door. My bedroom was just across from hers. As soon as my door opened, Auntie's bed was the first thing I would see. Bentzen's bed was nearer to the front door and opposite the second bedroom. The numerous clocks, placed and hung willy-nilly all over the sitting room, were still there. I used to amuse myself by counting them when I was a little girl. The clocks made their own cacophony when they all struck simultaneously throughout the house. The beautiful, see-through satin and lace curtains I had admired had been replaced by dark, plain-coloured materials. The house appeared sad, broken and bereft of its former welcoming appeal. Auntie also looked worn out, drained and fatigued. She had elephantiasis and waddled about in pain, her massively swollen legs bandaged from knees to toes. Her legs had become so huge they were almost wider than her torso.

As the predicted storm hit with heavy driving rain, the workers were taken home earlier than usual. Before the housemaids left, they warned me not to use the mirror in my bedroom and to always keep it covered.

"Why?" I asked, somewhat flummoxed by such a curious remark.

"You'll see," one answered as she quickly left the property.

The remains of the day whizzed by in a whir of hope and fantasy. Fading trepidation was replaced with joy. It seemed that in no time at all dinner was being served. Auntie, Bentzen and I sat down to the sumptuous meal her maids had prepared earlier. There was more food in front of me than I would normally see in a month. For a time I was mesmerised by the bounty and oblivious to the fact that Bentzen and Auntie were not speaking to one another. I was brought up with the rule that children did not speak unless they were spoken to, so I kept quiet and observed. Bentzen's heavy breathing was the next thing to catch my attention. Every time he inhaled the long grey hair on his arms and around his neck moved in the gust. It was the same when he exhaled. In between, he was snorting, wheezing and making noises from his nose and throat that didn't sound too healthy. He had once been a heavy smoker.

Bentzen wore a white, very old singlet pockmarked with small holes. A pair of dirty, faded blue shorts hid his ample beer belly. It wasn't exactly formal attire. As we proceeded with dinner, he suddenly startled me by springing from his chair and rummaging around for something. Quickly he found a small notebook and wrote a message that he gave to Auntie as if he was a mute. She shook her head and carried on eating. He wrote another note and gave it to her. She said no again and kept her focus on the meal. Bentzen was getting agitated. He finally told Auntie that he needed it, which only served to escalate her displeasure.

"You can't have butter before bed because it blocks your airways when you sleep. You might not be able to breathe, you fool," she yelled at him.

"I don't care. I can't eat my bread without butter," he screamed back.

"I told you never to interrupt me when I am eating. It is the only thing I do that I need total silence for. If not I cannot digest my food properly. So shut up and eat and try to control your damn breathing. It is driving me insane!" she shouted.

Bentzen slowly sat back onto his chair and pushed his bread away in a huff. Still irritated, he quickly scribbled something new, and with a flourish showed it to Auntie. I could see it said "Mean Ottilie." She dismissed it with a snort and a dirty look and kept on devouring her meal. From the corner of my eye, I saw Bentzen's irritation towards his wife but said nothing. It was also on that very first day I knew who the boss was. Although I was amused by their method of communication, I sensed trouble if my Auntie was crossed.

Auntie Tillie and her husband both wore hearing aids. It was most entertaining to watch when they had heated arguments. It was so loud that I was sure the whole district of Saleimoa heard them. Each would take out their hearing aids so they did not hear the vicious words coming out of the other's mouth. The insults were either in English or Samoan, depending on which language was most offensive for the circumstance. It seemed to me they got out all their anger and frustrations in bad language and cruel words without risking any lasting insults they might have regretted later in a cooler mood. It was their way of coping, but it was scary and bizarre at the same time. Mostly I didn't understand what they were really saying to each other, so I used their facial impressions and the tone of their voices to determine the seriousness of the situation. The louder Auntie became, her body language would also change into a scary person. Auntie and Bentzen had been raised in environments so foreign from my own that they may as well have come from the moon. I reasoned if they were to respect me then I had to respect their ways. So I watched them morph from yelling and screaming at each other, to later carrying on as if nothing had happened.

Borge Bentzen was his full name, but he was Bentzen to everyone who knew him. He kept reminding me to call him Uncle, but I preferred Bentzen. It suited him. He was a hard-working Danish man who started his career as a first mate on a ship while still a teenager. He then crewed on another ship of the Canadian Australian Asian Line, a subsidiary of the Union Steamship Company of New Zealand, in the late 1940s. His first encounter with Auntie Tilie was on the ship from Samoa to New Zealand. He was surprised that a Samoan girl was able to speak fluent English. He took a liking to her, but she was married and travelling with her husband Roy, a New Zealand national.

They didn't meet up again for ten years, when Auntie visited New Zealand to sign the sale contract of their house after her marriage to Roy ended. Bentzen was still keen to woo and court the fair maid, but she was going through a difficult time and not interested in forming a relationship. Settling for friendship with a hope of something more, he would stay at her estate when his ship docked in Samoa. He had been patient and persistent and ultimately his strategy paid dividends. Their relationship finally blossomed when Auntie trusted him sufficiently to share some of the tales of her anguished youth. To remove her from such painful memories, Bentzen offered to take her on some of his voyages. His company, his humour, his kindness and his ocean-faring adventures were a welcome distraction when she needed them most. It was almost a swashbuckling romance of cinematic proportions, and to me they seemed the perfect couple.

Bentzen was worldly, wise and down to earth, a solid rock for the volatile Ottilie to cling to. He introduced her to the wider world she had longed to see. He offered solace and serenity from the storms that clouded her life. To the adoring Bentzen she was his beautiful island princess.

In time, Bentzen was promoted to captain, and together he and Ottilie travelled the world as often as possible, collecting and buying antiques, furniture, fine art and expensive automobiles to return to Samoa. Life seemed a dream for them until Bentzen decided to retire in 1957, settling for a peaceful and unscheduled lifestyle with Auntie at her Saleimoa estate. He was ready for the change, preferring the laid-back island lifestyle. Auntie Tilie had reservations, as according to her the plantation carried too many bad memories. Nonetheless, they were a devoted and driven couple.

When Auntie decided to put all her effort and the money from Bentzen's retirement funds to expand their home, her husband supported her all the way. Together they transformed the bare house that her father Wilhelm had first designed into a palace. This was much more to Ottilie's taste and style. She added extra rooms, stairs and balconies. She decorated it with huge beautiful windows and installed red and green diamond floor vinyls throughout. Bentzen, being a worldly traveller, knew how to trade overseas and knew which countries harboured the best markets for their produce. His experience and funds, united with Auntie's one hundred acres of fertile soil, was literally a marriage made in heaven. Together they became owners of one of the wealthiest plantations on the islands of Samoa. Individually, Bentzen and Ottilie had been raised by families with strong work ethics and shrewd business practices.

Outside the wind was getting stronger, howling around the buildings. The only light on in the house was in the kitchen and dining area while we were eating. That night was my first opportunity to learn the routine of our evening meal at the farm. There was no official training; I just had to watch and follow. I did not even dare to ask because I felt that it was not the done thing. I had learned from my upbringing in the village about how to sense danger and about the right time to approach adults when we had something to say. It was only 6pm, but we retired to our beds straight after the meal. All the lights were switched off, apart from mine. It was pitch black outside because of the storm, but darker still inside the house.

"Turn your light off in half an hour, Jane. We try to preserve electricity here. Oh, and always close your bedroom window by 5 pm. We both turn off our hearing aids when we go to bed, so we will be completely deaf. Only if there is a fire or a crisis will you wake us up – by shaking us! Good night, my dear," Auntie chimed out.

This was all new to me. I had always been surrounded by a family of twenty people talking and laughing, but now I was sitting in this lovely room alone with no one to talk to. My bedtime in the village was usually late because the whole family slept together. Even when our kerosene light was put out, we all had each other close by. In the unfamiliar surroundings of Auntie's house, utter loneliness and uncertainty crept in.

In an attempt to distract my mind, I focused my attention on the bedroom. I vaguely remembered how the room had been when I was very young. It used to be Auntie's bedroom. I noticed that the furniture had been moved around. The mirrored wardrobe was by the window facing the door. The mirror was covered by a thick, dark-brown sheet. My single bed was against the wall and there were two small tables in the corners with Auntie's framed pictures on top. She was such an attractive lady in her younger years. A Samoan Bible was placed near yet another clock on the side table next to the bed.

It was not long before I heard Bentzen and Auntie snoring loudly in unison, as if in competition. Their snoring was so loud it even rose above the sound of thunder, gale winds and my bedroom door being closed. I imagined it must be lifting their beds off the floor. In my unfamiliar environment, I lay quietly on my bed in the darkness for a long time. Trying hard to fall asleep, listening to the loud sound of the rain hitting the iron roof of the house, punctuated by the snores of my Auntie and Uncle, my mind drifted back to my grandfather and I immediately became upset. Emotion overcame me in floods of unwelcome tears. While I was growing up we only cried when we were beaten or when someone died. Crying tears because you had emotional issues was seen as weakness for boys and baby tantrums for girls. In any case, we lived on top of each other. There was no space for privacy to contemplate or sort out feelings of hurt, anger or injustice. If we cried we would be teased for the rest of our lives, yelled at and mocked for showing such flaws. During the time of my abuse, added to the grief of missing my grandmother and my Puka, I cried silently inside. I carried on as normal without anybody being aware of the burden I concealed, a burden that was slowly grinding my sense of self-worth into tiny particles.

Lying in my room in my new life, such restraints did not apply. The long held back tears and inner pain came gushing out. I was on my own, and a deluge of emotions overwhelmed me, to the point that I was whispering to those I was enraged with, telling them how much I despised them. I forgot where I was and just cried and cried, cursed and cursed, pinching my skin hard to be able to feel something again. Between the storm, the synchronised snoring and my own grief, I couldn't imagine there was room for any additional auditory sensation in this symphony of sound. Yet again, I was wrong. As if it emanated from some otherworldly place, I was suddenly jarred from my grief by an extraordinary screech followed by someone else crying. The crying was combined with some strange voices in languages that I did not understand. They were coming from outside, seemingly from everywhere. It froze me in a bewildered fear. I assured myself it was the strong sound of the howling wind. By then Auntie's many dogs started yelping and barking hysterically. It was not unusual for dogs to act like that, especially when there was a storm, but this was something else. The dogs were terrified and frantic.

The voices became closer and clearer. I distinctly heard the cry of a baby as if it was just outside my window. Some of the voices were more extreme than others. Before long they were inside the house, upstairs and in the area where Auntie and her husband were sleeping. I could still hear them both snoring loudly. My room was completely dark, illuminated only by an occasional flash of lightning. The glow from the lighting effortlessly pierced through my window's curtains, briefly shedding light on the mirror and Auntie's photos.

Of course I was young, afraid, emotionally scarred and scared. I was alone for the first time in my life and bereft amidst an enormous storm. Who wouldn't imagine any manner of other worldly occurrences in such circumstances? Nonetheless, I know what I saw. In the glow of lightning, the mirror didn't look at all like it had looked during daylight. It almost seemed to be breathing, as if someone was there trying to emerge from beyond the looking glass. Auntie's photos reflected back from the glass, but they were not alone. Interwoven with those images were the images of other people: women, men, my dying pet pig's head and other horrifying images I could not clearly make out. I was not sure what was happening, apart from the fact that the atmosphere in my room and all over the house felt outlandish and eerie. The Bible's pages were flapping as if someone were turning them.

Fear consumed me. Quivering, I covered my head with the sheet, trying to block out the terrifying sights. Had the intrusions only been visual I might have been successful, but even cowering under my bed sheets I could not mistake the sounds coming from all over the house. It was like people being tortured, with an occasional spike of laughter piercing the night air. It then swirled around the house becoming faint, then louder than the first episode. The intensity was so overpowering that I thought the whole house was going to be lifted off the ground. Curtains flapped wildly, yet all the windows were closed. It was in this moment my grandmother came to mind. She had died in the previous ten months and persistently insisted that I should not to go to Auntie's estate. Perhaps she was upset that I had not followed her instructions. Fear turned into anger again. I found myself telling her, assuming she was there, to leave me alone.

"Please, Tina, you're dead. You can't protect me. You lied to me. Will you please leave me alone? I am so unhappy and scared."

I was still curled up in a foetal position, my eyes tightly closed and pretending I was talking to Tina when the sheet covering me was suddenly pulled away from my body by a strong force. I now felt there was something profoundly evil there, not my grandmother. But I also sensed her presence in the room, protecting me, not trying to hurt me, even though I did not see her. An urgent desire to pray filled me. Before that night I had never prayed so earnestly. In sheer terror, I started to push all my faith through my lips, asking God for his help. It did not happen right away, but the chilling voices slowly faded, the dogs stopped howling and the storm eased. The macabre, all-enveloping atmosphere was completely removed. Peace was restored. I felt as though I was being protected again. Nothing was going to hurt me after all.

I lay on my bed a while longer, bewildered, disbelieving all I had just experienced. Had the stresses of my day or the preceding years sent me into a state of temporary insanity? Reinforcing this thought were the loud snores still coming from Auntie and Bentzen. How could they have slept through all that? Still worried about my state of mental health, I finally slipped into a deep sleep.

Following the experience of my first night at Auntie's place, I awoke the next morning to the hum of conversation. Outside my room I heard sounds of people muttering and chattering, punctuated by busy clattering sounds from the kitchen. There were definitely people about. After the events of last night I was not sure of anything, but these activities and noises seemed normal and familiar. Just to be sure, I waited silently for ten minutes, listening intently to all that was going on from the kitchen. I then heard a familiar voice bark an order. It was one of the housekeepers. Exhausted but relieved, I gently opened my door and furtively peeked out. One of the maids came ambling by holding Auntie's bedpan, heading to the toilet near my room to empty it. Auntie Tilie and Bentzen were not there, but I assumed they must have headed out earlier to begin the day's business.

"Hello!" I shouted excitedly.

The poor maid was so startled by my loud greeting she jumped backwards, splashing the contents of the bedpan all over her clean clothes.

"Ooooh! Sorry if I scared you," I blurted out, feeling foolish and uncomfortable. "But where are my Auntie and my Uncle?"

Grimacing at what had happened, she restrained herself from admonishing me, angrily pointing outside before she stomped off. The curtains in the living room had been drawn, the sun was shining beautifully and all seemed intact, just the same as it had been the previous day. No disturbances had occurred, nothing was out of place, only Auntie and Bentzen's unmade beds awaited the maid's attention.

With my confused mind seeking explanations, I risked breaking Auntie's first rule. I went to the kitchen and asked the old cleaning lady, "Do you believe in *aitu* (ghosts)?"

"Yes."

"Have you seen any?" I asked cautiously.

"Yes."

"Where?"

"Everywhere in this place," she replied in such a matter-of-fact manner it seemed it was odd for anyone to even query it. She didn't even pause in her labours as she nonchalantly responded.

Still confused and debilitated from my last night's encounter, I decided to go back to school the following day. That morning was the first time I learnt what a working farm was all about. It was not what I had originally thought. What I had observed from the window was somehow different. The lorry had just arrived back from picking up the workers, and on the top of the steps stood Auntie Tilie with a large ledger in her hands. She was performing the daily roll call. Each worker answered briskly then stepped aside into their assigned groups. Bentzen stood behind Auntie, feeding and talking to the many dogs. Once this task was completed, breakfast was served from the same big pot of stew the dogs were fed from. Following the morning repast, Bentzen jumped into the passenger seat of the lorry and the driver sped away. In the back were the four groups of workers to be delivered to the various areas of the plantation.

Auntie Tilie and Bentzen ran the plantation like a Swiss watch, keeping a close eye on the smallest detail. The various roles included gardeners who tended to the inner compound, a worker who cared for the pigs and chickens and others who harvested coconuts. Each person was individually responsible for the task assigned to them. When the truck was gone, Auntie sat on the steps to play with her pets. Auntie Tilie and Bentzen had never been blessed with children so their many dogs became a surrogate family. They loved their animals unconditionally and the dogs loved them right back. It was another trait the couple had in common. The only time I ever caught them sharing a smile together was when they played with and fussed over the clamouring mongrels.

Although Auntie was still pleasant towards me, after a few hours in my new home I felt I should be in school. Auntie Tilie was exhibiting a darker side I had never before encountered. She seemed bitter, unpredictable and resentful much of the time. She could be a scary lady when her anger was aroused. Everyone feared her mightily – and with good reason. I had grown up knowing a kindly, thoughtful Auntie. Once I moved into the estate, I only occasionally saw glimpses of that nice Auntie through the all-pervading dismay she apparently felt towards life. She strode around with a confidence bordering on arrogance. She spoke with a clear, powerful voice and acted fearlessly at all times. Yet she cried like a baby sometimes for no reason I was aware of.

One burden she lived with, which no doubt fuelled her complex personality, was that fact that she was afflicted with severe elephantiasis. This grotesque, disfiguring disease infected her legs from knees to toes. Over time, it gradually worsened until she could no longer wear shoes or walk normally. She waddled from side to side like a duck, but stomped like an elephant. The constant smelly discharge from her sore encrusted legs was potent, pungent and unpleasant. Her elephant-sized legs were always covered with layers of bandages. When they were exposed they looked massively swollen and utterly disgusting. They were surely a constant source of agony for her, and a very understandable explanation for her erratic mood swings. Covering her legs were pockmarked holes that were constantly weeping puss. It was not uncommon to see fly maggots squirming in the ulcers. She would often sit on the front steps and allow her dogs to lick them clean. The chickens even crowded around her to peck out and eat the maggots from her sores.

Despite this major disability, Auntie and Bentzen were constantly busy in the fields, their loaded rifles close and constant companions. It was as though those rifles were part of their anatomy. Even when sleeping those rifles were close by, fully loaded and ready to let fly should there be a disturbance during the night.

As regular as the clockwork in Auntie's countless time devices, the enterprising pair would drive around the property in their car checking on the plantation's affairs and making sure the workers were not slacking or stealing. They were always busy doing something, from barking out orders to toiling through mountains of paperwork hunched over a desk in the corner office in the living area.

This place was industrious and bustling during the day, and terrifying as hell itself at night. I was nearly fourteen years old with no parents and no options. I had no way back, no way out and nowhere left to run.

Chapter 9

The Place of the Dead

As a child, it had never occurred to me that there was something sinister about the mansion and the surrounding plantation that I used to believe was a magical place. The stunning garden that overwhelmed my senses was the most perfect, blissful and serene vision that had ever met my young eyes. The high-set white edifice that Auntie called her home sat brooding and imposing on its raised mound as if it was a castle in the clouds. It was both impressive and intimidating. My grandmother used to advise me, as soon as we were closer to the second gate, not to look up at the house but to keep my gaze focused straight ahead.

"Why?" I asked, wondering at the reason for this strange request.

"It is not good manners to look up at someone's house, plus you might bump into a tree," she reasoned.

Even though I believed her, I never quite felt it was the whole truth of the matter. It was only after I was well settled in with Auntie Tilie that Mase and some of the workers told me about images of strange, dark, shadowy people watching from the upper level, and at times walking around as though they lived there. Those who witnessed these sightings knew these shadowy figures bore no resemblance to any resident or visitor to the estate. I now know my grandmother had seen them on many occasions during her time on the property. This was one of the secrets she took with her to her grave.

Downstairs was open for me to explore. Upstairs was strictly prohibited to me; Auntie was the only one with keys to the area. One room above my bedroom was always securely locked. Auntie kept that key permanently hanging around her neck. The housekeepers called it the secret room. They had never cleaned inside it, nor had they been permitted so much as a glimpse of what lay behind that mysterious locked door. Inevitably, some gossiped and speculated that Auntie kept all her expensive treasures and boxes of gold in there.

The upper level presented a breathtaking view of the mountains and sea surrounding Saleimoa. Fragrant cool sea breezes always wafted around that area. This made it far more pleasant than the frequently muggy and humid atmosphere downstairs, so I wondered why we could not live up there instead. It was laid out in similar fashion to downstairs: open plan with two rooms and a closed, louvered balcony area where Auntie and Bentzen used to entertain their friends and family. The rare occasions on which I went upstairs with Auntie were the only times I ventured there. The main living area was furnished as a family room with toys strategically and carefully placed in various areas. One in particular piqued my interest: a clockwork laughing monkey holding cymbals in both hands that sat whimsically on the piano in one corner. It would sound the cymbals and laugh when the key protruding from its back was wound up. From my room downstairs I sometimes heard this toy operating while someone was playing the piano. I lay quietly listening with a mixture of bemusement and fear. To my knowledge, no one was up there; I had heard no footfalls on the loudly echoing wooden floor.

All the walls were covered by expensive paintings with little design in their placement. A large and imposing grandfather clock stood in the front corner, further asserting itself through its loud, slow, rhythmic ticking. All of Auntie's favourite furnishings and objects were kept in that big room and laid out perfectly for show, not for function. The room was a display area, a showroom for what seemed to me a very elite clientele. Access to this upper area was by two sets of outer stairs, one at the back near the kitchen, the other at the centre in front. Both stairways were secured by hardwood doors, iron roofing and heavy locks. Both staircases had secure doors at the base and upper level, making them doubly impenetrable. Each door throughout the entire house had its own key. My wily aunt had reasoned that if the bunch of keys was stolen it would take longer for the thieves to find the right key for every door than was worth their time to rob the estate. The housekeepers carried no keys; Auntie opened the doors and they cleaned while she watched and waited. She didn't trust anyone!

The bathroom was near the kitchen. The laundry and outdoor shower were next to my bedroom window beside one of the huge concrete water tanks. Underneath the back staircase sat an old generator that clanked and coughed noisily day and night. It supplied electricity to keep the freezers and other essential appliances running inside the house.

This home should have engendered serene and relaxed feelings; it was opulent but comfortable and homely inside, if a little ostentatious. Instead, it induced no such feelings. Throughout the house I felt a strong unease. I was edgy and uncomfortable, unbalanced by opposing forces of good and what I felt was something palpably evil. It felt to me as though the darker forces were the stronger of the two. Evil was winning whatever battle was being played out there. The worst time was when the workers went home at 5pm, the sun dropped out of sight and that dark force shrouded the building. The house was literally taken over by these unearthly things, most profoundly when Auntie was extra mean or cruel that day. It was as if the evil forces were attracted to and fed from her negative energy. I also felt that the individuals who lived there, including myself, were more vulnerable when our spirits, emotions or state of health were at low ebb. It was usually between 8–10pm that the force would erupt.

The dogs would howl in distress and someone would knock at the front or back door. At times there would be tapping on my bedroom window, and someone seemed to be having a shower at the outdoor bathroom just outside my window. I would hear footsteps, slamming kitchen closets, a baby crying and little children giggling as if they were playing some secret game. Then there were loud, terrifying cries of anguished pain, weeping, screaming and laughter all orchestrated into this symphony from hell. The uproar could last from two to five minutes and sometimes repeated during the night, depending on what had happened in the house during the day. The voices were so extreme that I often slept with cotton wool plugging my ears and my pillow over my head in a futile attempt to block the horror from my senses.

I knew when the apparitions were about to arrive. The odour of the house suddenly changed to a strong overpowering perfumed aroma or a foul stench. None of us wore deodorant or perfume, not even Auntie and Uncle. The extremely foul smell was of burning, decayed, putrid matter. That stink was the most frequent one, as though a rotting carcass was being burned. Eventually I had to raise the subject with my guardian and benefactor.

"Auntie, I hear noises and see things at night time. They scare me," I told her one Sunday morning when she was not as stressed as usual.

"You heard them too? The bastards! This damned house needs to be demolished and burned to the ground. Do you know why I am deaf? The noise was so excruciating I pierced both my eardrums to avoid them. If you don't react to their menacing and cowardly behaviour, they will eventually give up and go away," she told me angrily.

"I see things as well," I anxiously confided to her.

"That is why I make you go to bed before 8pm. They are always here, but they will only bother you when you're scared and pay attention to them," she explained more calmly. It was as though she was instructing me how to handle wayward chickens not some terrifying force, supernatural entity, or things undead.

"What are they, Auntie?" I probed further, feeling I needed more information than she was offering.

"We will get someone to come to bless the house again," she replied dismissively.

By way of placating me, I was introduced to some small white pills, which I was advised would help me to have nice dreams. From then on Auntie gave me two of them before I went to sleep each night. I did not know what they were, but once I took them I slowly melted into another world, a world of not remembering, not caring and most of all not feeling. These amazing tablets not only took away my anxiety about the night ahead, they helped to suppress other memories and pains. They were the best magic ever. Now I realised how Auntie Tilie and Bentzen were able to sleep through anything. The instructions on the bottle read: "Take one tablet half an hour before bed." Auntie gave me two and they took six each with our dinner at 6pm. Those magic little white pills were dished out like lollies; within fifteen minutes we were comatose.

Mase knew more about the history of the house than most people. He had been working there from long before I was born and was the one Auntie turned to when there was a crisis. He was a loyal and trustworthy worker and I believed he would have died to protect my Auntie, even though she treated him shabbily at times. Mase once told me that his role was to keep Auntie safe, not only from any human threats but from the evils that resided there. He was like a peacemaker. He believed that his presence limited these unwelcome visitations, although I was to discover that in protecting my Auntie he had suffered horribly; in fact, he'd nearly died twice.

"Every time I get involved, when I fetch a priest or a healer, these things follow me and do all they can to hinder me," he whispered to me once.

It was 4pm on an ordinary Saturday when the next notable event occurred. Bentzen had returned with the truck from dropping the workers off after their 1pm knockoff time. Mase was always last to leave, usually walking up to the house to let Auntie know he was leaving before departing. Auntie would give him food and money for the Sabbath, but on this particular Saturday Auntie had wanted to relax and Mase was three hours late. In consequence, I was asked to take his things to him instead. I spied Mase from a distance sitting in the middle of his hut as if he wasn't going anywhere, which was unusual. Not thinking too much of it, I wandered over to him and noticed he was staring directly at the big house. His gaze was fixed and he was motionless. I had learned enough about this place to know something was terribly wrong. He did not even look at me or acknowledge my presence. It was as though he was hypnotised by something.

"Are you okay?" I asked tentatively.

Not only didn't he reply, but he didn't even turn his head. I gazed towards where his stare was fixed, but whatever it was he could see was shielded from my vision. With my heart now racing, I dropped the bag of goodies and ran back up to the house to tell Auntie that there was something wrong with old Mase; he was not moving. As Auntie could not walk that far, I waited impatiently fearing the worst while she got her car keys and then struggled to clamber inside the car. It seemed like hours before

Auntie and I finally arrived at Mase's hut, by which time he was having a full-blown seizure on the floor. He was shaking violently, foaming and gagging with a terrified look on his weathered old face.

"What's the matter, Mase?" I tried to talk to him, scared by how wretched and terrified he looked.

"He is there. He wears a black suit. He is very cruel. Leave this place – you are not safe here," he babbled, as though mad and in a voice different to his own.

He appeared to be hallucinating; certainly, he was not making sense about the apparition he was referring to. Auntie was still sitting in the car with the engine running, yelling at me to get Mase up and bring him to the car.

"I can't get him up! He is very sick!" I screamed back.

Mase was not a big man, but in the midst of that seizure it would have taken three or four people to get him to his feet, if that were even possible. Eventually the worst subsided and he was able to sit up. I tried to massage his shoulders when he complained his neck and shoulders were tight and sore.

"Mase, we have to take you to the hospital. Do you think you can stand?" I asked desperately.

Without waiting for him to answer, I tried to lift him. He stood up shakily and I helped him inside the back seat of the car. He told Auntie that he wanted to be taken home, not to the hospital. Not commenting one way or the other, Auntie turned the key in the ignition, but the vehicle stubbornly refused to start. The engine coughed and stalled. She tried again but to no avail. To our complete amazement, the horn then suddenly started beeping all of its own volition. This sent Auntie into a spontaneous blue-swearing fit. Mase also started cursing loudly, with his hands gesturing in the air like he was talking to people standing by the car that Auntie and I could not see. I sat terrified in the passenger seat, turning to look at Mase's weird reactions, then to Auntie who was about to cry from frustration.

Mase's abuse to the unseen appeared to help the situation as the car finally cranked into life.

"Are you okay, Mase?" I asked warily. He just nodded his head but he still did not look good.

Auntie and I dropped him off to his family, as he had insisted, and I explained to his wife and one of his daughters what had happened.

"I told him to stay away from that place," his wife blurted. "Do you know why no one lasts there? Because that place is evil! It's full of bad ghosts. They sometimes possess your Auntie too. Be careful Sieni, you will be next."

Her words stunned me to silence.

An overwhelming feeling of emptiness and dread came over me as we were driving back home and night began to fall. It felt like we were going to visit a cemetery where the evil dead were going to return. A lifetime later I realised the scene was like something out of a hellish theme park, but here there was no escaping through a turnstile back into the ordinary world. As we passed through each gate and I clambered out to lock them behind us, I couldn't help thinking I was cutting off our only escape route. I felt like they were watching us, welcoming us back so that their torment could begin again. This time I intentionally avoided looking up at the house while we were driving, but from the corner of my right eye I glimpsed the light on in the kitchen where Bentzen was reading a newspaper.

The dogs were barking as we approached the main house. I was looking straight ahead, our car lights were full on, and, to my horror, on the mango tree next to the garage I clearly saw a naked black man hanging from a rope wrapped tight around his neck. A month earlier I had a vivid dream of a man being hung.

One of his eyes had popped out and was resting against his cheek. The gruesome scene on the mango tree sent me into a state of hysterical screaming. Auntie stopped suddenly and my head shot forward into the windscreen.

"What is wrong with you, girl?" she yelled at me in confused anger.

"There was a man hanging on the mango tree, a black man," I replied with my heart firmly in my mouth, my skin crawling.

"What man? I didn't see any man," she protested.

"He was on that tree, Auntie – right there!" I argued forcefully, pointing at the mango tree in front of us.

"For goodness sake! I could have shot you straight through the windscreen," she exclaimed in agitation.

My head felt just fine, at least outwardly. Inwardly it was another matter. I had seen this vision as plain as day; it was as though someone wanted me to know about his suffering. The dogs remained wildly restless from then on and throughout dinner. As nonchalantly as sweeping a dead fly off the counter, Bentzen and Auntie simply turned off their hearing aids. I was the only one who would hear the howling and chaos of what was sure to follow. As I saw it, my Auntie really did care for me and had obviously noticed the desperation on my face. In the middle of her meal she left the table and returned a moment later with three tablets for me. She told me that the other one would help my head in case I had a concussion. I had no compunction about gobbling down those magic little lollies; in fact, I eagerly awaited them all day. After that, I just lay on my bed for that heavenly calming effect.

"It is all a dream and everything will be better in the morning," I repeated over and over to myself until, blissfully, I slipped into the peace of a deep warm slumber.

Mase returned two weeks after his episode. He never wanted to talk about what happened, but he did offer some words he thought to be consoling.

"Don't worry about the ghosts," he told me. "These things are not here to hurt me, you or anybody else. They can only hurt you if you lose faith within yourself."

"But you were sick, Mase. I saw you. You couldn't even move."

"That's because I got scared and allowed my fear to take over," he explained.

"But you saw something, didn't you?"

"Yes, but I can't tell you. I am not allowed."

Mase continued to work for Auntie for another ten years, but never once did he reveal his secret.

Chapter 10

Cruelty

It did not take long for me to learn the rules of the house. I was mostly free to do as I wished but I was forbidden to talk to the staff or any workers unless Auntie had instructed me to. The rules were simple but ironclad in their application. Provided I complied with the rules, all I desired was given to me freely and gladly. I had a car and chauffer to transport me to and from school. I was given money to buy lunch or anything else that my day required. Every second Saturday, Auntie and I went to Apia to buy clothes and any pretty things I wanted. Those trips provided a welcome respite from the routines of the estate, which amounted to an eclectic jumble of boredom and terror.

This material bounty came at a price. I was lonely and scared most of the time. School became my private refuge, my sanctuary of normality. Of course, I could have returned to my family, but when faced with the option of certain physical torture and rape versus an uncertain supernatural threat there really was no choice. I had cut the ties with my family the day I walked out. There was no going back, and while I harboured some silent guilt about deserting Tama, I had made a decision that this was my life. I had paid my dues in caring for Tina, now it was my time and felt I deserved all the generosity that Auntie Tilie was so happy to bestow.

At school, I had friends and was free to talk to whomever I pleased without fear of repercussions. There I did not need to take tablets to fall asleep, hiding from reality in a befuddled state. Each day as I returned home, a taut knot formed in my stomach dreading what the night had in store. It wasn't until the end of our second school term that, for the first time, the dread was actually surpassed by something positive. I was looking forward to returning home. I had my school report and was excited to show it to Auntie. Perhaps surprisingly, given my background of missed schooling, drugged sleep and ghostly companions, I had achieved an excellent grade. There was no doubt in my mind that Auntie would be proud and pleased that the money and effort she lavished on me was not in vain. She never failed to remind me that she had wasted a lot of her money on people who turned out to be useless, bad investments. She felt such people were just using her. I was so excited about my report and so determined to prove I was neither useless nor using Auntie that I had quite forgotten two weeks of school holidays lay ahead of me.

At the final bell I hurried out of my classroom. Bentzen and the truck driver were already waiting for me in front of the school. I squeezed into the middle of the bench seat and Bentzen handed me a bottle of ice-cold soda with a bag of sweet pancakes. I loved my Uncle; he was such a thoughtful, caring gentleman. If his inner charm had been matched by outward beauty, he might have been the perfect man. However, that was not the case. Outwardly, Bentzen could be downright revolting. It was a hot humid day and he was sweating profusely and had taken off his shirt to cool down. For a demure teenage schoolgirl, being squished between two stinky, sweaty men was asphyxiating. In fact, being bumped and jostled against hairy, smelly specimens of aging manhood was so repugnant I couldn't even think about eating the treats I'd been offered.

Bentzen did not care what others thought of him and I could look past his eccentricities because he was such fun. Despite the outward repugnance, he was a truly caring and decent human being. There was seldom a dull moment when he was around. I made fun of his broken Samoan and he would chide me about my jumbled English. We both thought each other's language sounded silly. When I had visited the estate as a little girl, Bentzen was always sitting on his favourite chair close to the front windows. At that time he was routinely nicely attired, sitting in the morning sunshine reading his international newspapers. Sometimes on my market days with Tina, I would see him in the capital, Apia, shopping, trading or going about the general business of the estate. I remember he would often drop by the market to give Tina and I cool drinks and food. He was always jovial, dapper and clean-shaven, a familiar and respected figure in the capital. Whenever we met he warmly greeted Tina and I, often rubbing my head playfully or lightly tapping it with his paper as he went by. I liked him a lot.

Bentzen considered himself something of a lady's man. He would alert the driver to honk the horn when he saw females on the road so he could enthusiastically and in good humour wave and blow kisses at them. I don't think he realised his better days were behind him and he was constantly coughing, hacking and spitting. Although I still loved him dearly, I could not wait to get out of the truck so I could wash my hands and be free of the stench to finally enjoy my pancakes.

Arriving back at the estate, everything seemed perfectly normal. I pushed open the back door and walked into the kitchen, itching to show Auntie my report from school. Nothing could have prepared me for the sight that met my eyes. Any thoughts of my good results were immediately swept into oblivion as, to my total horror, I saw a young female slouched in a foetal position under the dining table sobbing uncontrollably. The floor was soaked by her tears and sweat. A hangman's noose was pulled taut around her neck, the other end of it tied to the table leg. Her hair was dishevelled, bruises covered her face and a smear of blood ran from her eye to her lip. I immediately knew who was responsible for her plight and questioned one of the maids. This was taboo for me to do, but in the circumstances I felt the situation warranted the risk.

"Ottilie found out the girl may be pregnant by Bentzen. She is really, really furious. Ottilie said that when she returns she would hang her from the mango tree," the anxious maid replied.

"Where is Auntie?" I demanded.

"Ottilie was interrupted and had to rush to the plantation. The fences were cut and damaged by thieves, so she's gone to inspect them."

On hearing our conversation, the girl on the floor sobbed harder, denying the accusation. She was begging us to let her go. "It was not my fault. It was Bentzen. He gave me money," she pleaded.

My first reaction was to set the girl free, but I thought better of it and ran outside to get Bentzen. The dark frown and palpable expression of alarm on his face as he quickly untied the girl left me with little doubt as to his guilt. He was in serious trouble.

"Run home," he instructed her urgently. "Run home and never to return to the plantation."

I was standing dumbfounded in the kitchen, unsure whether to sit, stand, run or just dig a hole to hide in. The tension inside the household was intense. Then we all heard Auntie's car coming, and we knew that the situation was soon going to be a lot worse. I could almost feel the ground shake when she got out, slamming the door so hard it sounded like a shotgun blast. Terrified, I ran to my room, only to find Bentzen had beaten me to it. He was hiding in my wardrobe, peeking out through a tiny slit in the open door. He beseeched me not to say a word. I made sure Bentzen was well hidden and left my bedroom door ajar in case Auntie barged in. I thought that she would find me on the floor pretending to read and not be suspicious.

The fierceness of Auntie's rage when she found out the girl had been released by Bentzen enveloped the house. She had a high-powered rifle in one hand, the now-empty hangman's rope in the other and was pacing up and down the living area, bellowing out for her husband like an enraged dragon ready to scorch everything in its path. Every word that came from her mouth was loaded with bile and venom; every step she took was pounded into the floor with hatred and ferocity. I was certain if she entered my room in that frame of mind and found Bentzen there, she would have shot us both without hesitation.

Auntie Tilie's violent frenzy halted abruptly when she could no longer draw breath from the rigours of her exhausting tirade. She slumped herself down on a chair, yelling out to the maids in the kitchen for a lemonade. While Auntie was puffing and panting, trying to quaff her drink, one of the men came to tell her they had caught one of the thieves but the others had escaped. Despite her exhaustion, she abruptly arose, picked up her rifle and waddled outside. I ran across to a window and watched with dismay at what I was sure would not be a good outcome for the thief.

In front of the garage were two of Auntie's men, one restraining the thief, the other holding his getaway horse. It was obvious the animal was used to commit the crime. Both sacks on the horse's back were fully loaded with crops from the property. The boy was young, about seventeen. As soon as he saw Auntie stepping down the stairs towards him with a weapon, he became so distressed he lost control of his bladder.

"Please don't hurt me. It wasn't just me; others made me do it," he begged.

Auntie ignored his pleas. Without a hint of mercy on her face, she aimed at the horse point blank and shot it. The poor beast fell to the ground instantly dead, but Auntie pumped two more shots into it just to be sure. That done, she strode over to the thief, raising the butt of the rifle high, then with all her might she struck the young man square on the side of his head. Its heavy brass butt end crunched sickeningly into his cheek. His young body crumpled and slumped to the ground unconscious.

"I am not in a mood to kill two people today. The soil of this place has sucked up enough evil, repugnant blood," she shouted at the unconscious man with a contemptuous look on her face. She spat on the ground to add weight and authority to her point. "Pick up this piece of filthy meat, whether dead or alive, and throw him on the road outside the gate. Hopefully the birds and rats will feast upon his eyes. Oh, and cut up that horse to feed to my dogs," she barked to her workers before striding back inside. I would not have thought it possible for someone with her afflictions to stride, but stride she did.

Quaking with fear, I raced back to my room. Bentzen was not in my wardrobe anymore. He was awaiting his fate in the living area and Auntie did not disappoint. While Bentzen wriggled in his seat like a defenceless worm, Auntie beat him with the rope, then the rifle, then a chair and finally with her fists. I can't imagine where her stamina came from other than pure rage, perhaps magnified by the demonic forces that seemed to possess the house. Then I remembered Mase's wife telling me those forces at times also possessed my Auntie.

Bentzen cried out in Samoan, "No, Ottilie. Please stop. Enough now, Ottilie!"

His pleas only served to encourage her, much as mine had once done to the brutal minster that almost beat me to death. All the fear and pain of that damnable day came flooding back to me as Auntie carried on huffing and puffing, cursing and swearing, bashing and beating her husband. She was not as insanely ferocious as she had been a full thirty minutes earlier when she had commenced his admonishment. That fact alone comforted me in the knowledge she was human and not possessed. Nonetheless, the rage within her was sufficiently fierce to cause Bentzen to bleed copiously. As his pleas for her to desist became more desperate, she simply pulled out her hearing aid. At the same time, she made certain that his hearing aid remained at full volume so he could clearly hear every curse, threat and tone of malice she could muster. That poor pathetic and harmless old man was abjectly defeated, humiliated and abused. I could only stand by, powerless to help him. A few short hours ago he had jokingly flirted with females when we drove past them. Here was a man of the world, a former master mariner of his ship who had been highly respected by his crewmembers and passengers, reduced to a gibbering, pulverized wreck.

Thankfully, the assault came to an end. Auntie threw him one final contemptuous look of distain, picked up his set of keys and walked out.

"Be out of the house by the time I return from rollcall," she barked over her shoulder.

She returned before six o'clock and then went straight to bed. I was now in my room hiding, thankfully being ignored. I can only guess she blacked out, fatigued from the physical and emotional exertion of the day. She did not even once call out to see if I was home. Perhaps she did not care about anyone anymore. Dinner lay served but uneaten on the table. Auntie was fast asleep. There was no sign of Bentzen and I had no appetite. The house was in an eerie limbo.

Eventually I worked up the courage to crawl out of my room when I heard Auntie snoring. The place was already in darkness. An acute sense of loneliness and futility filled me. I was more scared than ever because Bentzen was not in the house, and I had no idea where he was or what condition he was in. It was about 7pm when I heard a car door slam. Quickly I rushed to the back door to unlock it, hoping it was Bentzen; innocently, I thought I could suggest he sleep in my room. To my dismay, I saw he was preparing his bed in the lorry. Making sure the door was unlocked from inside so I could get back in, I went to check on him. He was hurt, bruised, had a cut on his head and his nose had been bleeding.

"Why did you come out of my room? Auntie could have shot you," I said, knowing that was a silly thing for him to have done, especially when angry, vengeful Ottilie had a loaded rifle in her hands.

"I knew she had used all the bullets in the magazine when I heard her fire three shots," he told me simply while shrugging his shoulders.

"But she still beat you up," I pointed out. The comment didn't require a response. "Why don't you go to the guest house to sleep? You would be more comfortable there," I suggested.

"When your Auntie gets angry and kicks me out, she means out! She took all my keys so I could not enter any buildings on the property, not even the garage."

We two unfortunate souls sat in the dark truck for a while, not saying a word. We just sat silently staring at the dark house in front of us. It was the first time I had actually taken a good look at it from outside at night. It appeared a lot more eerie, otherworldly and hostile in the gloom. I shivered as I felt that gnawing chill pass through me, as if evil was already in the house watching us. Bentzen broke the silence, asking if I could go inside to get him some aspirin tablets. I looked at the house and then at Bentzen who was obviously in pain.

Putting my fears aside, I ran up the steps and pushed the back door open. As I entered, it was like stepping into a freezer. The icy chill bit deeply, stopping me in my tracks. To add to my unease, the door slammed shut behind me. It was a still, clammy, windless night with nothing to account for that forceful closure. Despite my unnatural strength fuelled by fear, the door would not open again. From inside the house, the throaty grating of Auntie's voice growled menacingly at me. Scared out of my wits, I managed to wrench the door open and run back to the car. Bentzen was sitting rigidly in his seat, his eyes transfixed in terror on the house as if he was watching a horror movie. I spun around and looked up to see moving shadows, dark silhouettes of people moving around on the top and downstairs levels. We were both entirely awake and witnessing precisely the same macabre scene. Entities were moving slowly from the direction of the second gate, passed the front garden and then headed towards the house. It was as if we were valets in a parking lot watching people entering a ghoulish private party to which only they had been invited. In between these apparitions appeared a brief vision of the naked, dark-skinned man hanging from the mango tree just to the left of where the truck was parked. It was the same image I had seen when Auntie and I drove back from taking Mase home two months earlier.

Among all of these shadowy yet substantive images was one far more disturbing than the rest. It was a little girl sitting on the downstairs windowsill, obviously looking directly at us. Strands of her hair were draped over her face, obscuring her identity. The dogs were in a total frenzy, running around, crying, whimpering and barking hysterically at the house. Bentzen and I were struck mute, hypnotised into a dumb, stunned silence as we witnessed this terrifying scene. I believed that we were meant to see these things, even though their purpose or meaning I could not fathom. I had no idea how Bentzen felt about all this, he just gazed in resignation as powerless to influence their progress as he had been to prevent his beating. I had seen, felt and heard strange things before, but this was a marked escalation of the occult calamity in this property of the damned. The scene was utterly overwhelming; it overpowered reason. One thing was clear – these entities, whatever they were, were extremely angry. We both saw a clear image of Auntie walking around in the living room among the spectres, which was odd in itself. Once Auntie had munched down her magic little white pills she was generally out. Perhaps she was so fatigued from her early violent display that she forgot to take them.

Without warning, Auntie turned and looked directly at us through the window. Her gaze was vacant, as though she was in a deep trance looking directly at us but straight through us. Goosebumps prickled all over my skin. I felt naked, vulnerable and completely bewildered. Thankful for the refuge of the truck, I inched as close to Bentzen as I could.

"What are those things? What's happening, Bentzen?" I asked weakly, trembling in fear.

Without saying anything, he jumped out of the car and marched up to the house. I sat protesting from inside my sanctuary, calling for him to come back.

"Turn the truck lights on," he yelled to me. The lights came on in a brief blaze but then fizzled out.

Bentzen, bravely and with all his might, attempted to push the back door open. Failing to budge it, he screamed as loudly as he could for the cursed house to go to hell. He was swearing, damning and threatening these things in between his usual severe coughing fits. I was convinced he was going to pass out or have a seizure. He acted like a wounded soldier at the front lines charging into battle with his feeble sword, knowing that he was not going to come out alive but refusing to surrender. He did not stop until it all subsided. I was still desperately flicking the lights on, but every time they turned off as before. All the while I was keeping my eyes firmly fixed on Bentzen.

The instant the entities dispersed, the headlights of the truck came on and stayed on. By then Bentzen was utterly depleted of breath. He motioned for me to come to him. I still did not want to go back inside the house, but neither did I want to be left in the truck in the dark by myself. I felt like my entire being had been turned inside out, as though I was a raw, insignificant nothing in a universe I was completely ignorant about.

Summoning what little courage I had I ran to Bentzen, knowing he was my only safe refuge. He was my hero. He had stood his ground and fought those dark forces after he'd been beaten savagely and in the midst of coughing his guts out. There was no doubting he was my hero. We cautiously ventured inside and turned the lights on to find Auntie Tilie half-naked and unconscious on the floor, splayed out near the front door. Bentzen gently shook her.

"What happened? I must have fallen," she mumbled weakly, as we struggled to help her back onto her bed a good five metres away.

I remembered what old Mase had told me: as long as people with good hearts were around and acts of kindness were performed, these evil beings would not be provoked. I did not understand at first, but after witnessing it first-hand I held Auntie's hand and prayed with her. She looked confused, disoriented. Without knowing how Auntie would react, I pleaded with her to allow

Bentzen to sleep inside. To my surprise, she nodded a yes and said that I should also go to bed.

Bentzen gave me an encouraging hug and whispered, "View those things as unwanted guests. Ignore them when they appear and completely put them out of your mind when they are gone. They thrive on human fear."

It did not take long for my magic pills to work. I neither knew nor cared what happened after that. Without the help of those pills I would not have made it through the night.

The next day, Auntie was hallucinating and acting as though insane. The local *taulasea* was called again to bless both the house and Auntie. Apparently the housemaids had found Auntie lying on the concrete floor on the front porch moaning and groaning when they first arrived in the morning. No one knew how long she had been there. Bentzen carried on business as usual in the plantation with the workers, utterly refusing to accept that the things we saw last night were more powerful than he was. I thought he was the bravest man ever. He later told me that he had witnessed similar things when he worked on a ship.

When the healer arrived, Auntie was sitting in her comfortable chair babbling away to herself and complaining about pain around her neck and in her stomach. Even as the healer started to work on her, she turned and yelled at her to go home. Fearing she might think me insane, I bravely decided to try and explain to the healer what Bentzen and I had seen the night before. To my astonishment, she simply shrugged and told me that they were still there.

"I can sense them, right now, right here," she told me.

I was instructed to fetch the gardener in case Auntie needed to be restrained. She was a big powerful woman with the strength of a man. Once everything was prepared, the healer started asking her questions such as, "What do you want? What happened to you last night?" Auntie's voice had somehow changed. One minute she was angry with a voice of a man talking in another language I did not recognise, the next she was quite chatty about someone named Alan in her own voice speaking Samoan. Moments later, a third personality emerged; it was a young girl's voice that abruptly changed to the cracked and slow voice of an old woman. At that time I did not know who Alan was, but his name kept coming up and Auntie wanted to be with him.

"Please leave us alone," Auntie begged the healer.

"Leave who alone? How many of you are there? Who is Alan?" this lady asked while smearing Auntie's body with pungent green leaves that had been mashed up to form a salve. It was supposed to disgust the evil spirits to a point of not wanting to be around the person being possessed.

"Damn you. I am more powerful than you," the man's voice spat angrily at her.

"If you were more powerful, whoever you are, you would tell me your name," the healer said without any hint of fear, continuing to confront whatever was torturing Auntie.

Auntie's face gazed at this woman in front of her with obvious contempt. She hissed at her as she spoke in those other languages, as well as spitting at the lady to add to the insult.

"This is my domain. I can do whatever the hell I like!" she yelled to the healer at the top of her voice, a cruel fire burning in her eyes. She then switched back into speaking foreign languages, in between puking out horrible slimy brown vomit.

The healer believed she was talking in German, so we did not understand what she was saying. Auntie refused to speak in Samoan after that, which made it difficult for the healer and for those of us standing around to know what she was talking about. We all guessed it was not good because of her hostile tone and fierce facial expression. The second dose of herbs Auntie was given was supposed to expel whatever was inside her and hopefully calm her.

Ruta, a well-known local spiritual healer, was reputed to be excellent at her profession and able to contain then condemn evil spirits in the local villages. She performed seeming miracles every time she was called into the farm. She knew her craft, which had been passed down over three thousand years to those with the gifts to practise it. I was told that her great-grandfather had been one of the most powerful *taulasea* on the island. The demons apparently feared him greatly. As soon as he knew who was inside a possessed person, he would order their graves to be opened by the family and cauldrons of boiling water were poured over the remains. If he felt the malevolent spirit was too strong, the bones would be dug up then boiled in the cauldrons until the evil spirit left the person. Doing this denied the entity a refuge from which to venture out among the living. This method apparently worked every time.

Now I watched his great-granddaughter with admiration. She was calm, fearless and knew what to say and do at just the right moment. This woman simply and resolutely refused to quit until Auntie was back to her normal self. Whatever possessed Auntie that day became powerless and departed – until the next time.

At last she fell into a deep but fitful sleep after three exhausting hours of Samoan-style exorcism. It was the first time I had witnessed anything like that and it was terrifying to watch.

"It is hard to get rid of something so evil that has lived right here. It should all be destroyed and have boiling water poured into those graves. It is the only way to be rid of these things for good. Otherwise they will never leave. This is going to be a long process for this place," Ruta remarked.

"What are they?" I asked.

"I can't tell you. You will have to ask Ottilie when she is awake. When I see these things, or when it is revealed to me by a person who is possessed, then I can get into negotiating between the dead and the living. Unfortunately, Ottilie speaking in another language made it difficult for me to be able to help her properly and these demons knew it. She is the host," Ruta explained.

Glancing furtively at Ottilie, Ruta took me aside and said I was susceptible to these things, so I should be careful. That wasn't something I needed to hear!

"How do you know?" I asked, feeling terror in my soul.

"I can sense them around you; they are very interested in you."

"Please Ruta, why me? I see and hear them at night. Are they angry with me, or was it something I did?"

"No, not all people can see and feel spirits. Sometimes they may hang around from the time you were conceived, or perhaps sometimes when the person is seeing someone suffering for a long time. It is usually when the person is vulnerable, in turmoil and in doubt that spirits use that person to either be a messenger or a host. Because of your kind heart, they are finding it hard to enter into you, but they are here waiting. You are lucky though, because you have a very strong ally who is protecting you. That is why these other things can't hurt you," she explained.

"What is it? Who is protecting me?" I asked earnestly.

"Your grandmother, I can see her being very fiercely protective of you."

"Oh, my Tina! But I don't see her," my eyes welled up with tears at the thought my beloved Tina was close by.

"She is there. You won't be able to see her because she is only hanging around to protect you. You might see signs, nice ones, though."

I was greatly touched and comforted to know Tina had kept her promise after all. I'd thought she had abandoned me.

Auntie still looked exhausted and confused when she finally awoke. The first question she asked was why the healer was sitting on the chair. Ruta explained why she was there, and even offered to stay the night to ease the house's disturbances. Auntie flatly refused.

Ruta looked at me and shrugged her shoulders. "This is the problem," she said.

Two days later, Auntie was on duty again, back to her normal self. She even chastised me for permitting the healer to sit on one of her chairs instead of the floor, as servants were supposed to.

"Servants are not allowed to sit on these chairs. Her arse belongs on the floor," she scolded.

I found this behaviour of Auntie's very disturbing. This woman had spent nearly half of her day trying to heal this ingrate, and her only concern was that Ruta sat on one of her prized chairs without her approval. I had always wondered why every time my grandmother took me to visit Auntie Tilie she was never offered a chair to sit on. She would always sit on the mat on the floor while we were on our comfortable chairs. My grandmother must have known the rules. Chairs were only for blood family members and special elite friends. I was quite upset to realise that my beloved Tina was always treated as a servant, right up to the time she died, while I had been given special privileges.

I could not imagine treating anyone as though they were a second class citizen for any reason.

Chapter 11

The Maids and the Bread

The school holidays were coming to an end. I would have to endure a few more idle days of being bounced around in the car while Auntie checked on the plantation workers. Then some level of normalcy would return to my life. After doing the rounds we returned home where I would routinely watch the unpleasant spectacle of the maids washing Auntie's rotting legs. This ritual was followed by the unremarkable activity of the dogs being fed, and then Bentzen and I played with them for a while. I was restless and bored witless.

Unable to face the thought of another day accompanying Auntie on her rounds, I pleaded to stay behind. I was missing my grandfather and cousins terribly, and thought if I could speak with the women in the kitchen I might solicit some news and reconnect with the flavours of village life. We often spoke in secret when Auntie was otherwise occupied, but at all times we remained cautiously aware of the ticking clocks. Our interaction was timed in short bursts, as we were all keenly conscious of the fact that Auntie knew precisely how long each task took and would exact a high price if she thought the staff were slacking off.

I was fascinated by their family stories. I understood their daily struggles. I had lived that harsh life and realised that my grandmother was absolutely right – nothing is given freely without consequence or some price exacted, one way or another. Towards the end of my holidays, the servants' tales inspired me so much I confided to them that I wished I could go back to my old life. They gawped at me in disbelief. I tried to explain that I had missed the friendship, community and intimacy shared at my village. It meant more to me than pretty dresses, wearing shoes and being stifled by a lazy and meaningless existence. I should have realised they would never understand. When I was in their position I would never have understood either. With a snort of contempt at my selfish plight, the elder maid then turned and reminded the younger maid not to forget the unused loaves of bread. They were always earmarked to go to the chickens.

"Why?" I asked, puzzled.

"Ottilie instructed us to feed her chooks the stale bread," she replied tersely.

I quickly examined both loaves. Apart from a few tiny spots of mould, they were quite edible. I was well aware that for a Samoan village family, baked bread was a rare treat. Everything they spent their hard-earned cash on was a privileged delicacy. Bread such as this, fresh or stale, would never be wasted. It would be a crime to throw away food while still edible. These two loaves would be so well received by the children that their smiles would brighten the night. Thinking that throwing them to the already fat and cosseted chooks was a sin, I told the women to take the loaves home.

"No! We can never do that. We would be punished severely. One of the maids was fired on the spot when she picked up a rotten mango from the ground to eat," I was told with wide-eyed fear by the older maid.

"But Auntie is not around. Here, take it home for your children, one loaf each. I won't tell," I persisted.

Seeing they were still wary, I reassured them that it would be okay. Auntie Tilie would never find out and I would certainly never tell.

"If she asks, just say they were already fed to the chooks," I suggested, believing I had every angle covered. Quietly I felt very smug about my act of generosity.

One of Auntie's conditions for working inside the house was to be hygienic and clean at all times. The housekeepers always carried spare clothes in case they soiled their garments, so each stale loaf was wrapped in these spare clothes. They did it with such care it was as though they were hiding the crown jewels. After the grand theft bakery was accomplished, they went on working as though nothing had happened, trying to erase from their minds what they had just done. They knew Auntie could smell guilt and hunt down the perpetrators like a bloodhound.

It was not long before the lorry full of workers rumbled and bounced back from the field with Auntie's car cruising behind them. It was the end of another day and the workers were impatient to go home. This was also the time of the day I would sit on the steps happily soaking in the social drama of it all, observing every little nuance that occurred. The simple act of them wiping away their sweat and clearing their noses using the hem of their *lavalavas* gave me amusement. I would laugh about it later, recollecting the scene in the solitude of my room. I felt keenly alone and vulnerable when the workers went home.

The bread incident was long dismissed from my thoughts. I sat in a shady spot on the steps while Auntie conducted rollcall, listening and watching the militaristic nature of the daily ritual. Perhaps she was testing my loyalty. To my absolute horror, she called out the two maid's names and ordered them to open their bags. Stunned at Auntie's powers and with a spreading nausea in my stomach, I shot the women a quick startled glance. Our eyes met in shocked dread and disbelief that somehow our plan had been rumbled. I tried to give them a silent signal I had not said anything by slowly shaking my head from side to side. Once the spare clothes were unravelled, the bread fell out instantly, landing in plain sight of all on the dirty concrete floor. The maids stood guilt-ridden and shame-faced, the undeniable evidence directly in front of them. The earth stood still. Everyone fell silent while Auntie reminded all assembled she had eyes in the back of her head and a psychic sense for treachery. No one would get away unpunished when they lied or stole from her! Only later, I learned Auntie would randomly conduct searches on workers, especially the women who worked inside the house. It was just an unlucky coincidence she busted us.

She slowly carried on in a voice that dripped with calm but menacing authority, "Because I am tired, you can take the bread, but you won't get paid tomorrow. I don't have the stamina or inclination to do anything else now," Auntie huffed, then gazed hard at the women as though daring them to respond. Neither of them did. Instead, they tried to catch my attention. I was cowardly hiding my face in my hands. I could not stand to see the blame glaring at me from their eyes. They were desperate for me to say something, to plead with my aunt to spare them. But I could not; I simply did not have the courage. They were going home but I was staying. I feared the dark, unpredictable side of my Auntie. I was too familiar with her wrath and its consequences.

The truck drove off as I sat with my head flopped down, trying to think of how to make this right. I knew how important it was for these women to get their money. I thought it very unreasonable of Auntie to dish out such a punishment. Two fortnightly pay packets for a couple of stale loaves of bread was not justice by any stretch of the imagination. Payday was every second Thursday, and these women toiled hard for Auntie to earn it. An hour earlier they were telling me how they always looked forward to their fortnightly wages. The money was never enough, but at least it helped out a little. Their children were going back to school the following week and school fees were due. It reminded me how lucky I was that I had everything paid for, which only served to deepen my feelings of guilt over the situation.

I knew that I was the cause of their dilemma, no matter how hard I tried to delude myself that they really should not have listened to me. I tried to tell myself they might have taken the loaves anyway without my intervention, but I really wasn't being terribly convincing. Guilt bloomed and blossomed inside me, rapidly overwhelming me to the point where I decided the only course of action was to own up. I would confess my guilt and beg for mercy for the two maids. Somehow I was as equally unconvincing in my self-talk about Auntie being forgiving as I was in telling myself it hadn't really been my fault. The mistress Ottilie had made it clear to me from the very beginning that her rules were never to be broken. One of those rules, of course, was that I was prohibited from speaking with the workers. I was faced with an unconscionable dilemma. I had overridden one of my Auntie's commandments in order to break another.

As I mulled over the situation, considering it from every conceivable angle, dinnertime approached. It suddenly dawned on me that I had completely forgotten about my school report. I had meant to proudly hand it to Auntie on the day school holidays had commenced and now they were nearly over. Events of the moment had taken over any excitement about insignificant academic achievements, insignificant in the scheme of malevolent spirits from the afterlife wreaking havoc in the homestead. However, with the supernatural activity having calmed somewhat and a distraction definitely in order to deflect from the sin of having broken my Auntie's rules, the time seemed right to present my grades. Besides, I wanted Auntie to know that I had huge potential and was a credit to her. I could only pray this news might lift her spirits sufficiently for me to plead clemency for the maids.

Over dinner, I fidgeted nervously as I sidled up next to Auntie while she was eating. With a flourish, I suddenly thrust my report letter in front of her.

"What is this?" she asked, only moderately curious as she carried on eating.

"It's my school report and I did really well. Thank you for everything, Auntie!" I squeaked timidly, the tiny puddle of courage I'd summoned instantly evaporating in her presence.

"I will have a look at it tomorrow," she said curtly, pushing it away.

Her uncaring attitude deflated me completely. I started crying, "I am sorry, Auntie. It was me who told the maids to take the bread home for their children. In fact, they did not want to so I hid the loaves in their bags. Please, I am prepared to work for you either in the field or here to pay for the bread, but please give the women their pay. They need it very much. Please Aunty, they did nothing wrong. It was all my fault!"

I was babbling and blurting out sentences one after another without pause. Auntie Tilie savagely smacked her hand on the table and yelled at me to shut up and compose myself.

"I thought you were different," she growled. "I thought if I let you be brought up poor you would come to appreciate law and order and the value of things. You would realise that obedience and discipline are the masters of all success. Now I see I have been wasting my time yet again. Tomorrow you will pack your things and go back to where you came from."

She turned her gaze away as though she could not stand the sight of me. Now on my knees sobbing, I felt I needed to explain my actions properly.

"Please Auntie, it wasn't their fault. When I was a little girl I was so hungry I used to faint at school. Rotten bread would have prevented me from collapsing. That was why I convinced them to take the loaves home. I am sorry I talked to the women, but I was so lonely," I blurted.

"I don't give a damn!" she screamed, standing up in a huff and roughly barging past me, knocking me over while I was still on my knees. No sooner was she up and I was down when she spun back and stopped, her finger pointing accusingly at me, so close it just about poked out my eye. "Just to let you know, I don't really have to care about anybody," she added coldly.

"But I have nowhere to go. One of my uncles raped and did horrible things to me. I can't and won't go back. I'd rather die," I sobbed, pleading with her to have mercy on me, without thinking I was telling her more than I wanted to.

She was just about to lash me with her acid tongue again when she paused, looked at me almost sympathetically and then stormed out of the dining room without another word. I looked up, feeling desolate and empty, to discover that Bentzen was staring kindly at me. He grinned and threw me a cheeky wink as if to let me know all would be well.

I cried myself to sleep yet again that night. It seemed that whatever my situation, I was still a lost and unloved waif. In seeking solace, I turned my thoughts to my grandmother and what the healer had revealed to me: Tina was my guardian angel. I talked and cried out to her as though she were sitting on my bed listening, but I was so consumed with self-pity that even the thought of my cherished Tina afforded me no comfort. The tears that flooded out seemed to be drowning my soul as I faced another night alone. I was in desperate need of Auntie's knockout pills to put me to sleep forever.

I was unable to calm my racing, confused mind. It was as though I was spiralling down into a dark, bottomless abyss, descending to a lightless place devoid of warmth or feeling. In previous times, when my uncle abused me or I'd been forced to endure other hardships in my village life, Auntie Tilie's farm had always shone as a beacon of hope. I had clung to the reassuring fact that Auntie was waiting for me. Now even she was abandoning me for a petty infraction made with the best intentions.

It was midnight and I was still awake still crying uncontrollably, trapped in the vortex of a bewildering life. I knew Auntie Tilie and Uncle Bentzen would have already removed their hearing aids; it was safe for me to be in a hysterical self-pitying mess. There was never any doubt of the time as the multitudinous clocks started to burst to life throughout the house chiming the midnight hour. It was uncommon to hear anything else at that hour, so I was somewhat befuddled to suddenly hear Auntie's heavy steps pounding up the stairs and entering the room directly above mine. As I continued to sob beneath the sheets, I came to realise that I was not the only one crying. Between talking and laughing, Auntie was also wailing. This brought my own tears to an abrupt halt as I tried to hear if she was crying over me. I could not make out her conversation, but she was talking in earnest to someone. She sounded like a crazy person, talking and wailing at the same time. This went on for a prolonged period, thankfully distracting me from my woes.

The next morning, after having slipped into a fitful slumber, Auntie barged into my room flapping a piece of paper in her hand. She yanked my curtains open and snapped, "I am not happy with this!"

Befuddled, I sat up, trying to shake off my sleepy state.

"What is it?" I asked blearily.

"Your school report," she chided, waving it in the air with a disapproving expression.

Having no clue what the problem was, I tried reasoning with her. "I have all A-grades. There is nothing higher than that!"

"That is not the issue here. Who was the stupid fool who gave you 'Karl' as your surname?" She stood ruddy-faced, waggling the paper at me as though I was a simpleton for not recognising this most heinous of errors.

Before I could say another word, she informed me that I should have my birthright, my true family name. I did not know what I was entitled to, nor was I ever told who my real father was. It was always a closely kept secret that no one, not even Auntie, seemed willing to share with me. If I asked, I was reprimanded for not having the courtesy to think about the people who have helped me. After many fruitless attempts to find the truth, I had given up trying long ago.

"When do you go back to school?" Auntie asked.

"Next Monday," I replied.

"We will go to Apia tomorrow and finally sort this all out. In the meantime you can help me in the storeroom after breakfast."

I think I felt my jaw drop to the floor as Auntie shot me a rare grin and left my room.

There was never a dull moment with my Auntie Tilie. There were many bewildering, confused and terrifying ones, but no dull ones (notwithstanding my own boredom when she was not around). During the previous night I had been left with no doubt whatsoever that I would be leaving the farm as soon as I awoke. For a moment I wondered if I was still fast asleep and dreaming. The Auntie who had just spoken to me was not the same woman who had verbally attacked me last night with unmerciful chastisement and bizarre reactions.

It was payday for the workers, so naturally the drama with the housekeepers sprang to mind. It was a great relief that Auntie had made peace with me, but there were two women who would have no money to feed their families or send their young ones to school because of my well-intentioned interference.

Over breakfast, Auntie sat at the table as though nothing had happened between us. There was no mention of me going anywhere, apart from Apia to change my last name and then into the holy of holies, the storage room. The woman who was at once my benefactor and commandant had once again transformed into a completely different and wonderful person. Nonetheless, I had learned to be wary, knowing she could revert again just as quickly. While I was enjoying a lovely breakfast, the maids were cleaning the floor and cooking for the dogs, labouring in the belief that they would not be paid for their efforts.

It was a good day with Auntie. We talked and toiled together seamlessly and congenially enough. My first bookkeeping experience was somewhat of a revelation. I was shown how to stock take, to balance the four separate books with what was purchased two weeks earlier, what was used for our food, what the workers bought on account and how to balance what was left over. After that exercise I understood why it was impossible for anyone to steal from Auntie. She had every minute detail recorded. She knew everything right down to how much bread we ate, the weight of the ham that was sliced for our lunch, what remained (in ounces) and how many grams of jam were left in the bottle. Nothing was allowed to be missing -- everything was balanced and accounted for. I was astounded at how thrifty and exacting she was.

Before that day I frequently saw Auntie going in and out of the storeroom, but I did not realise that she noted everything down in such pedantic detail. She had everything that was needed to survive in that storeroom: boxes of bulk food stacked up, filling the entire area. There was also a big freezer chest full of enough meat to feed a large family for a year.

"We would be the luckiest people on the island if there was a sudden ten-year famine in Samoa," I joked.

She laughed and agreed with me. It was the first time we had fun together, even though we were working. I really enjoyed the interaction with her and asked if I could help her more. I even suggested that I should be attending to her legs instead of the maids.

"All right, but listen closely, my girl. I am the only one with a key to this room. If things don't balance or go missing I will be looking at you," she assured me with a frown of distrust on her face.

"You can trust me," I promised.

The storeroom and the worker's accounts became my job when I came home from school and weekends. Auntie congratulated me when it was all balanced and told me off if I made mistakes. Eventually, everything was done perfectly – her way.

During that first day of bookkeeping I kept away from the kitchen, trying to avoid eye contact with the maids. I felt awful. Towards the end of the day I sat on the steps and amused myself by watching the men de-husking hundreds of coconuts in front of the constantly smoking copra house. There were six of them having a race to see whose pile was going to be completed first. It was an incredible sight of dexterity and speed. I had never seen anything like it before and imagined myself as the judge of a competition. I was so absorbed in what these men were doing I did not notice Auntie standing behind me and then quietly going back inside the house without uttering a word.

A few minutes later she called out from her office. Once summoned I dutifully obeyed. She handed me a big envelope and told me it was mine. Surprised, I asked what it was for.

"It's for you. You worked hard today and you also did well at school," she explained.

"You don't have to pay me," I gasped. "I am more than happy to help, to do things around here. I am very grateful for everything, Auntie."

Even as I spoke, tears of appreciation were welling in my eyes. Auntie was in such a loving mood I could not possibly risk spoiling the moment by mentioning the women in the kitchen or anything about the day before, even though my heart ached to do so.

"Open it," she abruptly demanded, looking at the envelope.

Again, I dutifully obeyed. Inside, to my surprise, I saw two small envelopes, each with one of the housekeeper's names on it and the amount they were being paid – their full wages. Before I could utter any words of gratitude, she ordered me to summon the ladies to sign for their wages. Great waves of relief overwhelmed me. This moment was the beginning of my real relationship with my Auntie. I learnt a useful lesson on that day. Auntie was the boss, the mistress and the regent of the palace with a hard-nosed and partially distorted view of all other members of the human race, yet deep down she was a kind woman. Through the darkness of her cruelty still shone a light of kindness and generosity.

Chapter 12

The Girl with No Eyes

Five months after Mase's illness and Auntie's exorcism, a bee landed on my shoulder and stung me as I was washing my clothes one Saturday afternoon. Aside from the pain of the sting I felt fine, until around dinner time. By then I was feeling distinctly unwell and asked Auntie if I could be excused to go to my room and rest. My fever worsened as cold chills swept my body. By the time I heard Auntie and Uncle getting ready for bed, I was freezing and shaking, desperately needing blankets, something heavy on top of me to ease the tremors. I rolled myself up inside my foam mattress, huddling in a foetal position trying to keep warm. My only comfort was when my severe reaction to the sting eventually rendered me unconscious.

I was awoken later by the sound of Auntie gagging. It sounded as if she was gasping for air. This was out of the ordinary, beyond the snoring and other bodily functions that elicited auditory responses from their room. Even when there were other disturbances in the house, these normal but unpleasant sounds were signs they were still alive and sleeping deeply. Oddly, those sounds gave me comfort. In an instant my room felt bitterly cold. I assumed it was just my body's reaction to the bee sting. Drawing the covers more tightly to stay warm, I lay silent and still in the safety of my cocoon mattress, deciding that Auntie was having a bad dream. The clocks startled me when they began to chime 10pm. The one next to my bed was also chiming, although it was not supposed to. I had turned the chimes completely off weeks before so that it would not disturb me as I slept. Still wrapped inside my mattress I reached out for my clock. To my horror, something was out there waiting for me.

For a moment I stopped breathing, rapidly withdrawing my arm when I felt the bony hand of a woman grasping my own. I instinctively knew it was a woman because the hand was small and dainty. Fully awake by then, I jumped up and turned the light on. Almost immediately it went off again. In that brief moment of light I saw the little girl on my windowsill facing me. She was about seven years old, maybe a little older. She had long, straight black hair with stringy wisps hanging down covering her face. She was wearing a dress decorated with large, vibrant red hibiscus flowers. The red of those flowers seemed unnatural, as though it was a living thing that to this day I feel unable to fully describe. Through the wisps of black hair I could see the features of a young girl. I stood transfixed in a cold sweat with waves of fear pulsing through my body. I tried frantically to make the light come on but with no effect. The dogs were running around in nervous circles outside, barking and howling at the house. Completely terrified, I opened my door preparing to yell out to Auntie and Bentzen, caring little that they would not be able to hear me. The sight I saw struck me mute.

Standing over Auntie were two men, one black, much darker than a Samoan, and another I could not make out clearly; he was just a shadowy form with no distinct features. On the windowsill next to Auntie's bed sat the pale girl I had just seen in my room, her gaze fixed on Auntie and the men. Even though I couldn't see her eyes, I somehow knew where her gaze was directed. My eyes physically hurt by the overwhelming redness of her dress. The window was open, allowing the breeze to move the curtains and enough light from the full moon to sweep in so I could witness these figures and their actions more distinctly. The black man, I guessed in his forties, did not appear to have any clothes on. He had fire seeping out from holes in his face and body, much in the way holes punched in the side of a brazier allow the fierce internal fire to be seen. He was straddled directly over Auntie Tilie and was strangling her. Auntie was still in a deep sleep, but her arms flailed wildly in the air and her body convulsed as she tried to breathe. My entire body felt heavy. I was trembling so uncontrollably I felt my heart was going to give up on me. I was beyond fear; words cannot fully explain the experience. This was a terror without comprehension. All nerve systems came to a halt and I just waited, resigned to whatever would follow. I felt I had no power over anything, especially over myself. Since I arrived at Auntie's house I had experienced extreme fear before, but this took it to a whole new level.

Inside the living area where Auntie and Bentzen slept, the atmosphere was filled with an overpowering foul stench. The odour was so repugnant I could barely breathe without retching. I sensed true evil all around me. I had no control over my body anymore; I stood frozen in place. Inside I was screaming, but no sound would come out. I heard Bentzen snoring, but I was unable to turn my head to the source of the snores. My eyes could only focus on Auntie, who was being attacked while the apparition of the little girl was grinning, taking perverse pleasure from the assault. Now I realised her satanic gaze was directed not at Auntie but at me. Her position and the extra light enabled me to see more clearly through the hair concealing her face. I saw in detail the seemingly bottomless black holes where her eyes should be, two formless dark voids in place of eye sockets.

The more scared I became the more events escalated. I felt they wanted to make Auntie suffer and that I should bear witness to it. Knowing that I could not move my lips to speak, I silently asked God for help, praying in earnest and with all my might. I was by then well practised in praying, and the first thought that came to me was to help my Auntie. That was what my prayer focused on. As I was praying for God's help, the men immediately vanished. They had never looked at me or acknowledged me once throughout the ordeal. They were gone but the little girl remained, her evil grin now transformed into an angry grimace.

She slid silently from the windowsill and began walking towards me. Her steps were slow, measured and menacing, as if to prolong my terror. Frantically I kept repeating my prayer in greater desperation and urgency. I tried to close my eyes, thinking that whatever was going to happen I did not want to see it, but against my will, my eyes remained stubbornly open. I saw the shadow of another spirit dart in front of me. It was as though it was blocking the girl from reaching me. As soon as this happened, the light in my bedroom came back on, the little girl vanished, the awful smell abated and the pervading sense of evil from another world disappeared. The shaft of light now coming from my room enabled me to see Auntie. She was asleep, coughing a bit but breathing normally. Trembling in deep shock, I silently and slowly closed my door. It was only 10.06pm. I was bewildered. It seemed as if many long hours had passed while Auntie and I had been terrorised. However, according to my clock only a few minutes had ticked by. I decided to leave my light on and just lie in bed, trying to erase what had just happened from my head as Bentzen had once advised me. It was a good theory but impossible to put into practice. I was in desperate need of some of Auntie's magic pills to knock me out. As I had a fever, Auntie had given me aspirins instead. They obviously did not work as well as the potent one's she usually gave me.

I thanked both God and Tina for not forsaking me.

While I was lying on my bed shaking, I recalled that I had seen this girl twice before when I was about six years old. Auntie Tilie had asked me to stay over one night, making a bed on the floor in her room because I did not want to be alone in the spare room. While I was asleep, the little girl whispered to me and I awakened to see her sitting on the windowsill in the room. Auntie was not on her bed, so I asked her where she was.

"She will be back soon. She is upstairs," the girl told me.

I was curious. The girl's eyes were covered by her hair. She was friendly to me, but when I asked her if she could pull back her hair so I could see her properly she vanished without answering. The next day I saw her again when I was running around in the garden chasing butterflies. This time she was not facing me. She just walked past me amid the butterflies as though she did not see me. I remember finding it odd that the butterflies flew away from her as she passed. I called out for her to stop but she did not respond. Instead, she disappeared into the humid mist among the trees. As I recall, these incidents did not scare me. I just wanted to play with the mystery girl and have a friend. When I told Auntie about her, she said that the apparition was not real and was all in my imagination. I believed her but I was still puzzled by the incident.

I also mentioned the girl to my Tina. She abruptly ordered me never to ask to stay with Auntie Tilie again. Stretching further into my memory, I recalled more disturbing aspects about this girl. When I was sleeping under my grandmother's hospital bed, I caught a glimpse of her outside the ward. My pig was killed the next day. I thought of the girl then as if she was my friend who came to warn me that my pet was about to be slaughtered.

Another memory returned to me of my grandmother a few weeks before she died. She seemed to be hallucinating and pointing at a girl with no eyes who she said was outside our hut at night. Because she was close to death, the family suspected she had gone senile and was seeing things. But what was this same strange girl doing at Auntie's house?

After I said another prayer for God to wrap me in his kind arms and protect me, sleep came without difficulty.

At 7am the following day, the maid knocked at my door telling me that my Auntie wanted to see me in a hurry. She was having her breakfast in the living area.

"I want us to go to church," Auntie blurted.

I was still struggling to regain my sanity and strength after what had happened the night before, so Auntie's shocking announcement dumbfounded me. I did not even know whether she believed in God or not. She had never displayed any religious inclinations before. I had never seen her pray or read the Bible, although she did own one. I spied red welt marks around her neck, so I could not resist asking her if she remembered anything from the previous night.

"No! Now go and get ready. We should go to church today," she said, brushing me off.

"Which church?" I asked, still thinking that maybe Auntie was not serious.

"Any church that God lives in. What is your village church like?"

"Not good," I quickly answered. "Perhaps we can try the Catholic one on the other side of the village. Can I ask the housekeeper what it's like and the time of the morning service? I believe she is Catholic."

Auntie gave her permission. The housemaid was in the kitchen boiling water for Auntie's legs when I approached. She assured me that her church was good, but doubted Auntie would have the patience to sit through an entire mass. As I considered that comment, a vivid image of the little girl kept flashing through my mind.

This was an opportunity to ask the maid's opinion. I changed the subject deftly without pause so she had no time to consider whether it was wise to answer me. "Have you ever seen a ghost of a little girl with no eyes here?"

"Yes," she replied without hesitation. "I couldn't see her eyes because they were really dark and hollow. However, if you see her in the mirror she appears a lot more mean and scary. She has the body of an old woman sometimes. A lot of people have seen her," she added as though it was nothing unusual. Then her tone changed. She continued in a whisper to tell me that some of the workers had suffered from encounters with demons in the house. One lady had apparently been possessed.

"It was a very busy cocoa season. I was one of the women chosen to work around here to help with the processing. I wasn't working inside the house then, but this other lady did. She had been here for quite some time and was alone working inside. Ottilie liked her and often accompanied her to Apia. We heard frantic screaming for help one Saturday afternoon. Myself and two others rushed to see what it was. Ottilie was out in the fields and Bentzen had gone to town. We found her in Ottilie's room writhing on the floor, foaming from her mouth while struggling as if to release something from her neck. She was gasping out that someone was strangling her. We didn't see anybody, but when I looked up I saw a reflection in the mirror. It was that little girl just standing there grinning from ear to ear. Her hair concealed the rest of her face, but when she turned and slowly walked away, she looked like an old woman. The other two couldn't see her. She was wearing a fiery red dress. Shortly after that, the sick woman's voice and face changed."

"What happened to her?" I asked, now fascinated as well as vindicated about what I had seen the night before.

"She was apparently possessed by that girl. She never came back to work again," the housekeeper hushed.

"What do you do when you see these things?" I asked.

"Don't look at them. Just pretend they are not there. They only hurt people who don't respect things around here. This place is full of bad spirits; everyone knows it. I believe that woman was possessed because she was standing in front of Ottilie's mirror vainly combing her hair. The girl didn't like it for some reason and made her pay. Some believed it was Samauiafi, the well-known demon girl of Samoa," the maid told me.

From what this woman explained, I thought maybe it was a good idea we attend a church after all. Besides, the way I was feeling, any positive prospect to be closer to God in any way possible was preferable to being at this hellish farm. I was excited at the thought of basking in the warm, nurturing cocoon of a Christian fellowship again.

In preparation for our church hunt, the maids washed, disinfected and bandaged Auntie's legs. Following the cleansing ritual, we both dressed smartly, as if we were going to Apia for the day. We had not yet settled on which church we were going to grace with our presence, but to me it didn't matter. The plan was to drive around and decide solely on how it looked from outside. Auntie said that she would be able to feel which one was right when she saw it. So off we ventured to select a church.

Our first stop was the Catholic church in the village of Leauvaa, four villages from my village, Salepouae. The service had just begun, so we politely waited until the first hymn was finished. Parked outside of the cathedral, we sat listening to the powerful harmony of the choir resonating from inside. Auntie was really soaking it up, sitting with her eyes closed and humming along. As soon as it finished she instructed me to go inside and offer a donation of ten tala and return to the car. "We have to leave to search for a better one," she told me.

We drove off again looking for another church, this time stopping at the Catholic church in the village of Lotosoa, near Salepouae. It was the church attended by one of our housekeepers. We did the same thing, just parked outside and listened to hymns, donated money then drove off again. We did this at four different churches, which took three hours in total. It was actually an enjoyable experience, and in between we stopped at stores and purchased cool drinks and pork buns to keep our strength up. The hymns really did something to lift my spirits. I felt the presence of God even though we did not enter any of the churches. Because of my bad experiences growing up attending church in my village, our method of church hunting suited me just fine. Auntie, I felt, really wanted to go in, but something inside her prevented it. She was almost hyperventilating every time we stopped in front of any house of God, then the powerful sound of a choir floating through the air seemed to calm her.

After our last stop on our way home, she unexpectedly drove out of our way to see Mase. That was surprising in itself, but her request to him amazed me even more. She wanted Mase to invite his reverend and a choir to the farm to perform a service. She would donate a handsome sum to the church if they complied. Since Mase was one of the deacons, he said that he would try, but if they did come it would be after lunch. Assuming his fellow church members would accept the offer; we stopped at the local store and bought a carton of ice cream and other treats to demonstrate our hospitality.

Watching Auntie cheerfully stock these supplies, I couldn't help feeling sad for her. I knew underneath she was a good person. The brusque and scary demeanour that the world saw was her protection against further injury. Despite occasional – in fact, rare – outward bursts of cheerfulness, something about her seemed desperate, tired and sick in spirit. It was as if something was eating her away. The image of the man trying to throttle her and the leering little girl taking pleasure at her pain sprang again to mind. These images were still raw. I felt that maybe she did something awful to these people and now she was searching for forgiveness. We were two confused, tormented souls, driving back into the lion's den with no real armour or weapons to defend ourselves.

Several hours later a car pulled up in the driveway. It was Mase with the minister of his congregation and two fellow deacons. The choir could not come on such short notice they explained. Because Auntie had invited these people, seats and cool refreshments were offered on arrival. She was genuinely and obviously happy to have them in her house, and was more than capable of playing the consummate hostess when the occasion demanded it. The men commented on how splendid her mansion and the estate were. They said that driving into the property was like entering a different world. These men had obviously heard of the place and its owner, but this was their first introduction to the fabled and feared Ottilie. I watched their faces with fascination as they praised her, showing their delight and honour to be invited there.

"I hope you brought God with you," Auntie suddenly blurted to them.

They apologised immediately for making themselves at home and not immediately attending to the work of the Lord. "Yes, we really must begin. I have a Bible study in few hours' time," the minister responded, his relaxed demeanour quickly evaporating.

They began by singing a hymn to praise the Lord, after which his two assistants read and quoted passages from the Bible. Finally, the three men took turns in prayers and blessings. It was all quite beautiful. Mase accompanying the other men singing a hymn combined to create a powerful and moving resonance that reverberated throughout the entire room. It was as though the music acted as a cleansing aura. I could not hold back tears of joy and relief, realising then how much I missed my family's prayers each night and the fellowship of the church. I would have done anything to convince them not to leave.

The job of serving ice cream, cakes and sodas fell to me. Auntie gave each man money for their beautiful service, and asked them to promise they would visit once a month and organise the choir to join them in future. Meanwhile, I could not help noticing the minister's changing attitude. He kept looking at the windows directly opposite him, as if he was seeing something disturbing. He was no longer as relaxed as when he first arrived. He had become restless and anxious to leave. Goodbyes were said and hands were shaken.

I followed them outside and out of curiosity asked, "What is wrong? Did you men see anything?"

"A scary little girl with no eyes sitting on one of the chairs by the window looking at me," the minister replied, immediately looking horrified at his own admission.

Mase and the other men claimed they had not seen anything. Mase joked that maybe the minister needed his afternoon nap before Bible study.

"There is something really evil about this place. It just didn't feel good at all," the minister added, rapidly becoming pale.

Mase whispered to me, "The real reason the choir didn't come was because most of them are scared of this place. Don't worry; remember they won't hurt you."

As they drove away I stood there for a while feeling empty as the loneliness filled me once more. Mase returned to Auntie's farm on his usual working days, but the minister and the others never ventured across the threshold again. A few weeks after this, Mase confided to me that the day I found him sick in his hut was the day he saw the girl without eyes and she had explained to him why she appeared that way. He told me that much but no more.

"Maybe she is trying to tell us something," I suggested. "I have seen her in various places, even my grandmother saw her before she died. She is not hurting me; perhaps she needs my help."

"All I can tell you is that I think she was killed here. Don't tell your Auntie I told you this," he whispered, seeming to be heartbroken over what he knew. Whatever else Mase had seen and knew about the girl went to his grave with him.

Chapter 13

The Boy in the Room

There was never a moment when Auntie didn't have her guard up. She was always on edge, mistrusting of people and their motives, but that did not stop me from trying. In reality, she was the only person I had in the world so I had to try, but moreover I wanted to. I had started to develop real feelings of love for my Auntie, and I wanted to show her that I was grateful for everything she had done for me. After many failed attempts, Auntie finally surrendered to my nagging insistence that it should be me who washed her legs. This was so distasteful yet so intimate that I felt sure it would bring us closer together.

The queen of the palace was unsurprisingly self-conscious about those repulsive and foul-smelling legs. It was a constant source of embarrassment and humiliation for her. Nonetheless, she conceded the point to me. She watched closely as I removed the bandages with tender loving care and was overwhelmed when I refused to wear gloves. Tears spilled from her emotionally charged eyes. In the fourteen years I had known this woman I had never seen her sensitive, vulnerable side.

"No one has ever touched my legs like that before," she wept.

"Auntie, I used to remove poos from my grandmother's bum when she was in pain. I never wore gloves. This is no hardship; it's the least I can do for you," I assured her.

She dabbed her eyes with her handkerchief and unexpectedly burst out laughing. "Your grandmother was very lucky to have you," she cheered.

"We were fortunate to have each other," I replied firmly.

Sunday was our Sabbath, a day of rest and reflection for Samoans. On the estate it was still a working day, but at a more relaxed pace. It was the only full day of the week on which the labourers did not come in to work. Bentzen would laze around, reading newspapers, playing with the dogs and take turns with Auntie driving around the property to check on things. As I had taken over one of the maid's chores in tending to Auntie's legs, the maid no longer needed to come in on Sunday. Conducting this cleansing ritual was not an easy process, sometimes taking up to an hour, twice a day. Originally the leg washing area was set up by the laundry at the side of the house, directly opposite the big concrete water tank and the chicken coop. Once I took over this chore, I considered a change of location was in order. To relieve Auntie from having to look at a depressing, mundane view, I persuaded her to adopt a position in the front of the house near the stairs. This area overlooked her vibrant, magical garden.

"I never realised quite how exquisite those flowers are," she exclaimed to me one day, pointing at her orchards as though she was seeing them for the first time.

I was so pleased with myself at suggesting this relocation, but it was better yet that it had served to take my Auntie's mind off ugliness and refocus it on beauty. She had lived there all her life but had never appreciated the true beauty created by her long endeavours in the garden until that day. Our Sunday routine became our bonding time, the most treasured for me and the happiest for Auntie. It was nearly three months into this ritual before she really started to let her guard down, then we talked and laughed and shared stories and secrets in a manner I would have previously believed impossible. Some of our discussions centred on her world travels. She was proud of her adventuring and I listened in awe to her stories, which she freely shared with obvious delight. She proudly declared that there were only six countries in the world she hadn't been to. Jerusalem and Egypt were some of her favourites.

Full of enthusiasm, she told me about Mele (Tina) and how fond she was of her, pointing out she was once the best friend she had ever known. "I remember one day when I went to pick her up in my car. We took a drive to Apia to introduce her to some German soldiers. No one knew she was my maid as we sat on the beach drinking cola with the fellas. I even gave her a pair of my shoes to wear that were far too big for her tiny feet. We laughed about it so much because they kept slipping off as she walked," Auntie laughed as she fondly related this beautiful memory to me. "Mele had a beautiful heart." She paused in reflective sadness. "Just like yours. No matter how hard I was with her, she never said no when I needed her. When she smiled, her tiny eyes shone and I could see her soul."

It was a perfect description of my beautiful Tina and it filled me with pride that Auntie had really seen the true beauty of my wonderful grandmother.

During the time I spent at the farm there were good days and bad days with Auntie Tilie, but the more we shared stories and family secrets the closer our relationship became. I also learnt very quickly how to react when Auntie was in a really horrible mood. When she fell into one of those foul tempers I would disappear into my room to read the Bible or study. This escape was usually sufficient for a temper tantrum, but when she descended into depression that was entirely another matter. This transformation seemed to happen randomly and instantly, often taking days before the condition seemed to remedy itself.

Bentzen and I both knew how seriously we had to take these slides into an emotional abyss as dealing with the Auntie who had had enough of life. It was infinitely more problematic than dealing with raging Auntie. She would resolutely refuse to get out of bed, eat or drink. During those times, I would voluntarily take time off school to help the maids with her care. On one such occasion, a few days had slipped past without her foul legs being cleansed. The stench became so awful it actually made it difficult to breathe in the house even when all windows were opened. It was one of those times when Auntie Tilie had decided she would rather die than endure life any longer. During such episodes, Bentzen had to be in control of her pills, as she had tried to overdose more than once.

"You know, I will not be going back to school until you are better," I exclaimed, trying to reason with her so she would at least permit me to wash and disinfect her legs.

"Leave me be. I am ready to go now. I hate this life," she moaned.

But I wasn't letting her go anywhere. I would sit beside her, reading stories of Jesus from the Bible, talking to her and breathing in that wretched odour, desperately trying to convince her to eat something. After days of unrelenting persuasion, I finally broke through. She woke up on a Sunday morning and wanted to have breakfast outside on the front porch. That was a demanding day for me.

The maids did not work on Sundays any longer, so I became both nurse and housekeeper. After I helped Auntie into a nice warm bath, dressed her and cleaned her legs, it was already 1pm. I set her up at the front porch to get some fresh air and sunlight while I prepared a meal. As I toiled in the kitchen, Bentzen joined the dogs and a far more relaxed Auntie, who was laughing while the animals licked her hands. Happily serving them the meal, I excused myself so they could enjoy their repast while I tended to Auntie's bed. By the time I had finished and hung up the sheets it was nearly 2pm. Auntie was dozing happily on her chair and Bentzen had gone to check the plantation, when the dogs started acting very strangely. They were wagging their tails and jumping up and down as if they were playing with someone. As I spread the sheets on the clothesline not far from where Auntie sat, I noticed the unmistakable shape of a head-like shadow on the sheet. I quickly moved the sheet to see what it was. In the clear light of day with no fever or night shadows to blame the vision on, no violent lead up to the event, I could see as plain as day a little boy standing behind Auntie as if he was touching her face. I stood there gawping, wondering if he would turn to look at me, but he just disappeared. I had never before seen an image of a little boy, but I had heard a boy's giggle, either from upstairs or somewhere far away, echoing throughout the house.

Early that evening when I was tending to Auntie's legs again, I could not resist telling her what had happened earlier on that day. She said nothing in reply. As we waited for another day to end and the darkness to slowly creep over what was left of the daylight, I was burning with questions. It wasn't until after twilight when I was helping her into bed that Auntie suddenly grabbed my hand and asked if the boy I'd seen was happy.

"What do you mean, Auntie?"

"Was he smiling? Did he look happy when he touched my face?"

"I didn't see his face, just the back of his head. But he appeared content. The dogs were playing with him. Their tails were wagging," I told her.

This information seemed to please her as she laid her head on her pillow with a faint smile on her lips. The incident left me with more unanswered questions.

The following weekend, on a perfect Sunday, Auntie suggested that we go upstairs to tidy up. This was not our usual routine but I complied happily. Following her strenuous struggle to move her big legs up each step, I couldn't help wondering how she could walk up alone at night in the dark. I followed in fascinated silence. The next surprise was when I noticed she didn't hesitate for a moment to find the correct key on her jangling jailor's key ring of a hundred keys. It was the deft skill of someone who had done it a thousand times before. As soon as we entered, and with that special key hanging around her neck, she unlocked the door to the most secret room of the estate. I stood behind her, rocking on my heels impatiently.

The door swung open and a wave of apprehension gripped me. The faded, thick, blue-black curtains were fully drawn. The atmosphere was dark and eerie.

"Wait here while I pull the curtains," she ordered. "I don't want you to accidentally bump into anything."

As I waited, Auntie stamped towards the windows. I could not understand why the lights were not turned on so she could see where she was going. It was creepy, and it felt like an age before she finally reached the windows and quietly opened the drapes. After my eyes adjusted to the light, I found that I was standing in the middle of the room. I immediately saw a little boy's toys on the floor. On top of a wall of shelves sat a large brown teddy bear. Toy cars were neatly placed in rows on the other shelves.

At first I thought Auntie was collecting toys as well as clocks, until the chilling realisation set it. This room was a nursery. A rocking horse stood in one corner by an antique wooden bassinet. By the wall was a single bed with a mosquito net over it, as though someone were on the bed sleeping. I could not clearly see what was on the bed, as a white sheet was hanging over the mosquito net on my side blocking my view. On one section of a wall were

133

three framed pictures. One of the photos was of a young and attractive Auntie Tilie sitting on a chair with a little boy. The other one was of the toddler on a rocking horse in his sailor suit, the same toy as in the room. The boy looked about two or three years old. By the bed sat a wooden rocking chair of the type that wealthy people sat on when nursing their babies. Everything was in pristine order.

As I stood there trying to figure out the purpose of this room, as Auntie did not have any children, she walked towards the bed and released the sheet from the netting, folded it neatly and hung it on the rocking chair. I held my breath, partly curious and partly terrified in anticipation. I watched intently as she lifted one side of the mosquito net. There on the bed was a glass box with something lying in it. At first I thought it was a large white doll.

"Hello, my darling. It's only me, mummy," she spoke to the doll. "Wake up. There is someone I would like you to meet." She turned to me with a proud smile on her face and motioned for me to come closer. "This is Alan, my precious little boy. He is such a lazy little man. He doesn't run up to his mummy when she comes to see him anymore like he used to. Alan, wake up! This is Jane, your cousin Karl's daughter. Remember I told you about her?" She carried on talking to what I came to realise with growing horror was Alan in his coffin.

My mind was reeling, my powers of speech struck mute. What I saw was so bizarre and unsettling it defied description. In a sealed glass coffin, the size to fit a small child, lay the embalmed corpse of a little boy. His face was white as chalk. Cotton wool was stuffed in both his nostrils and in his mouth. His eyelids appeared to be glued together. I could not comprehend what I was seeing. I had seen corpses before, but nothing like this. His mummified face was plastered so thickly with some kind of white powder or paste it was difficult to discern whether it was a real child. The rest of his body was covered. He appeared to have no hair on his head and he was wearing a white baby bonnet.

It was not traditional Samoan custom to preserve dead bodies. I was not scared of the corpse, but rather deeply troubled by how Auntie treated it, as if it were still alive, responding to her every word. It was too much for me to comprehend. There had never before been a hint that Auntie had born a son.

I shifted my attention to the photographs on the wall. There were no similarities. The boy in the pictures was smiling, vibrant, almost laughing, a picture of youth and life. I did not want to say anything inappropriate so I opted to remain standing in silent witness to the strange tableau.

"Mummy has got to go now, but I will see you again tonight. I love you, Alan," she chirped like a songbird.

After replacing the mosquito net, she turned on a music box by the coffin. It tinkled out baby rhymes, setting the mood for Alan's naptime. Before covering him with the white sheet, she made sure everything was neat and orderly. With saucer-like eyes, I observed the macabre scene, praying we would soon be leaving the room.

"Good-bye, Alan," I said without thinking. For a moment I felt I was also losing my mind by believing Alan was there. Nonetheless, it accidently proved to be a politically expedient gesture, as my accepting farewell solicited a kind smile towards me from Auntie.

"My dear, go and get us some soda from the fridge. We shall sit out on the balcony and enjoy the cool breeze. I am going to tidy up Alan's room. I shall join you shortly. That darling boy of mine never puts away his toys after he's played with them." She made the statement so convincingly I almost believed it. She bustled about, making sure the room was perfect before the curtains were drawn once more and his room relocked.

The view from the upper balcony was magnificent and serene. It was a perfect sunny day with brilliant white clouds dotted about the vibrant blue sky. I could still hear Auntie talking to Alan as I waited, admiring her stunning garden. I thought how that little boy would have been running around down there, happily chasing butterflies. His bedroom and toys gave the impression that he must have been spoiled and adored by his mother. The photograph of mother and son on the wall certainly depicted a story of how happy they once were. Inevitably, the image of the little boy standing behind Auntie touching her face affectionately while she was napping a week earlier came back to me. Why had she not told me then who he was?

I heard Auntie shut then double lock the bedroom door before heading towards me. It was peaceful as we sat quietly sipping our drinks, cooled by the ocean breeze. For a while we just sat in silence, savouring the amazing view spread majestically in front of us.

"Auntie, what happened to Alan?" I finally and bluntly asked. I did not want to use the words *die* or *death*, in case she believed he was still alive.

"He just died. He was very young. One day I found him dead on his bed. He had complained about pain in his chest and I told him to go and lie down. He wasn't even sick." She wiped away tears at the memory, obviously angry about the senselessness of his early demise.

"I am so sorry, Auntie. I didn't know," I sobbed, no longer able to hold back my own tears.

"After Alan was buried, I still saw him everywhere," Auntie continued. "He was playing like he was still alive. I saw him when I slept, during the day, at night, in my car, in the garden, always calling for me to bring him back home. He even followed me when I was travelling overseas. I decided to bring him home to be with his dogs, toys and all the things he loved."

According to Auntie, Alan visited and waited for her in the bedroom at night. She would read him stories, sing songs and talk with him. The room where Alan's body was preserved for all time was just above mine. This explained the nocturnal movements I'd often heard and, of course, her frequent and uncontrollable sobbing.

She went on to tell me that she once fell asleep and forgot the time. It was 1.30am and Alan was standing by her bed shaking her, but he was in the form of a man. As she did not remember him as anything but a little boy, she did not like this manifestation at all. As a fourteen-year-old girl, I listened, riveted, hanging on her every word. I saw the face of the saddest woman on earth. I now know her devastating loss became the essence of how she lived her life thereafter. She wanted to buy others' love just to fill that void. I had no trouble believing her when she told me she would trade everything to have Alan by her side once more.

When she finished her confession, I stood up from my chair and gave her a kiss on the cheek to show her that I loved her. She patted me on the back, flashing me an approving smile.

"I hate this place, I know it is bad luck and evil but I can't leave because of my son. He visits me here, he touches my face when I am asleep, he whispers to me when I am sad." Auntie exclaimed.

Auntie told me that Bentzen had learnt about body mummifications when he worked part time at a funeral parlour in Denmark. He apparently suggested it, thinking it would help Auntie and Alan to be in peace. It was her and Bentzen's intimate secret. Auntie believed she would pass before Bentzen and so made an agreement with him to place Alan's corpse on top of her in her coffin. If she outlived Bentzen she would then rebury Alan's body in her plot where Alan was initially buried. She didn't trust her family to do the right thing once she had passed on. I listened intently with an ache in my heart for my Auntie; I promised her I would carry out her wish if I was around.

During my research while writing my book, I found out that Alan was born on the 15th of August in 1925 when Auntie was only twenty-three years old. He died before his fourth birthday. I remember bursting into tears when I discovered that Alan and I shared the same birthday – mine was in 1961. Could this be the reason why Auntie Tilie never forgot my birthday and I was extra special to her?

Chapter 14

Secrets

Auntie Tilie was bitter towards her mother but despised her father. She would refer to him as Will or Willy, never father or dad. Whenever she mentioned her father's name, it was accompanied with resentment and hatred. I could see her cringe in disgust at his memory, which was somewhat surprising, as he'd left the entire estate to her.

"I was so furious when my mother left me. I was the only girl. She should have taken me with her to keep me safe," Auntie bemoaned to me one day.

Whatever memory she was reliving, it so enraged her that she was literally shaking. She displayed the same face as the Auntie who shot the horse and nearly killed her husband. In desperation to change the subject so she might breathe in some calming air, I confessed to her that perhaps if my mother had taken me to New Zealand with her, I would not have been raped by her youngest brother while I was taking care of their mother. Recounting all the ugliness, the hatred, the shame and the agony of the emotional turmoil inside me provided release for the first time in my life. It felt agonising yet empowering to finally tell someone everything I'd been through. Rage filled my soul as tears streamed down onto my dress while my Auntie listened.

She tried to console me, but it was my turn to be bitter and vengeful about how unfair life was. The sensitive, compassionate side of Auntie that only emerged on rare occasions came to life and gazed directly into my soul. She listened intently and offered encouraging, sincere and kind words that fortified me with a sense of hope. She understood exactly what I'd endured, how vile it was to be terrified during the night time hours and in any moment of solitude. She knew what it meant to have someone you used to love and trust suddenly become someone you feared and hated. Auntie Tilie was probably the last person I thought I would be turning to for a sympathetic ear and shoulder to cry on, but once again what she shared with me left me speechless. In truth, she knew more about how I felt and the traumatic after effects of my uncle's abuse than I understood myself.

"When a member of a family that you trust hurts you like that, especially as a little girl, the pain does not go away. It will never go away. My father did the same to me," Auntie revealed solemnly, then paused with a frown for a while as if she was thinking.

I could not believe my ears as I tried to imagine someone like Auntie Tilie being scared of anyone. I'd always thought she was invincible. "You saved me, Auntie. I think if I didn't come here there was a possibility I would be pregnant by my mother's brother," I interrupted.

"My own father was an evil man," she uttered with remarkable control, as if she wanted me to listen and understood. Then she became withdrawn and silent, her eyes disappearing into a total void. She stared for a while over her garden to where the graves lay and pointed out her father's tomb.

"I hated him! For years I wanted to dig him up and place his evil bones at the back near the pig sty," Auntie stated.

I didn't know what to say next. While I had been struggling to endure my own suffering in silent secrecy, my Auntie Tilie had been going through precisely the same quandary. I guess we were both broken inside. I am not sure why she felt the need to tell me about her secret relationship with her father, because she struggled to even mentioning his name, I'd thought she was going to pass out. Perhaps she thought it could help me with the pain and the shame I was carrying, or Auntie Tilie had finally released hers to me knowing that I of all people would understand.

My wily and wounded Auntie suddenly looked up to heaven and asked, "Do you believe in God, Jane?"

Despite what had happened in my life, my experiences with the church and the people who were supposed to practise what they preached, I had often prayed ardently to God. When I read the Bible about God's love and healing of the sick and taking away pain, and yet looked upon my grandmother's terrible suffering for years before she died, I did sometimes question where he was. It would have been entirely reasonable, I considered, for me to answer "no," but instead I heard myself saying, "Yes, I believe there is a God."

Auntie paused for a moment, contemplating my response. "Do you believe that God really forgives bad people?" she asked me calmly.

I wasn't sure how to answer, but instinctively felt there was a right and wrong answer to that question and I dare not pick the wrong one. I remained silent.

"This place needs to be burnt to the ground. It hides horrible secrets. When I am gone, I do not want anyone in the family to come here. The suffering should end with me and my children," she declared forcefully.

I was left in no doubt this was how it would be, although I did wonder about the word *children*.

Chapter 15

My Identity

Over the eight months I lived with Auntie, whenever she had visitors I was sent to my room and told to close the door. I complied, reading quietly on my bed or happily daydreaming about the wonderful future I imagined for myself. I could hear Auntie chatting and laughing with her visitors and offering the children sweets and drinks. No one ever knew I was there. Of course, this edict served to add to my feelings of isolation; it fed my insecurities and made me feel just plain worthless. Auntie had her own skewed reasons for treating me this way; her overpowering fear of betrayal clouded her thinking and judgment about my welfare.

For as long as I can remember, I felt that I did not belong anywhere or to anybody. In my extended family and village, I was the only child burdened with many surnames. This caused me constant confusion. It was never explained to me why my name needed changing time after time. One year at school I was known as Sieni Ta'ateo (my grandfather's first name). The following year I was labelled with something completely different. I remember running home crying to my grandmother one day after the children said that I must have been conceived by many fathers. As always, Tina knew the right things to say to calm me down.

"They are jealous because they are not like you. You are special. Only important people in Samoa have many names. If only those naughty kids knew who you truly were, they would be staring at you with admiration."

I did not completely believe her but it made me feel better. "What is my true identity, Tina?" I enquired timidly.

"You have Chinese in you on my side, and China will one day rule the world," Tina told me with an air of finality. I saw an uncomfortable expression of guilt in her eyes but her tone succeeded in forcing me to cease and desist in my line of questioning.

Growing up, I used five different surnames and had two birth certificates, even though I was fairly certain I had been born only once. At birth I was named Sieni Kalo. When my mother left for American Samoa to work, my grandparents had to register my existence so I could attend school when I was old enough. Children who were born out of wedlock in Samoa had birth certificates that only recorded their mother's names – "father unknown" was written in the father's part of the certificate. My grandparents did not want that for me. That label on a birth certificate would have meant that I was a bastard child, and in Samoa that branded you as a child of shame. Fortunately, they knew of my father but they did not know his family name or how to spell his first name, which was Karl. They decided to simply put down what they thought it was, hence the name Kalo. In those days in Samoa, the parents sat down with the village mayor and told him the information they wanted on the child's birth certificate. The mayor filled in the necessary forms, added his signature and authorised stamp, then filed them with the birth registry. If the parent had told the mayor the child's father is Darth Vader and his mother Princess Leah, that's what would have been recorded.

When my mother had me legally adopted out by her eldest sister Salaki and her husband Aukuso, my surname became Aukuso, although in school and around my village I was still known as Sieni Ta'ateo. When my grandfather received his chief's name, Fasia, my last name at school changed yet again. My Karl surname was resurrected later when I started high school. My Auntie Sia, whom I lived with after Tina died, had a smart idea. If I used a European-sounding last name, it would probably guarantee me a good job after I left school. She saw my potential and thought a European name would secure my future when my mother failed to take me with her yet again. Those days in Samoa, people with German or any European family names seemed to be guaranteed better-paid jobs. It was not always the best applicant who secured a position. In fact, more frequently it was one's networks of influence that meant more than skills and experience. I simply went with the flow and embraced whatever name people decided for me. It all became so confusing I just gave up bothering about it.

Following the drama with my school report, when Auntie Tilie discovered that Karl was the surname I used, we went to Apia to sort it out as she promised. At that time I still had no idea what my family name was going to be and didn't think to ask, reasoning I would find out soon enough. Perhaps, I mused, I would also find out more about this Karl person.

In those days, people started queuing as early as 4am to get anything done in government departments. Some slept there overnight to reserve their place in line. There were no appointments, people just patiently lined up hoping that someone would be able to see them. If you failed, you would try again the next day. I had experienced this dreadful system before when I accompanied Auntie Sia from the village to sort out Uncle Migao's birth certificate. It was his turn to travel to New Zealand.

We were in the line for five hours, taking turns standing while the other sat to rest her legs, going without anything to eat all day in case we lost our place. I was dreading this day, especially as Auntie Tilie could not stand for a long time.

We arrived just after 10am, replete from our delicious breakfast at Aggie Grey's fancy restaurant. Auntie and the great Aggie Grey knew each other well from as far back as 1940. Aggie had turned her hamburger joint into a boarding house and Auntie was travelling back and forth to New Zealand when they became firm friends. Later, when Auntie met Captain Bentzen, she introduced sailors and other overseas visitors to Aggie's establishment. According to Auntie Tilie, she was the unrecognised orchestrator of Aggie Grey's business success. During the Golden Years of Hollywood, Aggie played host to many visiting dignitaries and celebrities, Marlon Brando among them. Her legacy has made her name a leading figure in Samoan tourism. Over the years these two powerful women had developed a deep friendship, so it filled me with both joy and pride to be introduced to Aggie as Ottilie's favourite family member.

On demand, Auntie's chauffeur parked our car right in front of the Registry office. After struggling out of her seat she strode purposefully in as I followed meekly. She stomped and huffed straight past all the unfortunate people weary from standing many long hours already. Not a single one spoke out against her queue jumping; they just averted their gaze to the pavement. Auntie did not know anybody in the office, but she walked right up to one of the counters as if she owned the place, and with her loud voice demanded to see the manager. The girl behind the counter was busy serving someone. I could see everyone's eyes fixed on us in amazement, even those of the office staff. Hesitant but taken by surprise, the lady paused for a minute, looked at Auntie again and did exactly what she had commanded without complaint. I swelled with pride. It was obvious this lady did not want to comply, but decided to err on the side of caution with this scary lady. Within moments we were escorted inside the manager's office where he politely offered Auntie a chair. I was in awe, I had never been with anyone who could walk into such a place, make demands and receive such respect.

With my report in her hand and twenty tala thrown to the man, Auntie stated, "I need to change this girl's birth certificate to her rightful family name. She is my niece and I've just taken over her care. Another twenty on top of that if you do it right away. I don't have time to wait."

Twenty Tala was probably all the manager earned for a day. He glanced hungrily at the money, briefly to the name on my report and asked me for my date and place of birth. The information duly imparted, he asked to be excused as he hurried into a room where all the files and documents were kept. Within a heartbeat he returned carrying two copies of my birth certificate and placed them in front of Auntie.

"There was no Sieni Karl, but I was able to find Sieni Kalo and Sieni Aukuso," he announced none too confidently.

"Who the hell is Aukuso?" Auntie demanded.

"That is a problem. She was legally adopted by these people. The family court was involved. Therefore we are powerless to issue her another birth certificate with a different surname unless her adoptive parents or her mother signs over their rights," he timidly explained.

Quickly I explained to Auntie who the Aukusos were. She pondered these details for a moment before removing herself from the chair and thanking the man for his help. He politely opened the door for her and we marched out again in plain view of the people waiting to be served, their children lying bored and listless on the dirty floor. I had learned another valuable lesson that day, observing closely the manner in which Auntie worked the system to her advantage. I would be sure to make use of these tactics in the future. She was not, to my mind, demanding or bossy; rather, she was efficient and concise. Later she explained to me that to get what you want in life you have to simply let people know from the start that you will not accept no as an answer. It seemed perfectly acceptable for her to behave this way – to simply walk into an office with a bag full of cash and expect people would have no choice but to say yes.

Marching out of the office, Auntie explained that one of her friends was a barrister, suggesting he might be able to assist. She did not want anyone to know what she had in mind, but with money and powerful friends at her disposal little if anything was going to stand in the way of her objectives. She was right about that of course. Her barrister friend assured her the matter would be dealt with in a few days. That was that – impressive!

My new name became Jane Olida Schwalger. Schwalger was one of the better-known and respected German names in Samoa. I often saw the Schwalger name on some business signs in town. For me, the new name was the essence of belonging, a tangible symbol of my new future and it was rightfully mine. Auntie had just gifted me the most beautiful treasure of my life – my true identity. Much later, I discovered that Olida was Auntie Tilie's middle name.

Chapter 16

Grandfather's Revelation

As we prepared for Auntie's seventy-fifth birthday celebration, a message was sent from my village family that my grandfather Tama was seriously ill. Having not seen him for eight months, a consuming guilt swept over me. He was calling to see me urgently, fearing the end might be near. This news did not sit well with Auntie Tilie. She didn't need to voice her concerns; they were etched into her frowning expression so clearly she might have been shouting them out loud. Before she could reply to the messenger, I blurted out that I was going to see Tama. My tone was so adamant even the iron-fisted regent didn't attempt to object.

"Don't forget that you start your new school soon," she reminded me sternly before acquiescing to my demand.

A week earlier I had a fight with one of the girls at my old school and we had both been suspended. Instead of telling Auntie what really happened, I pleaded to attend a better school for my future education. She took some convincing but eventually I'd won the point. Of all the colleges in Samoa, I'd chosen St Mary's College in Apia. It was a girl's only school and I had always envied their striking uniforms (white blouse and a smart blue pinafore). It might have been a shallow basis for the decision but it seemed to me that all the best-looking girls on the island attended this facility. Although Auntie had some reservations about the distance, she decided I could be dropped off in the morning at one of the local shops and I could catch the bus to and from school from there. As usual, when we went to enrol, it was not quite as simple as we hoped.

"Where are your parents?" the female principal asked, scrutinising my application.

"My Auntie is waiting outside," I replied.

After coldly eyeing me up and down, the principal decided not to accept my application on the grounds that I was not a Catholic. I believe she used it as an excuse. I felt perhaps because my mother was not with me for my enrolment, she recognised my unworthiness. Such were my insecurities. Again, my hopes were dashed. I shuffled dejectedly back to Auntie, who was waiting impatiently in the car. The moment she saw my unhappy face she knew things had not gone well. When I explained what their criteria demanded, she silently exited the vehicle and stomped into the school like she was going into a prize fight.

"I bet you she will be coming out with your uniform," the driver remarked, smirking widely at what he knew the headmistress was in for.

We waited fifteen minutes before Auntie returned victoriously brandishing papers in her hand as though they were the spoils of war. The driver leapt out to open the door, throwing me an I-told-you-so raise of his eyebrows as Auntie re-entered the vehicle grinning from ear to ear.

"You will start next week," she told me triumphantly.

"Thank you, Auntie," I offered in sincere humility.

"Have you learnt a lesson today?" she asked. "You don't deal with servants. You see the person who makes decisions. If she doesn't listen then you go to the top."

I had been talking to the principal so I wasn't sure how much higher I could go. In any event, I had to know. "What did you say to them?"

"I told her that I was a very good friend of the Pope, and if I pleased I could buy the entire school then have the whole lot of them fired," she said, bellowing with laughter.

With pride and amazement at her brash lie, I burst out laughing too. I did not know if Auntie really said that to the school principal but frankly it wouldn't have surprised me. Auntie Tilie did not look like a woman over seventy. She had the stout, stocky build of a man, and something in her Germanic ancestry made her damn intimidating when she entered a room with a mission in mind. She exuded an aura of extreme confidence, facing all obstacles without a hint of fear or hesitation. This was certainly a woman not to be trifled with and I really admired her for that. Those times with Auntie Tilie taught me many valuable lessons that helped me enormously in later life.

Arriving back at my village, I had that familiar burning knot in my stomach. My beloved grandfather was indeed terribly ill. He was pale, sick and frail, far worse than I had imagined. On hearing my voice he sat up, tears of joy flooding into his eyes. Apparently, he had been living under the belief that I had left him because of his decision to have my pet pig Puka butchered to feed the minister. On top of this, he'd been burdened with a gnawing guilt because he'd given Tina his word he would look after and protect me. He felt he had failed because he did not dare to come and rescue me from Auntie Tilie's place. He apologised profusely, and we both cried, hugged and kissed, and forgave each other. The truth of the matter was we were both so happy to see each other there was no need to discuss the past. As I looked around, it dawned on me that though my village and people I grew up with, including my family, were still the same doing the same village routines, I was somehow different. I felt I no longer fit in that life anymore, although I missed my cousins and the company of other children immensely.

Tama interrupted my thoughts. "What does that mean woman feed you? You've put weight on."

Auntie Vaitogi joined us at that point, telling me she had not seen him this happy for a long time. Tama and I talked, shed tears and caught up with family news, one piece of which caught me quite by surprise. He told me he had sent an urgent message to my mother to come and extricate me from Ottilie's farm. She was arriving from New Zealand the following week.

"Perhaps, she can take us both back to New Zealand with her," Tama exclaimed with great hope.

I had very mixed feelings on the subject, but never more so than when I learned with sickening horror that my Uncle Faalua had already joined my mother in New Zealand. My mother had apparently paid his fare three months earlier, this very same uncle who destroyed my innocence and twisted my perceptions about myself. This man was the reason I had run away from those I loved, yet he was living free in New Zealand. I feared him more than I feared the vengeful dead at Auntie's place. All the terror, pain and anguish of Faalua's assaults came rushing back to me, shattering the fleetingly happy reunion I'd been sharing with Tama. The woman who had given birth to me had been fully appraised of her brother's crimes but clearly didn't give a damn about it. In fact, she had rewarded him with a much-coveted move to New Zealand.

I was beyond furious, beyond rage, at my mother's actions. The injustice of the whole situation seemed more of an affront and uncaring than the crimes my uncle had committed in the first place. The betrayal stabbed me as solidly as if it had been a spear to my heart. This was it. I wanted to return to Auntie Tilie's place.

Auntie's place was now my home, and at least I knew exactly where I stood there. In the deepest part of my soul, I wished she was not the person who gave birth to me.

I could not utter a single word. Impotently, I broke down and sobbed while Tama and Auntie Vaitogi looked on, puzzled and worried. Due only to the severity of my grandfather's condition, I summoned every ounce of self-control I could muster to contain my fury. Eventually, I composed myself and assured Tama nothing was wrong. Deep inside I was raging at the injustice of it all. For Tama's sake alone, I reluctantly agreed to wait until my mother arrived in Samoa.

During the period prior to mother's arrival, Tama was curious about what I had encountered while away from the village. He insisted on being told every detail, asking some extremely odd and probing questions. It wasn't hard to assure him that I was treated like a princess and that Auntie Tilie really cared for me, but his fears didn't seem to abate.

"Perhaps she has calmed down a bit," he mused uncertainly. "But aren't you scared at nights there?" He tilted his head, watching my reply closely.

"Was she that bad?" I asked, pretending not to know what he was talking about.

"Oh yes. Very bad indeed," he assured me. "She used to whip workers and threatened to hang them. Do you remember that poor old man in our village who walks with a limp? His injury was a result of your Auntie's bullet. She shot him point blank in the leg when he was caught stealing. The *taulasea*, Ruta, has also told me about what happens at Ottilie's farm. She pleaded with me to get you out of there."

"You worry too much," I replied flippantly.

"When I found out you had gone to Ottilie I was worried sick for you. I know the place better than you do. During the day everything seems okay, but at night it becomes something else entirely," Tama said icily. My ruse hadn't fooled him. He knew I had seen things.

I wanted so badly for Tama and my family to think that I had the best life. I wanted them to believe I was the luckiest girl in our village to be living in such luxury. No one needed to know about the dark side. We were all drugged before seven o'clock at night, so when the ghosts took over we were fast asleep and mostly never cared about them. They were not hurting me, so their presence became normal, almost routine.

"I know that place. I know there are ghosts there," he insisted. "Tina and I have seen them ourselves when we worked there."

This was the first time in my life that Tama had shown any level of willingness to discuss anything that involved Ottilie. While I wanted to maintain the facade of everything being fabulous, I could not allow an opportunity to learn more about Auntie's estate slip by.

Tama explained he had once worked at the estate, and seemed only too willing to finally reveal all the awful truth he knew. I listened in shocked disbelief as he recounted the most ghastly tale. He had been a regular workman for Ottilie over a five-year period when he was in his early twenties. This was during the time of Auntie Tilie's first husband. He was there when Alan was born, and when he died, after which the farm had been closed for nearly a year. Tama went back when the grieving parents returned from overseas and left when he met Tina two years later.

"My real father was a German man who came here with Ottilie's father, when Germany sent Samoa some of their agricultural experts to help establish our economy with farming," he explained. "When Viliamu (Wilhelm's name in Samoan) first bought that wretched place it was thick, wild jungle. My father worked with him to clear it with the help of foreign black men they employed. The two German men were friends – and I have to say not very nice human beings. Workers were hung for minor infractions; some were thrown alive into the copra house furnace to save bullets and to hide the evidence. Some of those killed were cooked in a huge cauldron to feed the other workers and their dogs. It was well known in the village because nothing could disguise the stench of boiled up human remains.

"Those were horrific and tumultuous times in our land. In those days, Samoans were so involved in trying to establish sovereignty and stability in their own country during the civil wars and the Mau Movement revolt (Indigenous opposition movement when Samoans began to assert their claim to independence), they just ignored what these men were doing. Mostly, the people they were abusing, murdering and cannibalising were not Samoan. That farm was a killing field for many of those workers. For some reason he spared the Chinese, but Viliamu hated the blacks."

My eyes were wide as saucers as I listened, but my heart felt as cold and black as ash.

"When we worked at the copra house at night we saw terrifying images. That place is justifiably haunted. No human should ever live there," he mused distantly. "Terrible things have happened there, some from the ancient days. It is cursed ground and ends up destroying any who live there."

After absorbing and analysing Tama's story, it seemed consistent with what had been happening at the farm. Until that moment I'd had no idea that Tama's father was German, much less a friend of Auntie's father. Everything he was telling me was tantamount to a deathbed confession, one he felt he had to make for me to understand why it was so dangerous to live at the estate that I used to believe was a magical paradise. It also occurred to me I had German blood on my mother's side as well as my father's.

"My mother, Matalega, was a local girl," he went on to enlighten me further. "Her family lived on the boundary of Viliamu's acres. That was how she met my father Salu (Saul, his German name). Unfortunately, my father returned to Germany while we were young and uneducated. We never found out what his surname was. Samoan *matai* names were more important to our mother's family, so we didn't bother with it anyway. Mother always suspected my father had another wife and children in Germany and that he escaped back to his country because of the killing in that place."

"How come our family doesn't have any money?" I suddenly asked, wondering where all our *Palagi* wealth was.

"When my father left, he didn't even say goodbye, never mind leave any money for our mother to help with our care. It was extremely hard on her. That is why we are the few poor half-castes on the island. We are half-breeds with no last name and no money. My mother later married a Samoan man from Savaii who helped bringing us up."

He was struggling with the entire saga, but forced himself to continue as long as he was able. Apparently, many people had died at the estate over the years for no apparent reason. Some were possessed and withered away, dying weeks later. Others, including Tama, were taken over by an overwhelming urge to jump in the furnace. In his case, it happened when he worked in the copra house and saw images of men screaming for help. His fellow workers grabbed him and held him down, saving him from a fiery fate when they spotted him acting strangely. Without the help of Ruta's grandfather, the renowned healer, he said he would not have survived.

"I can also assure you that Ottilie's son and her father did not die from illness or natural causes. The house had something to do with their deaths. Viliamu suffered greatly. He was rotting away for years before he died. No medicine or all his money could arrest the decay," Tama said chillingly.

"But these things aren't hurting me, Tama," I insisted, defending my privileged position at the estate.

"They will, Sieni. You have the blood of two evil men flowing in you and, as Ruta said, you were conceived on that farm. It makes you dangerously susceptible to these things; you have a deep connection to that place."

I waited until we were alone before asking another question that had been burning on my lips. Tama was studying me to assess if I believed his tales and accepted how serious the situation was when I asked, "Did Auntie Tilie have a baby by her father?"

His eyes fixed on mine for a heartbeat. In that instant he realised I knew more than I'd been letting on. With a sigh, he decided I needed to know it all.

"That was supposed to be the deepest secret of them all. My mother, being Viliamu's best friend's lady, was the only one allowed to go to help when Ottilie was pregnant and suffering badly with morning sickness. Ottilie was very young, a teenager. She was my age. My mother was also there when Ottilie gave birth to a baby girl. The infant was apparently killed by Viliamu shortly after her birth by smothering her with a pillow. She was buried on the farm. My mother cried for days after that.

"I met Viliamu a few times when my oldest brother Salu (named after his German father) and I went to the farm to meet with our father. He was a heartless brute of a man. He was cruel even to his own children, especially his older sons. When his first wife left, taking the two older boys with her, they were banned from the estate. The mother never visited the other children, out of fear for her life. The wife's family threatened to cut Viliamu's head off with bush knives, but he had guns. It's no good bringing a knife to a gunfight. No one intimidated Viliamu."

Tama was finally making his point. I agreed I would wait and see when my mother arrived.

Chapter 17

Meeting My Dad

My mother arrived in Samoa a few days before Auntie Tilie's birthday celebration. Auntie sent one of her workers to remind me to return for the celebrations on Saturday. My mother, with an expression of disdain, told me we would be going together.

"How ungrateful you were to leave Tama," was her greeting remark to me on returning to Samoa. "He took care of you and you abandoned him. After Ottilie's party you shall come back here and take care of your grandfather until he dies."

As much as I feared and loathed my uncle, I don't believe I had ever hated anyone with the pure white-hot hatred I held for my mother. I was not at all thrilled to go to the party in her company.

We arrived at Auntie Tilie's around 2pm on her birthday, hot and exhausted from the long arduous trek under a merciless sun. As we passed the first gate of the place I had called home for nearly a year there were cars scattered everywhere. It looked like a parking lot. We were the only ones arriving on foot. Many people I had never seen before were relaxing around the front porch; others strolled around admiring the garden. As we drew nearer my heart was pounding. I was uneasy about two things. The first was Auntie's reaction to my not returning as agreed. The second was I had a strong feeling my father would be among the guests. I wondered what Auntie expected of me when I finally met the man she had hidden me from for fourteen years. I braced myself, planning to use the expression on Auntie's face as a guide for how I should react.

The celebration was already in full swing when we entered. It was a sophisticated affair, quite different from village celebrations I'd attended. Most of the guests seemed to be of mixed race, some were pure European. It was the first time I had seen how people with money and position celebrated. These were rich and well-educated businesspeople having real fun, casually drinking, eating and socialising, with none of the *Fa'a Samoa* nonsense spoiling the proceedings. Lawyers and Samoan government ministers were invited. I was pleased to see that everyone, including children, were treated equally and all was laid out for everyone to help themselves.

Auntie stood centre stage in the gathered throng, a glass of wine sloshing wildly in her hand. She was glittery, gleeful and in an uncharacteristically merry mood. Never before had I seen her so happily animated. Thankfully she was delighted to see me, which was a huge relief. She even gave me an unexpected quick hug. I had no money to buy her a gift. Instead, I wrote her a loving letter. It expressed my gratitude and apologised for not returning a week earlier to help with the preparations for her birthday. She placed the letter unopened in her dress pocket then told me to get something to eat and we would talk later. That suited me. Auntie was happy. All seemed well and now I could relax and have some fun.

Looking around to find where my mother had disappeared to, I spotted her with Auntie Vaitogi and a man I'd never seen before. My heart skipped a beat. He was large and imposing. I did not have to ask who he was; instinctively I knew he was my father. A moment later, my mother excitedly introduced him to me as such. My initial impression of him was of a healthy, stocky, fit-looking man. His heavy weight surprised me at first, but then I noticed his good looks and curly hair. He had a cheeky, easy smile and appeared shy, squirming in his seat as though he was unsure how he should react to me. For the first time in my life I finally believed I had actual parents. Neither of them had been involved in any part of my life, yet together they were conspiring about my future – without considering my opinion, and disregarding the feelings of the decent people who had cared for me. They hurriedly reached a decision while I was talking to Auntie Tilie: I was to live with my father and his family. My mother would return to New Zealand to her family the following week. For mum the problem was solved; that was it.

"But I thought you came specifically to take me with you," I complained accusingly. "And yesterday you demanded I returned to care for Tama."

"Your father wants to take care of you from now on, so you can get to know him and your other siblings."

"What about Auntie Tilie? She is going to be very unhappy about this," I warned, hoping to sway them from this path.

Of course, the co-conspirators were already well aware the mighty Ottilie would be displeased, and hence they had hastily concocted a plan to divert her attention. My mother was to request permission for me to return to our village with her. She was leaving the following week and we needed to spend those last precious days together. In the time bought by this deception, we would meet my father in Apia at the Birth Certificate Office to apply for a new certificate for me. From there I would say goodbye to my mother and go directly to my father's home. It was a cunning, underhanded plan. Auntie was relaxed and compliant. Having imbibed a little too much, she agreed without hesitation. I don't know why I didn't expose their deception and throw myself on Auntie's mercy, perhaps something about my two biological parents charting a course for my life gave me some hope for the future. In any event, I fought against the tears that tried to flow as I said goodbye to my Auntie Tilie.

On Monday morning, with more pain in my young heart, I said goodbye to my beloved Tama. I was glad my mother was taking him back with her to visit New Zealand; four of his children lived there. It should be a good place for him. I knew he'd enjoy the family reunion and he might receive decent medical attention. He was relieved I was not going back to the "evil farm," as he called it.

While we were sorting out yet another birth certificate for me, I could not shake the thought of Auntie Tilie from my mind. I relived all the many good things she'd done for me, our heartfelt conversations, and her confusing, complex character. Now having more knowledge of what took place at her estate, I felt a deep sadness for her. Waves of guilt rippled through me. I knew my departure would break her heart. She would be none too pleased at the new name chosen for me either. She had always called me Jane or Janey, but mother decided I was to be Sieni Jane, which was ridiculous because they meant the same thing. Mother seemed to be making all the decisions, father just smiled and signed. A few hours later I was legally renamed Sieni Jane Schwalger and a new birth certificate was issued. An official thumped it with a stamp and handed it to my father.

My mother and I parted once more as if merely strangers. She left with her sister Vaitogi, and I jumped in the passenger seat of my father's utility truck. From that day I was to call him dad. I was beginning to feel a little dizzy with the number of legal names I'd had and the number of residences I'd called home. Who truly wanted me?

Chapter 18

My Addiction

Another chapter was about to begin. Armed with legal proof of my latest name, the stranger I was now to call dad took me to enrol at the Church College of Samoa – a Mormon school. Dad had chosen this educational facility, as his wife was one of the teachers and the family were members of the associated church. Standing at attention in front of the short, stocky vice-principal of the school, I was introduced to my new regent-in-waiting, Brother Tausoga. Without report cards or any documentation from my old school, he decided to put me in Form 2C, the bottom rung of the academic ladder. I argued that I had been in Form 3A due to my excellent grades, earning me a seat in the school's top class. Brother Tausoga was unmoved. Without papers to support my claim, he dismissed it. Agitated and annoyed, I told him I'd been rushed out of my Auntie Tilie's house and could not pick up my things. Dad intervened, asking the vice-principal whether he would change my class if we provided proof to my claims. Dad told me he would go to Auntie and collect my documents just to calm me down.

As we drove away from my latest school, dad chuckled to himself, speculating I had stayed too long with Auntie Tilie. I was exhibiting her bad temper, fighting spirit and contempt for authority. Little did he know I was fretful to the point of a nervous breakdown. Even in the hot Samoan heat I was shaking inside. There was no doubt about it; I desperately needed some of Auntie's calming pills, especially after my dad told me he knew all along his auntie played a huge part in bringing me up; he was too scared to interfere.

My father and his family owned a nice home in Lotopa near Apia. My new school was located conveniently across the road. It was time for me to become acquainted with my latest domicile, my stepmother and my many siblings, all younger than I. Some were still infants. To my relief, I was warmly welcomed by my new family and discovered I gained a new grandmother! My father's mother was called Mama. I was to learn that my other grandfather, Martin (Ottilie's youngest brother), had died when my father was only fifteen years old. Mama became the matriarch of the family after that. She was highly moral and strong in spirit, a good example for the family. She adored her children and grandchildren, and it appeared to be an affection freely reciprocated. My stepmother was a lovely, attractive and smart lady. She treated me well and seemed perfectly comfortable with my dad conducting himself as my father without any interference from her. I liked her straight away. She was always fair and asked me to call her mum, which I still do to this day. To make things less complicated for the narrative, I will refer to her as my step-mum.

My life at my dad's home was my first real family experience. What a relief. What a pleasant surprise. Having lived most of my years on earth dealing with one horror after another, I couldn't believe my luck. It seemed too good to be true, and based on past experience I found myself wondering when the earth was going to open up beneath me. The family was reasonably affluent – they ate and lived well. They had a maid to do our housework and a nanny to help with the little ones while we were at school.

Although my dad and his family were born and brought up in Samoa, they did not live like Samoans. Their main priorities were taking care of their mother (Mama) and to give their children the best life they could. None of my dad's family held *matai* titles nor supported the *Fa'a Samoa*. At last I was in what I thought a family should be.

When I joined the family group, dad was a more domesticated man compared to his wilder, younger days. He was a respected bishop of his ward in the Mormon Church and, according to my step-mum, I came into his life at the perfect time. He had not always been a stable family man, but now he was hard-working, spending every day at his plantation in Aleisa, high in the mountains. The property was not as big as Auntie Tilie's farm, but there were cows, passionfruit, peanuts and bananas. Dad turned out to be a good provider – we never wanted for anything. Every Saturday night all we kids used to go to the movies in our church hall. Each Thursday evening we would be taken for a drive to buy ice cream in town after our family meal. It was all a new and wonderful experience to me. In fact, it was the life I had always dreamed of. Then the crack in the earth appeared, and it was in me.

I arrived as a teenager, full of conflicting and distorted emotions. This was compounded by my addiction to painkillers (although I was innocently unaware of the condition at the time). I did realise I was suffering from an insatiable craving for Auntie's pills and realised that wasn't a good thing, but "drug addict" was a term I'd never heard of. The last thing in the world I wanted was for my new parents to discover my shame. They might disown me! As the withdrawal symptoms appeared I became fearful, guarded and paranoid. I began reacting to normal situations in a most abnormal way. My body's intense urgency for tablets had taken control of me.

Every Sunday morning and again in the afternoon, we attended the Church of Jesus Christ of Latter Day Saints. As the bishop of his ward, dad immediately arranged missionaries to give me lessons so I could be baptised. There was no discussion on the matter. As it turned out, bible study with these young men was just what I needed. My new family, new school, new church, new legally acquired name and missionary studies, all blended to bring stability to my life. Amid my inner turmoil, the church and its teachings gave refuge against my fevered thoughts.

When I first arrived in this new life, I had assumed my dad owned cars and had money because he was one of the bishops of his church. The missionaries explained to me that no one was paid for serving God in their church, not even themselves. In fact, every member – even bishops and high leaders of the church – pays tithings. I felt a surge of pride for the man I called dad. On Sundays he wore his white long-sleeved shirt, a crisp tie and long black pants. The other six days of the week he dressed in rags to work on his plantation to feed his family.

Life at last was really, truly good, even through trying to wean myself off Auntie's magic tablets was a dark cloud hovering overhead threatening to rain on my parade. At first I didn't know what was wrong with me; all I knew was I was overpowered with the urge to continue taking those tablets. I had no idea where to locate some magic white pills. In agonising desperation to ease my opiate withdrawal, I shamefully stole from my dad to buy aspirin or any pills that might help. As an addict, nothing mattered more than quenching that awful raging need.

One Saturday night after my parents dropped us all off to our movie outing, I was tasked with watching the little ones. Instead, I raced to the bathroom and did not return. It was simply impossible to tolerate being in the company of others while going through withdrawal. The day before, a boy named Arthur had promised he could procure some tablets for me. His mother was on some kind of medication and he was certain it would help me. I had first met Arthur in my village the year Tina died. His mother was also from Salepouae. His father was half-European and half-Samoan from Apia. We'd spotted each other and both knew there was a mutual attraction, but we had never managed to speak during those days. I didn't see him again after that. Arthur was my age and extremely handsome. To me he looked very much like the actor Ryan Gosling in *The Notebook*, except with an exotic complexion. He'd left school at twelve years old, not the sharpest tool in the shed. Luckily, he had a father who could assist him with his future. His father was a mechanic who ran a successful business and was able to teach his son a trade.

Our first introduction was . . . interesting. I was walking to town one morning, suffering on one of my bad days. Arthur stopped and offered me a lift. Paranoid and restless, I jumped in, asking if he could take me to the hospital. Of course he was concerned at such a request, but I fobbed it off, telling him I was merely suffering with a severe headache. When we arrived at the hospital dispensary, I realised I had forgotten my money. Arthur kindly paid.

"What sort of headache do you have?" the man behind the counter enquired.

"A sharp, throbbing one, my vision is affected. I need something urgently. I frequently get these bad migraines; sometimes the pain is so intense it travels right down my spine." I exaggerated wildly in the hope of getting something strong.

He suggested a packet of tiny white pills. "Take one once a day, but only when symptoms occur," he advised, adding they would not make me drowsy.

In utter desperation to function normally, I took out two and swallowed them with relief. A few minutes later I felt better, in fact more alive than I had ever felt before. These things were pretty good. I could not stop talking. I suggested to Arthur we go to his house; it was close to my school and home. We could hang out, listen to music and he could drop me off just before my school bell rang. The handsome and congenial Arthur sat behind the steering wheel, nodded his head and flashed a cheeky smile in agreement.

By the time we arrived at his village next to my new village, I was sprightly, full of confidence, and extremely high. Arthur may have had other plans on his mind but I was in a party mood. With his grandmother's disapproving eyes fixed on me, I turned on the radio and started dancing alone in the middle of their living room. Spinning and flailing about without a care in the world, it must have been a bizarre sight. It was the middle of the day and I was still in my school uniform. Fascinated and aroused, Arthur just leered at me with his hypnotic hazel eyes. He had never seen anything like it before. Even I was surprised at myself; I certainly had never acted like this before. The tablets the pharmacy gave me were the opposite to the intended effect. Instead of calming me down to a normal level, they turned me into a dancing fool.

His grandmother eventually turned off the radio to end the spectacle and told us to go. Once in the car Arthur tried to work his charm. It was the first time I had faced him like that, but in spite of his good looks I could only see the thickest dullard of a boy. Conversing with him was excruciating, which was crushingly disappointing. Demurely I asked him to drop me home, citing my headache as a plausible excuse. From that day on he was in my power. Accustomed to girls falling at his feet, my uncaring attitude threw him out of his comfort zone. Arthur became hopelessly infatuated and would do anything to please me.

So here I was, at the movies and strung out, aching for some pills to lift my mood. I'd spied Arthur's car waiting as soon as dad dropped us off. He was there with one of his sisters and two male cousins, planning to head to Saleimoa to drop off his sister and pick up some tablets for me. If all went well, by the time we returned the movie would still be playing and I would rejoin my siblings as though I had never left. Sadly for me, I had not inherited my Auntie's precise ability to calculate time. The plan quickly descended into chaos. Not only was Arthur unable to find the pills, but by the time we returned the hall lights were off. The movie had long been over and everyone had gone home.

Agitated and scared, I knew I was in deep trouble. I asked Arthur to take me home immediately. It was dark as we entered our driveway. The house lights were off and it appeared that everyone had gone to bed. Unknown to me, my father was angrily waiting in the front lounge area. Thinking I could sneak in and wait until morning when tempers might be cooler, I quietly opened the car door. This was Dad's cue to spring his trap. He rushed out like a mad man, threatening Arthur with horrible retribution in language one would not expect from a bishop. To add weight to his threats, he started throwing a barrage of rocks at poor Arthur's prized automobile. Whatever valour Arthur possessed quickly evaporated under the weight of this onslaught. He revved the engine and took off, nearly running me over in the process. In the haze of dust and smoke Arthur's wake left behind, Dad grabbed me by the scruff of the neck, hauled me into the house and proceeded to give me a sound thrashing with his belt. I stood there silent and contrite, taking my punishment but feeling no pain. I was in greater agony from the dreadful withdrawal symptoms of my unresolved addiction. In fact, the thrashing probably released endorphins that helped calm my cravings. After that disastrous evening I never saw Arthur again.

Not a day went by when I did not think about Auntie Tilie. I missed her even if I did not miss going to bed lonely and scared of what the night held in store. I needed time to retrain my brain to believe that nothing bad was going to happen to me at my new home. This wasn't a transition that would occur overnight or without a great deal of emotional healing. On top of that, school was tough. Although I possessed a keen mind, I could not function under the distraction of my dependency.

My typical day involved attending two or three lessons out of the seven. I was constantly suspended for skipping class and not obeying school rules. I was even suspended for not attending to my suspension duties of weeding the schoolyard or whatever other chores were doled out as punishment. It wasn't that I wanted to be naughty; something in me was struggling to do the right thing. In reality I was battling to take control of my will and failing miserably. It was deeply exhausting and nearly saw me expelled for committing so many transgressions. I had no conception of how powerful addiction was. How could I understand that which had never been explained to me and of which I had no knowledge?

One of my subjects was music. I soon realised that not only was I not musical, but my state of mind at the time needed peace and quiet. Imagine having a thumping hangover and being surrounded by people tunelessly tootling horns and banging out of time on drums. That's what it was like going through withdrawal, except maybe a little worse. Grasping at straws, I decided I might be better suited to playing the piano. At least it was a gentler instrument. Sister Burgess shot that down after only my sixth lesson. She was a brutally strict piano teacher. By the end of a lesson my head and fingers were sore from the edge of her ruler. It was starting to feel like my brain had ruptured and my already damaged mind was slowly rotting from decay. So I skipped one class. The next day worse was in store.

Suffering extreme anxiety, a throbbing headache, anger and fear without rhyme or reason, I was also facing being in a class with one of my least favoured teachers. Waves of heat were thrashing through my body as I tried to focus on what Sister Burgess was saying. I paid attention to my fingers pressing on the keys of the piano and tried to remember the notes in my book. The more frustrated Sister Burgess became with me, the more my agitation escalated. As I was sitting on that infernal wooden chair staring blankly at the notes in front of me, Sister Burgess yelled until her puffed cheeks turned red. She reached for her famous ruler and raised her hand to strike me; I sprang up, snatched the ruler from her hand and broke it in half. She was struck mute, her eyes bulging out in their sockets from shock. I was unmoved and simply turned and walked out. I don't believe any of her students in twenty years had ever done such a thing. There was truly no doubting I was related to Auntie Tilie!

Needing to calm myself, I sat down on the grass behind our gymnastic building, gasping for air. In the distance I could see Sister Burgess striding furiously to the school administration office. I knew I was in big trouble but I felt violently sick inside and out. I had to wrestle this demon in me to submission. I tried to breathe in and out as hard and as fast as I could to release the tension. The sensations were a combination of extreme fear and intense rage. If the earth had opened up and swallowed me whole I didn't doubt it would have provided pure and blissful release. I continued to sit there until the next period bell rang. Rising unsteadily to my feet, one of my classmates spotted me.

"You're wanted in the office," he yelled at me.

Brother Tausoga was about the worst man to face if you were a student who'd broken the rules. He was short, not blessed with good looks and he carried a sizeable tummy. He reminded me of the actor Danny De Vito, although there was absolutely nothing funny about our vice principal. He hardly ever smiled and always carried a whip. Whatever was coming, I knew it wouldn't be good.

Waiting for what seemed like an eternity in his office, I tried to focus my full attention on his qualifications displayed on the wall and a picture of his family on his desk. I was reading some of his certificates when the door flew open and he made his grand entrance.

"Sit down," he ordered.

I sat.

"There is a report that you threatened to hit Sister Burgess," he growled, straightening his tie.

"No, I wasn't feeling well and she kept on hitting me because I wasn't focusing," I muttered.

"How many detentions have you been given for not listening to your teachers?"

I opened my mouth to answer but wasn't given the opportunity.

"You yelled and teased Sister Rao, you skip classes and I just came back from talking with your mother. What do you think I should do with you? We don't tolerate disrespectful behaviour in this school," he told me sternly, peering over his spectacles.

"I apologise, but I didn't feel well and I still feel sick," I whined pathetically, trying to hold back vomit from reaching my throat.

My migraine struck me hard again. My head felt like it was about to split asunder. The temples of my forehead were in extreme agony. It felt like I was breathing in volcanic fumes. I would have done just about anything for some pain relief. Thankfully, Brother Tausoga could see I was not faking and told me to quickly go to see Sister Wright, our school nurse, then to come back with a report from her. I rushed outside, one hand on my stomach and the other over my mouth to stop me from throwing up all over his office floor. I barely made it outside before vomiting in the school's well-maintained flower beds. With the hem of my blue pinafore, I wiped my mouth as I staggered towards the school nurse's room.

Nurse Mamele Wright was a big woman who could instil fear into the heart of any student. Thankfully she was a professional and had empathy towards her patients. She was also well experienced and proficient at her job. She suspected I was addicted to sleeping and pain tablets. I had been to her office many times begging for pain tablets for severe headaches. She would feel my forehead, take my blood pressure and give me two tablets, telling me to rest for a few minutes before I could go back to class. This time she was very concerned. As soon as I entered her room I threw up again, fortunately in the bin by her door.

"Are you pregnant?" she asked before examining me.

"No. I have those bad headaches again. Please, I just need some pain tablets and I'll be fine," I begged.

She gently lay me on the patient's bed, pulled the curtains and lifted up my uniform. With her enormous cold hands she none too gently started to probe and knead my stomach, then my breasts.

"Hmm, you are not pregnant," she confirmed with obvious relief. "What did you eat today? And why do you get all these headaches?" she asked with a suspicious look.

"I had an avocado sandwich, but I had the same thing yesterday. Pain tablets help me when I suffer like this. Please, I need some desperately."

"You can't have these every time you have a sore head. I will give you some now to stop you from feeling sick and to ease the pain. Unfortunately my girl, you will need to try to overcome these symptoms yourself, without having to depend on the pills," she kindly advised me, plopping four pills into my trembling hand.

I had to wait until she thought I was stable before she signed a medical slip for the vice principal. She reminded me in a stern tone this would be the last time she would give me any more pills.

I felt much better, almost normal again. It was amazing how those pills could have such a profound effect on me. I walked back to Brother Tausoga's office to finish where we left off, now armed with my little medical slip. He read the note that confirmed that I was in fact sick. After much consideration, he stood up from behind his desk and ordered me to go home to rest. That was thankfully the end of the Mrs Burgess drama. It was also the end of any hope of my becoming a famous concert pianist.

No one at home knew what I was going through, and I was too fearful of the consequences to ask for help. It was hard on my dad; as my new mum was a teacher at the school, he always knew when I was not attending. In a fit of desperation he pulled me out of school for a week to stay home and work, hoping to instil discipline in me. It did help somewhat, as I had the work to focus on and I felt safe at home with no one watching me. Dad was busy at the plantation with his workers; step-mum and my siblings were at school. I was slowly recovering with the nurturing support of the maid and nanny; they decided I was suffering from a strange virus. Both took good care of me, allowing me to rest when overwhelmed, only waking me when they heard my father's car returning. Slowly and painfully the addiction passed; I made a promise to myself to never take pills again.

Two months after settling in with my father and his family, Auntie Tilie finally found me. I was outside hanging up washing and dad was relaxing in the shade of the bamboo grove talking with his elder brother. I didn't notice Auntie's car creeping up, but dad did. With a startled cry he shouted out, "Oh no! It's Auntie!"

Before he could stand, Auntie's car accelerated then skidded to a halt right next to him. She threw open her door, and without a greeting or any pleasantries she laid into him with her venomous tongue.

"How dare you? You have not spent a cent on this girl and you come and steal her from under my nose like a thief. Where are your manners? Have you no shame? Are you a worthless, cowardly dog?"

She then strode over to me. I was sheepishly hiding my face behind the wet clothes, hoping she would not see me. The nasty Auntie Tilie I had seen many times before stood next to me, and in plain language told me she never wanted to see my face again. I understood and respected her pain and justifiable anger.

"Your father only wants you now because you are old enough to babysit and clean his kid's arses," she spat out with naked contempt. Before I could utter a word in my defence, she jumped back in the car and sped off.

For a good while we all just stood speechless. Then, as if nothing had transpired, my dad turned around and carried on speaking with his brother. My step-mum had ignored the entire scene and kept right on doing the washing. I stood limp and stunned behind the dripping wet clothes, allowing the soaking sheets that danced in the breeze to envelop me. They felt soothing.

Chapter 19

The Setback

A few months after Auntie Tilie's surprise visit, I came home from school to find both my step-mum and dad dressed in church clothes as though they had just arrived back from an event. Dad's older brother was at our house in good clothes too. Jokingly, I asked who had died.

"We just came back from Bentzen's funeral," my dad replied, as though they had just returned from the shops. He might as well have taken a crowbar and whacked me in the guts.

"When did this happen? I didn't know he was sick," I stammered, feeling my heart plummeting into my belly.

"The housekeeper found him dead on the floor the next morning. No one knew what really happened to him. The funeral was a very small gathering, just us really," Dad informed me without a hint of sadness.

I wanted to ask why I was not told, why they hadn't taken me to his funeral to say goodbye. Profound sorrow rendered me mute. I rushed to the bathroom, locked the door, and sat under a cold shower still fully clothed, crying like a baby. Collapsing on the floor, I wept and wept and wept. I loved my Uncle Bentzen with all my heart. My mind flitted back to the farm, thinking about Auntie Tilie being in that terrifying place at night all by herself. This only served to make me sob harder. My eyes, my gut, my heart and my soul throbbed with pain. Only when one of my siblings rapped on the door wanting to use the toilet did I shift my grief to my bedroom. The urge for pills came clawing back with a vengeance, anything to ease this pain.

I had only just really started to feel good about my life in this new home. In fact, Dad had commented a week earlier that I looked more settled and not so tired all the time. He was right. I was participating more at school. My female PE teacher was impressed with my loss of embarrassment around the other girls in the changing rooms. We weren't marked on how well we played a game, but rather for having the self-esteem to shower with bare butts in front of our peers. Previously my teacher had taken me to her office and informed me I was one of the prettiest girls with a very good figure, so she couldn't understand why I seemed ashamed of my body. The truth was that I hated my body, and I didn't like myself that much either. I felt disfigured, not wanting to reveal myself to people in case they saw the parts of my body that Faalua had violated.

After six months and many detentions for skipping class and not obeying PE rules, I finally plucked up the courage to bare it all in front of my class and jump into the cold shower. It felt quite empowering to have overcome one more fear. Jumping this hurdle was a milestone, and the emotional reward felt magical. Every night I prayed to God to give me the strength to get undressed in front of the other girls. Every morning I kept telling myself that if I went into that shower it would be like washing away all the filth my uncle had planted on me. It was exhausting, but my inner strength had proven to be more potent than I imagined.

I received a big tick from my teacher that day. She even whispered, "You could be a Miss Samoa." I took the compliment as a positive step forward and felt rather proud of myself.

Before Bentzen's death, I had taken part in our culture day at school. I volunteered to be a Taupou of our forms house where I had to squeeze and present the kava. I also joined our school's marching group as a pompom girl, which saw me marching and dancing with hula hoops and pompoms at the front of our school band. We were practising to compete at the Samoa independence celebration to be held in a month's time. That was a pretty big deal. The eyes of the country would be on us, and our school reputation hung on the performance. The Church College of Samoa was well known for being extremely competitive when it came to marching and band competitions. Brother Toouli was one of the best musical teachers in the land, his techniques and prowess having been acquired in the land of marching bands and cheerleaders – the good old USA.

Music was one of the subjects in our school that was encouraged. It was something they were proud of, considering ourselves to be superior in this arena over any other school in the region. As I'd already established I wasn't particularly musically inclined, I jumped at the chance to wave pompoms and cheer once Brother Toouli posted a notice asking for volunteers. I loved dancing, and quickly discovered it was fun learning and practising the routines. It was my big moment to shine. Following the usual pattern of my life, the glorious opportunity was dashed while I was quietly and secretly mourning the death of my Uncle Bentzen.

The next day, overwrought with emotion, I set off to school as normal, with no intention of making it the distance. As soon as I was away from watchful eyes, I jumped on a bus that went back to my village. I had to get away and decided Auntie Sia's place would be as good as any.

Auntie Sia welcomed me back, but I didn't feel I belonged there anymore. I was a sad, lost and emotionally drained teenager.

Dad didn't even come looking for me. It was a week after being back in village life, working, cooking and helping my Auntie Sia, that the Samoan independence celebration started. It was in its fifteenth year and a major, proud event for every Samoan. Apart from the sick and the elderly, almost every Samoan was in Apia to celebrate. Every village in the island participated. Dancing, marching, bands, comedy shows, agriculture shows and many other contests were all part of the festival spirit. My dad was also preparing his prize cow to enter. The celebration lasted a full and very hectic week, and I was in the village labouring for my Auntie Sia and her family. Listening to the radio, I heard an announcement:

> Now the Church College of Samoa is entering. The female leader with her baton is followed by beautiful looking pompom girls wearing yellow and blue matching outfits with white socks and blue shoes. The band is settling in behind them. Now they are forming a circle. The leader is commanding and the girls are dancing perfectly, swinging their hula-hoops. It's amazing! Wow! They are so good …

Through the radio I heard the cheering of the crowd. It was a joyous uproar – and I was washing dishes. I couldn't help feeling I'd let myself and everyone else down. I hated myself for being so weak, so incapable of controlling my erratic emotions. I felt worthless and unworthy. It was at that precise moment I decided I was going to make something of myself – or die trying. I knew in that exact moment if I didn't shape up and get myself together, no one was going to help me. I was not going to depend on or trust anyone ever again.

I asked Auntie Sia if she could take me back to my dad. The irony of this request did not escape me. I had run away of my own free will, yet I needed an adult to deliver me back. Back at my dad's house, there were no lectures. It was like I never left.

During the final term of school my dad made a deal with me. If my school report was good I could join my stepmother on her church trip to New Zealand at the end of the year. With my addiction receding and my thinking clearing, I knew I had the intelligence and drive to secure the grades I needed. It was simply a matter of focus and discipline. I concentrated on suppressing the past, using an almost physical effort in an attempt to bring some peace into my life. I wanted to make my father proud of me. These efforts were not in vain.

I received A-grade marks in all subjects. I was so overjoyed and excited about the trip I could hardly contain myself, but my jubilation was premature. My father sat me down and, contrary to our agreement, he told me I had to ask my mother in New Zealand to pay for my fare. Getting the A-grades was infinitely easier than convincing my mother to pay for my plane ticket. She stubbornly refused and never replied to any of my letters.

When I told Dad that my mother was not even answering, he asked if someone else in my family could help me. I felt suffocated and nauseous at this suggestion. Instead of responding, I rushed to the bathroom, locked the door and sat in the shower crying like a pathetic child yet again. For the umpteenth time in my life, I felt utterly lost, unloved and unwanted by both my parents. I begin to feel that dad had had enough of me. He needed to channel his attention on his other children, which by then included four other young souls he'd taken into his home to offer them a chance in life. As for my mother, she had made it crystal clear from the time of my birth – she did not want me at all. Over the years, she had paid for three of her brothers and other people's children to join her in New Zealand so they could find a better future. I, on the other hand, was treated with less value than a dung beetle – at least they had some use in this world.

With only a few weeks before the trip, I urgently sent a letter to my sister Agnes asking if she would be kind enough to pay for my fare. She was my last remaining hope. Agnes and I had been in contact and she was now the only one who appeared to care for me. She had sent me a watch, a school bag and other gifts when I went to live with my dad. I loved my sister and I had high hopes we would become best of friends. A week later, Agnes replied she would cover my airfare. I should have been walking on air except for the sting in the tail of that letter. Agnes informed me that our mother had mentioned she was not happy with my father. Apparently she'd complained that the least he could do was pay for my fare as he had promised he would take care of me, making up for lost time. My mother was also very unhappy with my sister Agnes for paying my fare. I felt betrayed by both my mother and father.

It was around this time Auntie Tilie became seriously ill and was admitted to hospital. A message was sent requesting that Dad bring me to see her before I leave for New Zealand. While news of Auntie's illness was upsetting, something inside me said, "This is the last you are ever going to see of Samoa, so this will be your only chance to heal the rift before you say goodbye forever."

Auntie Tilie was the most extraordinary person I have met in my entire life. I loved her. I admired and respected her. As I did with my grandmother, I felt I had a special place in my Auntie's heart. I was profoundly grateful to her. Granted, at times I was terrified of her, but I was proud she was my kin. The last thing I wanted was for there to be bad blood between us. To my relief she felt the same way. We hugged, we cried, we reminisced and spoke of my future. She was delighted I was leaving in search of a better future for myself.

"Don't let people take advantage of your good heart," she advised me. "Remember, you don't owe anybody anything!" She made that last remark most pointedly, glancing towards my dad.

I thanked her for everything. Without her my life would have been very different, if indeed I'd still be alive at all. I wanted to say how sorry and saddened I was about Uncle Bentzen. But I could not bring myself to mention his name; it would reduce me to a blubbering wreck. There were pauses and exchanged glances. I'm convinced she knew what I wasn't saying. Auntie Tilie and I had shared some intensely intimate moments. We'd shared laughter and tears, triumphs and tragedies – our bond was beyond mere words. She knew what I wanted to say. Moreover, she knew what was in my heart.

That hospital visit was the last time I would see my beloved Auntie.

It was around this time another piece of the Ottilie jigsaw puzzle was revealed. Shortly after Bentzen's death, my Auntie had set fire to the plantation, quite close to the house. It was a grandiose but ill-conceived attempt at suicide. Apparently, the plan had been for the fire to engulf the house with her in it as she lay on the bed comatose from an overdose. The fire had been extinguished before it caused any real damage and Auntie had been forced to see another sunrise, whether she liked it or not. How drastically I had misconstrued her life of plenty as one of joy. I now knew nothing could be further from the truth.

When I was alone with dad, consumed with a burning need to ask him about Auntie Tilie's estate, I reopened the subject. I wanted to hear it from him. I knew he had stayed at Auntie's before I was born. Perhaps he harboured some additional insights.

"Yes, Auntie's place is haunted," he said solemnly. "I often heard someone knocking, and when I opened the door an image just walked away. I could clearly see the figure had no head."

"Did you see anything else?"

"I saw lots of apparitions, disturbing images, and I heard noises at night. Even Auntie sees them. She said that sometimes they torture her, but she refused to say any more about it." He paused. "I suspect Auntie Tilie and her father (my grandfather) killed some of their black workers. Those were the images often seen there. My parents said they were ruthless and at times unspeakably cruel."

I was left wondering if the woman I both admired and adored was a maniacal murderer, a genius and a butcher, or a tormented soul lost between two cultures, as I was. In the end I came into a conclusion – my auntie Tilie was also a victim and a survivor.

Our flight was at 6pm on 7 December 1977. The airport was crowded with church members and their families. My step-mum and two baby brothers said their goodbyes to dad and the other siblings, knowing they would reunite after Christmas. I was not sure whether I was included in that plan. I was not sure I wanted to be.

I stepped onto the threshold of the plane and turned back for my last farewell wave. A surge of relief swept over me. At last, at long last, all the occult horrors and emotional miseries were finally behind me. It would be much later in my life I would discover the terrible truth. Those spirits from Auntie's followed me.

My grandmother (Tina) with some of her many grandchildren.
I am standing on the top, far left wearing a white dress. (1969)

Me sitting on my grandmother's grave
few weeks before I ran away (January 1975)

My grandfather (Tama 1977)

Auntie Tilie (beautiful 18 year old)

Auntie Tilie and her son Alan.
Alan died shortly after this picture was taken

Uncle Benzen when he was a captain of a ship

Auntie Tilie and Uncle Bentzen (1975)

Auntie Tilie's estate house (taken 2013)

Me in my Church College of Western Samoa uniform (1977)

My mother (NZ 1969)

Chapter 20

My New Life Awaits

The Polynesian Airlines plane started taxiing down the runway. My heart beat furiously with excitement and anticipation. I sat in the middle aisle struggling to hold one of my screaming baby brothers; my step mum sat next to me wrestling the other. By the time we were airborne it was dark outside. I tried to catch a glimpse of the island home I was escaping, but all I could make out was the occasional flash of the navigation light. The take-off had been both thrilling and terrifying, not for me alone but for the flight full of Mormons. For most of us it was our first experience on a plane. The entire cabin hummed with excited banter as though a group of children were watching a magician perform his wonders.

The captain spoke in a reassuring voice. "This is your captain speaking. The weather is calm and we should be arriving in Auckland in five hours – 10pm New Zealand time. Enjoy your flight."

Finally, I was on my way to reunite with my mother. Not that this fact brought me any particular joy. I was, however, also going to meet my other siblings and, more importantly, I was going to a place everyone dreamed of going. To Samoans, New Zealand was a place with plenty of money, plentiful food and beautiful white people with stunning clothes and perfect speech. At that time it was so different and alien to us we may as well be going to another planet.

The lights dimmed and the plane fell silent. My step-mum and brothers drifted off to sleep. I closed my eyes but I could not close my mind. My thoughts travelled back to Samoa, to my Auntie Tilie and my grandfather Tama. The memories of Auntie entered my mind like a force of nature. Staring out into the dark heavens around me, I earnestly made a promise to myself. I was going to do well at school in New Zealand. I was going to secure a well-paid job and I was going to buy myself a house. I would send for Tama and Auntie Tilie to come and live with me. I would take care of them and the three of us would live happily together. That was my plan.

On arrival in Auckland, after the happy greetings and meetings had come and gone, the lights died out and with them my dreams. My cruel destiny awaited me.

We were met at the airport by my mother, stepfather, Agnes and a female cousin. My step-mum was collected by her brother, Paulo, and his wife, Sea. In a week's time I was to join my step-mum for our two-week trip to the Church temple. Following that sojourn, it was organised for me to return to my mother where I would remain for an additional two weeks before returning to Samoa. So everyone thought.

My mother and her husband's home was big and pleasant with four bedrooms, two of which were huge. It stood right at the top of Cockburn Street in Grey Lynn, a prized location close to the city, beaches and bus stops. Charming red steps lead onto a front balcony. As the main door swung open, a long hall way was revealed. I shared one of the big bedrooms with my sister Ceal, Rowena and Kina. The other massive bedroom opposite ours belonged to my mother and her husband. My sister Cinta and my brother Laurie, the baby and the only boy of the family, had the two small rooms. Laurie was five years old at the time. My sister Agnes lived at the hospital hostel where she worked serving food for patients.

The large living area was next to my mother's sewing room, which contained a commercial sewing machine and overlocker. Boxes full of material lay tucked away in the corner of the living room. My mother was an excellent machinist and hence never short of work. She had a day job, after which she would cook dinner for the family before sewing through the remaining hours of the day, or rather, night. The house was always buzzing with customers dropping off and collecting their seamstress requirements.

A pleasantly framed door with a small glass window separated the front section of the house from the back. The walled-off kitchen itself was very tiny and narrow, but the size of the dining area made up for lack of space in the culinary department. Apart from the dining table, which sat eight, there was a two-meter chest freezer and a separate fridge, suggesting no one ever went short of food in this place. Opposite the fridge and freezer were a fireplace and four plump red chairs for those lucky enough to steal some relaxation time to flop into after dinner. Walking towards the far side of the house was the laundry room and a separate toilet. Stepping out from the back door, a single lockup garage stood a few meters away from the house. My stepfather's yellow station wagon was always parked outside; the garage served as an entertaining area for his mates. Other properties were located to the left, right and behind us, but the boundaries between each were surrounded by a corrugated iron fence for privacy.

Mother used to boast they scored this house because of her. One of the ladies she befriended shortly after she arrived in New Zealand lent her the deposit to buy this solid, big home. Although her husband helped to pay the mortgage, if it wasn't for mother's deposit and her extra hours sewing to bolster the household income, they would never have been able to secure it and would certainly not have managed to maintain it. The home was also walking distance to the children's school, parks and shops. Such a prime piece of real estate was my mother and her husband's pride and joy. From my perspective, they should have been floating on cloud nine. Instead, my mother incessantly complained about a lack of money.

Things were not good from day one. While I was ecstatic to be in New Zealand, I was still blind to the truth. My stepfather never knew I existed. The first he heard of me, "the other daughter," was when my mother buttered him up a few short days before I arrived from Samoa. My very existence had been hidden from him all these years. It was therefore unsurprising for him not to be enthralled at the prospect of my lobbying up in his home. My mother had no intention of sending for me. Apart from Agnes, my other five siblings had no idea I existed either until I showed up that day. Fortunately for me, they didn't seem to share their mother's mean spirit. They were good kids and we managed to bond well under very strange and difficult circumstances.

At Agnes's insistence, my mother and stepfather agreed to keep me in New Zealand. Through various connections, she found me a packing job at Nestle's chocolate factory. I begged her to send me to school for just one year so I could learn English properly, reasoning I would then be able to get a better job than packing chocolates. My pleas fell on deaf ears. My other five siblings attended Catholic schools, but it was too costly for me to go. Years later, I deduced she could have sent me to a government school; it would have cost her close to nothing. Unfortunately, I wasn't aware of this at the time. Instead, she just kept reminding me that her husband had to sponsor any New Zealand residency, and for that a lawyer needed to be engaged – and that took lots of money. If I truly wanted to remain, I was bluntly informed, I needed to earn money to help out. That was that.

It was a bitter blow to later learn that back in Samoa I had earned the school's honour medal. I had been promoted to the A class and was entitled to wear the badge that proclaimed my academic achievement for the following year. All of this was announced in my absence. With my parents uncaring attitudes about my worth, I kept any excitement at my achievement to myself.

So here I was in the workforce earning my own money, but my pay envelope was not to be opened by me. To this day I still don't know how much I earned a week. Out of my weekly pay packet, my mother would give me $5 for my bus fare, and if a bus driver forgot to take my fare, I had a few spare cents to be able to buy a pie for lunch from the factory's canteen. During this time, whenever my mother and her husband fought, which was constant, my stepfather would kick me out of their house. My name was yelled out between them in the most horrible way. All the plotting and the things I never knew about my life came flying out from their mouths as if I wasn't there. All I could do was listen in mute, impotent, devastated disbelief.

"Why didn't you tell me about her? How many more children of darkness have you spewed out? Isn't it bad enough I took in one? What kind of slut are you?"

"What do you want me to say? She was an accident, and I didn't tell you because she was not my child the day my parents took her."

My sisters and I sat on our beds forced to hear this bile. Soon enough my stepfather would yank the door of their room open to pace the hallway yelling. He wanted to make sure I could hear every vicious, hurtful statement spewing from his lips. He had a deep powerful voice. When he spoke it was like thunder, but when he was angry he could make the walls tremble. I had no doubt the whole of Cockburn Street was learning about the circumstances of my conception and that my mother never wanted me.

"I don't want bad blood here. I don't want her in my house. She is going to be a bad influence for my kids," he bellowed.

My mother suddenly burst into our room crying, asking me to come with her. I followed her to the laundry where she passed me blankets, a pillow and sheets. "Take them to the garage. We will sleep there tonight. This is my house too. I worked to pay for it, but this is what Sinafoa wanted, to see you freeze outside."

My mother made her statement loud and clear for her husband to hear, hoping to manipulate him into guilt-ridden remorse over what she was going to do. I wasn't sure if this was about some genuine affection towards me, or whether she was using me as a device to win an argument. Experience had taught me to believe it was far more likely to be the latter. I later learned the garage was used as the punishment bedroom routinely. Agnes had apparently slept there many times before.

In the middle of my first New Zealand winter, I was preparing my bed on the dirty, freezing concrete floor of the garage. The garage didn't have any lining. The roof, sidewalls and door were all made out of corrugated iron. My mother had a thin island mat that she lay out on the floor in one corner away from the door. I tried to wrap my body and my head with as many blankets as possible to ease the cold piercing my bones; it was so damn cold I could not stop my teeth from chattering. I had never experienced cold like this before. It was excruciating. On top of that, the place stank of alcohol, drunken men's urine and stale vomit.

"Listen, I will talk to Sinafoa tomorrow when he is calm. I don't blame him. I owe a lot to him for bringing me to New Zealand and helping with my family back home. Now they all work, have good futures and help their families. That had been my plan. If it wasn't for him, everyone would still be eating shit back in Samoa. I will go inside to sleep in the spare room. There are not enough blankets to keep us both warm," she reasoned.

With that, she turned the light off, pulled the garage door down and left me. Trying to get warm, I lay in a foetal position, my legs touching my chin. I realised now how horrible my life was going to be. This was a new low in feeling completely and utterly unloved and unwanted.

Unlike me, their dog was allowed to sleep inside. In the dark between my heavy blankets trying to keep warm, once more I cried like a baby. Crying gave release to my despair. It was so bitterly cold my tears felt like ice water as they dropped on my cheeks. Even though the door was shut, the biting wind crept in through gaps between the roof, walls and underneath the door. The door was also making a clanging noise when the wind pushed it, making the blissful release of sleep even more elusive. I loathed my parents, I loathed my life and I loathed myself. Wallowing in self-pity, I attempted to survive through the night.

Early the next morning, I was jarred awake by my stepfather's car engine as he left for work. After my rude awakening, mother pulled up the garage door and ordered me to come inside and get ready for work.

"Oh, and bring all the bedding back to the house," she added.

About the last thing I wanted to do was separate myself from my layers of blankets. The morning cold snap was bad. There was ice on the grass, and the inside of the garage was no warmer. My siblings were up, buzzing around the house getting ready for school, some eating breakfast. Everyone went about their morning routines like nothing had happened. It made me feel like screaming, "Do any of you have any idea what I'm going through? What I've gone through all my life? Does anyone even give a shit about me?" But I said nothing. I quickly dressed and freshened up just in time to catch my bus so I could arrive at work before 7am.

Work was now my sanctuary. Factory work was not what I had in mind, but for now I had somewhere to escape to. The problems and emotionally cruelty of home life were replaced with the aroma of cocoa and sweet chocolate. That was good enough for me. The first floor was a production and packing line. I was one of the packers. Our canteen was on the top floor. I don't know what else was in that building. It was only when the bell went off at 4.30pm that I noticed how many people worked there. There were close to a hundred workers from different multicultural backgrounds, many from the Pacific islands. The place ran twenty-four hours a day, seven days a week, with night shift arriving just as we were leaving.

Standing in front of the conveyor belt packing chocolates all day demanded attention and focus. The belt was continually moving while twenty or more girls and women stood behind it, handpicking and packing different chocolates into their correct boxes. We had to be very fast and look out for rejects to throw in bins for recycling. Our line supervisor was always walking around, checking the efficiency of our work. I was the youngest worker, but my Maori supervisor regularly congratulated me for being the fastest.

I came to look forward to seeing my new friend Nauru in the factory. She was an island girl from Rarotonga who was a bit older than me. We stood next to each other on the production line and during breaks in the canteen we were able to freely talk and laugh. Nauru lived with her boyfriend, Tess, in their nearby apartment. She told me he was a great guy and I'd be welcome to spend the weekend with them. To my lonely heart, nothing would be more wonderful than staying at a friend's place, talking and laughing into the night. It was something I'd never done before in my entire life, but I wouldn't even waste my breath asking my mother if I could go. Instead, I drew comfort from seeing Nauru five days a week, eight hours a day. It was sufficient to sustain a glow of happiness in me. Even though Nauru lived a reasonable distance from my home, sometimes she and Tess would drop me home so I could save money for an emergency. I would save $2 a week under my mattress and never counted my stash when my sisters were looking. The way things were going at home, I knew I needed to be prepared.

On the home front, constant arguments between my mother and her husband became increasingly dysfunctional. These fracases were not only disturbing me, they were inflicting an obvious toll on my sisters and brother as well. While under my mother's roof, I lived with a perpetual knot in my stomach. One minute the folks were laughing and interacting civilly with each other, the next they were verbally assassinating each other with vicious tirades. On more occasions than I could count, my mother would pack us all up, load us in a taxi and take us to other members of her family. These family members apparently loved my mother dearly and were only too ready to open their doors and take care of us whenever she needed refuge. The kids would miss school and I would have to find a new bus route to get to work. Everything about the situation was deeply unsettling.

Routinely, after a week or so of settling into a new environment, my stepfather would come to take us back. A month later, we would do it all over again. It was a sick and twisted game. My sisters knew my mother could easily call the police and have him removed from the house when he became abusive. She could kick him out and give her children stability, but she never did. I think she enjoyed the drama and attention of it all. Turning up to her family feeling all sorry for herself, she would receive love and support, knowing soon enough her husband would come back crying, begging for her to return home. No wonder my poor sister's Ceal and Cinta would jump out of bedroom windows in the middle of the night to escape the madness. They told me that their parents had been doing this since they were little. It was a bizarre rollercoaster without end.

Despite all the turmoil and abuse, every Sunday we all dressed up for church. There was extra shouting if one of us didn't want to attend the mass. We would sit together as a family feigning normality until, almost inevitably, a fight broke out right inside the house of worship. Usually this centred on my stepfather accusing my mother of looking at someone else's husband. My stepfather was allegedly a devout Catholic, although I was never once a witness to him practicing what his church preached. It seemed that he believed once he had confessed his sins he was absolved and free to do it all over again the next hour or the next day.

The first time we were yanked from our beds in the middle of the night I went with the flow of it all. I'd experienced and witnessed so much in my young life, little was capable of surprising me any longer. At least some of the past horrors had been left behind and I had my cunning plan, combined with my meagre savings, to escape and live my own life one day. My cunning covert mission brought me some peace until a dreaded union occurred. There, in Uncle Migao's house, where we sought refuge from my ranting stepfather, was Uncle Faalua, my rapist tormentor.

To finance the cost of rent, these two uncles shared a three-bedroom house with their wives and little children. Uncle Migao had two little girls, while Faalua had a son. It seemed they had opened their doors so many times to my mother and her kids they were quite accustomed to the charade. There were no questions asked, but rather big smiles and open arms. My uncle Migao was so happy to see me, he gave me a huge bear hug in front of everybody.

"I love this girl because she cared for my mother until she died. I was there and saw it with my own eyes," he announced with pride to the assembled throng.

As Faalua also headed towards me to give me a welcome cuddle, I awkwardly stood there not reacting, frozen with a fake smile plastered on my face, wondering if he could hear the pounding heart in my chest. Thankful for the company of my sisters, I was able to feel protected from any attempted renewal of his assaults. He acted very friendly and I felt wretched and unclean. I wished I had power to make myself disappear.

In the sitting area, we heard our mother pouring out her heart to her brothers and their wives about her terrible husband, yet again. They had apparently heard it all before and joked about it, which made everyone burst out laughing. While the adults were engrossed in light-hearted happy chitchat, I felt dejected.

Behind a closed door of our bedroom I felt compelled to tell my sisters Ceal and Cinta what Uncle Faalua had done to me and how furious I was with our mother because she knew what had happened, yet brought me to his house. Seeing him forced me to relive the nightmare, to smell his stink again, to hear his whining voice – all the things I wanted so desperately to forget. What was she thinking?

My sisters listened to my tale before confiding their own accursed secrets to me. Faalua had raped our youngest sister, Kina, when she was only nine. Kina was now ten and she and her sister Rowena were in Uncle Migao and his wife's room playing with the couple's babies.

"Does mother know about this?" I gasped.

"Yes. Kina came crying to mum that Uncle forced his penis into her pipi and didn't stop until he finished. She bled and was in physical pain. Uncle didn't stop even when she cried and begged him to stop," my sisters told me.

"What did mum do?" I asked, knowing the answer before it came out of Ceal's mouth.

"Nothing! She just gave him a good hiding. But Faalua is big, mum's blows didn't even faze him. The next day they were family again."

My heart bled for my little sister that night. If our own mother thought it was okay for one of her brothers to rape her daughters and all he would get was a slap on the wrist, what chance did any of us have? My mother wasn't simple. In fact, she had a fierce and sound mind. Even when she fought with her husband and ended up leaving him for attention, she had the fighting spirit of a dragon. Once she was driven to the point of getting the broom and hitting her husband on the head until he bled. Evidently, she was capable of protecting her daughters but she never did. Why? I didn't know the answer then and I still don't have a clue how any mother with a maternal heart can allow anyone to hurt her child.

Uncle Faalua, who raped me and my sister Kina, moved to Tokelau with his family. Kina's whole life has been affected by what happened and she struggled every day with relationships and her self-esteem. She uses drugs to numb the pain. What causes her the most suffering is our mother's betrayal. No matter how much time passes, she cannot forgive her or find peace. In Tokelau, our uncle lives a free man who has never been prosecuted. Kina and I live with the knowledge that in Tokelau he will have found new victims and that it is our mother who had betrayed them.

Chapter 21

The Mean Sister

My sister Agnes was three years older than me. I'd always looked up to her as a big sister. She was shorter than the rest of us but still very pretty. When I arrived in New Zealand she'd already left the family home, unable to deal with the dysfunction and disagreements. The hospital hostel where she worked and lived provided a convenient haven at first, but once she met the man of her dreams, without her parent's knowledge she moved into a de facto arrangement with him. They were planning to marry in a big Samoan ceremony the following year, and for that they needed money. My humble factory job paid better than hospital work, so she left the hospital to join me packing chocolates. I loved and respected my big sister, and was forever grateful that she paid my fare out of Samoa.

My sister's beau, Tavita, looked like a Samoan warrior when standing next to Agnes. Yet despite his fearsome appearance, Tavita was a gentle soul. He adored Agnes and would do anything for her, but this wasn't enough for my mother and her husband. They thought Agnes was too good, too pretty and too young for Tavita. On top of that, Agnes was brought up in New Zealand and couldn't speak a word of Samoan. Worse still, Tavita's family were dedicated to the *Fa'a Samoa*, which meant the couple would always be struggling. They say love conquers all, and Agnes was determined to marry Tavita with or without her parent's permission. I was simply happy for her, and if truth be told, that happiness was bolstered by the thought that once they married I could move in with her. What a great partnership we would have. We could support, help and protect each other.

According to Agnes, our stepfather – whom she called "dad" – had often beaten her violently when she was young. He also tried to rape her when she was a teenager. The whole time these events took place our mother sat crying, but did nothing. When the police finally intervened, after Agnes jumped out of our stepfather's car to alert passing strangers, mother begged her to drop the charges, reasoning that she needed her husband. Her children needed their father. Agnes conceded to our mother's wishes but lived with burning resentment as a result. This manifested in vicious anger outbursts. I couldn't imagine how fortunate I was to have caught her in a rare moment of benevolence when she purchased my air ticket for me. Whatever the reason, I was grateful for it, but I was to discover the price for this kindness was high indeed.

The relationship with my sister slid into anarchy after her engagement was accepted and she moved back home to prepare for the wedding. I can't recall how it all started, because her resentment and malice towards me seemed to blossom from nowhere. When I asked my sisters Ceal and Cinta if they could make any sense of it, they both told me that although I was receiving the brunt of Agnes's vicious outbursts, they had also endured her animosity and jealousy over time. When she really let loose it was as though she'd been possessed by the devil. Every spiteful sentence issued from her mouth was full of hostility and expletives. If we went to the shops and were five minutes late she would rip into us. She was the one sleeping with her boyfriend behind the folk's backs, yet we were the "fucken sluts of Auckland."

Agnes completely took control of us, apparently revelling in our pain and distress. The more upset we became the more her cruelty seemed to give her pleasure and power. Once she moved back home, Agnes and my stepfather acted as the household chieftains. It was a curious dynamic, knowing that once she had been the victim to his aggression, but then again I had to remind myself that Auntie Tilie had inherited her great wealth from a vicious and vindictive father who had raped her and then murdered her incestuous bastard child to hide the evidence. I felt helpless.

Mother merely and mutely viewed the spectacle of ongoing abuse as an impassive observer. She believed she owed Agnes her approval on holding the key to my life when Agnes agreed not to send her husband to jail. My sister and stepfather would doll out harsh punishment from unfair judgements with complete impunity. Agnes's lies were never debated or questioned. The sister who had once, and for inexplicable reasons, been my saviour had descended into the latest in a long line of tormentors. She had spiralled downward from a delight to be around into a vile creature incessantly yelling and cursing with facial expressions of the purest spite and hate. I have never forgotten those looks. If I believed in reincarnation I might have been wondering what terrible thing I did in a former life to deserve all this misery.

After seven months of drudgery packing chocolates, my friend Nauru whispered to me that there was a Nieuan guy named John who liked me. He had asked Nauru if he could meet me. Nauru and I giggled about it like a couple of schoolgirls. I asked her to point him out to me when we had a break. After seeing him I thought he was handsome, but in truth I wasn't even looking for a boyfriend. My family life was so dysfunctional, my time with my girlfriend was as much as I could maintain to stay happy and be positive. I was also too busy walking on eggshells around Agnes;

even a smile would set her off without notice. She could smell if I was happy and would hurl insults within everyone's earshot to embarrass me – calling me a bitch, or worse – and that was on a good day. It was as though she wanted everyone to know that she had power over me. She did; I feared her and was very cautious in her presence.

As John was still trying to pursue me, I continued to avoid him but he refused to be dissuaded. As I was coming out of the toilets one day he stood waiting for me around the corner. Without a word, he pinned me gently to the wall and gave me the most magical kiss. I had never been kissed by a boy before. I stood motionless, both stunned and thrilled. The world around us fell away. We were the only two people on earth. I was drenched in his embrace, ecstatically giving him the power to kiss all the fear out of my heart, mind, body and soul. In that instant, any problem I had ever had or could even conceive of was peeled away. It was as though he was breathing life into me anew. I don't know if that is what love at first sight was, but it was the most wonderful thing that had ever happened to me. The adrenaline rush was so heady and intoxicating I didn't want him to let go.

"I really like you," he whispered.

I could only gaze at him adoringly in reply. He winked at me, and I shot him a smile that could have illuminated the entire factory. Frolicking like a spring lamb back to my work section, resplendent in my white smock smeared in brown chocolate, my oh-so-seductive hairnet falling off my head, I could not wipe the grin off my face. I whispered to Nauru what had just happened and she burst out laughing. Agnes spotted this in an instant. She was glaring from the far end of the conveyor belt with a suspicious, evil expression. As I was walking on air, basking in utter fantasy that John could save me from her and my horrible family, I didn't have a care in the world.

For a while, John and I managed to steal moments here and there when we would meet for a chat. Just the sight of his smile made me melt into pliable pool of gooey golden liquid. Nauru covered for us initially, but my fears over this liaison were soon to be realised.

It was a Thursday when Agnes marched to my side.

"You're a fucking slut! You've stolen my friend's boyfriend and you're going to pay big time!" she yelled in front of everyone.

Before I came along, John did date the older sister of the woman who would be Agnes's bridesmaid. According to John, they had only been out once and she had become infatuated with him, telling everyone that they were still an item.

With every fibre in my being I wanted to crush the life out of my sister. Her humiliating words made me feel like dirt.

On that day, John offered to drive me close to home, reasoning I could save money on bus fare and it would give us a chance to talk about things. He wanted to make our friendship official and was happy to come and ask formally for my parents' permission. I really liked him. We concocted a plan whereby Tess would drive me to the top of the hill away from the factory workers rushing to catch their bus; John would be waiting around the corner for me. Thursday was also payday, so everyone was excited and somewhat distracted. I truly feared the worst if Agnes caught on.

After Nauru and I collected our pay, we left via the side door of the factory. Already waiting for me, my sister stood menacingly flanked by her cronies, the ugly Tokelauans, including the woman who claimed John as her boyfriend. Without a word, they all dragged me by the hair down onto the gravel at the side of the road, beating and verbally abusing me. Agnes's shrill menacing voice rose above the cars driving by and the noise of machinery from the factory. The commotion was so loud it also attracted workers from nearby factories who all gathered around, spurring my sister into a frenzy. Little did she know I was feeling no pain. I had switched off and was almost enjoying the beating, a technique I was well versed in from many years gone by.

Nauru tried stopping them. It was a valiant but vain attempt – there were too many of them. Instead, she ran back inside to alert our supervisor. By the time she returned I was in a bad way, my body shook with rage and humiliation as the kindly manager helped me up. I tried to remove some of the gravel stuck into my knees, not acknowledging the fact that my brutal big sister was still hovering like a vulture waiting to scavenge the dead carcass.

"I should never have paid your fucking fare to come to New Zealand," she screeched like a banshee. "You should have been left in Samoa to fucking rot."

The evil, insane glare in her eyes scared me more than anything else. It was there and then I decided I was not going home – ever. I didn't know where I was going, but I didn't want to be near this person. I wished I had not known her.

"Nauru," I whispered to my friend. "Can I come home with you?"

She nodded a sympathetic yes, but then my stepfather's car screeched up with my mother sitting in the passenger seat. Agnes had called them, spilling her bile, filth and lies to eager recipients who needed little excuse to inflict further pain and punishment upon me. Without a word, I was ordered by my mother to get in the car. Agnes sat next to me, mocking me, belittling me as if I was a piece of shit all the way home. I saw John's car patiently waiting for me as we drove past, but there was no emotion left in me and no ability left to run.

Naturally enough, more beatings and more tongue lashings awaited me on the home front. I sat like a zombie taking it all.

"You are a fucking embarrassment and you will not be going back to work there," Agnes screamed.

"I think she has been punished enough," mother attempted to intervene. "She didn't do anything wrong at work; she was not sacked. It is not easy to get jobs these days," she tried to reason, of course thinking more of the money than my welfare or Agnes's sensibilities.

"No! That slut is not fucking going back there. If she does, I will leave," Agnes threatened.

Mother said no more. Agnes won and I was out of work. The next day my mother and sister dictated what my life was going to be like, as I tried to draw whatever energy I had left to look at them with intense hatred. I was issued with the most demeaning and arduous home chores and I was not to use the phone. As their evil tongues wagged endlessly at me, I could only think of my grandmother and my Auntie Tilie. I no longer had any doubt they were the only people who had ever truly loved and cared for me. Tina's voice was telling me to be strong, and Auntie Tilie was reminding me I did not need to rely on anyone – I had all it took to make a life for myself.

As soon as the adults left for work and the kids were at school, I frantically searched for my passport and any documentation that maybe useful. I wanted to get hold of both Nauru and John, but at the factory workers were not permitted to use the phone while they were on shift. I packed a towel and my few meagre belongings, including treasured photographs of my life in Samoa, in a plastic bag, collected the money I had been saving and walked out of that horrible place. In their mailbox, I left my mother a note saying that I was not anybody's slave. I must confess I felt cold comfort and even a little smugness in effectively saying "fuck you" as I walked out on them all.

I caught the bus to K Road, and from there walked to Domain Park at the back of the Auckland hospital. I planned to wait there all day away from people. I would later walk to

Nestle's factory to see if I could spot John's car, or if Nauru would come out of the door we used to exit every day. For five long hours I waited at the park, thinking about what might happen to me. I had a fierce survival instinct, and even though I was morose, I was still aware of the world around me. I noticed a mother duck protectively and lovingly leading her ducklings around a pond. The sight of them caused me to weep. Wasn't maternal instinct supposed to be natural and overpowering in every female creature on this beautiful planet? What had gone wrong with my mother? Perhaps she'd been born with a genetic defect which omitted this most basic and primal urge in all species. The world was bleak. I was utterly alone in an ocean of humanity who didn't know or care I was alive. To the passing world, I was invisible.

At 3pm I gathered my things and set off on my hour walk to the factory. The sun was still strong and I was thirsty. I wanted to preserve my money in case I could not find my friends. From the $22 I had saved, I had $21.50 to keep me alive after paying the bus fare. I arrived at the factory at 4.10pm and looked around for John's car. It wasn't there. By the time the bell rang for the end of another work day I was well hidden, watching intently for my friend Nauru. There was no sign of her either, but I did see Agnes leave with her friends. They were joking and laughing, which infuriated me.

My stepfather and my mother's yellow station wagon had arrived to pick her up. She left, waving cheerily at her work colleagues. I waited until there was no one else about and the factory door was locked from the inside. Feeling deflated, I trudged back to the park to consider my next move. One thing I knew, I had to stay away from the main road or bus routes in case my family came looking for me. Agnes's fiancé was a daytime bus driver – he could be driving any of the buses hurrying by.

It was getting dark. I was cold and depressed. Where would I sleep for the night? I knew turning up at any of my mother's family would be bad. Doubtless they would call my mother, and I had no illusions as to my fate if that happened. I would rather be homeless and die on the street than to give them that satisfaction. I also knew the park was not a safe place for a young girl at night. I had heard about rapes and murders there in the past. It seemed to me the safest place to be would be where there was constant activity. The bus terminal in the city came to mind.

It took nearly two hours walking the back streets of the city to arrive at the terminal. By that time, I was famished, dehydrated and very tired. I had walked for three hours that day. My knees were still raw and my body ached terribly from the beatings. None of which thwarted me from limping onward to sort myself out before the day ended. There had been water taps in the park so I'd been able to keep hydrated through the day, but I needed something sweet to keep my energy up. I spent a precious fifty cents on a bottle of coke. It was the best thing I'd ever tasted!

For what seemed like an eternity, I sat watching buses coming and going as though I was waiting for someone. Eventually exhaustion won. I lay down on a hard bench, using my plastic bag as a pillow and plunged into sleep. It was 11pm.

"Hey wake up. You shouldn't be sleeping here," a female Maori bus driver in her green uniform cried as she shook me awake. She was plump and had false teeth. I could tell because her top teeth kept popping out as she spoke. It might have been comical if the situation wasn't so serious. I tried to focus on her eyes. They seemed to be kind and concerned rather than angry.

"I am sorry. I was waiting for someone but he didn't turn up," I blurted a lie in broken English as I sat up rubbing my tired eyes.

"Well you can't stay here, sweetie. It's Friday night and very dangerous. Go and ring a friend or your family to come pick you up."

"I have no family. I ran away. I don't know my friend's number or address. He lives on the North Shore. Please, it is only for tonight. Tomorrow I will find him. I have nowhere else to go," I begged, starting to cry again.

"There will be a lot of drunken pigs coming this way. It's not safe for you here. Come with me."

I followed her to a bus already parked up for the night. She reopened the door and waved for me to enter. "Sweetie, you will be safe in here and the seats are more comfortable. I will lock the bus from outside and leave a note on the dashboard for the morning shift driver that I let you stay the night on the bus. We are not allowed to do this, but I would rather get into trouble than to hear on the news tomorrow morning that something bad happened to you."

Something about the tone of her voice made me feel warm and safe. "By the way, is your bus driver friend a Samoan?" I asked, in case she was referring to Tavita, my brother-in-law.

"No! She is a European driver. She will be taking this bus at 6am. I am going to lock the door now."

I sensed she was tired herself – probably wanting to get home to her own family. I thanked her from the bottom of my heart and climbed inside. Instinctively I went straight to the back. Besides, that's where the long bench seat was so I could stretch out. Thoughts were tumbling through my befuddled brain. I cursed the day I was born. I could hear my Auntie Tilie's angry voice telling me I was made of stronger stuff. Then I thought of this kind Samaritan who had taken pity on me. She didn't even know me and yet was more concerned about my safety than her own job. She had reminded me there were plenty of good people in this world. With that final thought, I was at peace in the sanctity and security of that big yellow bus. The next thing I knew it was morning and a big male driver was opening the door.

"Hey, how did you get in here?" he asked angrily.

His overpowering aftershave hit me before I opened my eyes. Blearily I forced my heavy eyelids open and saw him standing all puffed up and ready for a fight. He was quite an intimidating sight towering over me. It was 5.45am and still dark outside.

"Uh, sir, it was the lady driver who let me sleep here for safety. She left a note for you. She said that another female driver was coming in this morning."

"What lady driver let you in? What did she look like?" he asked with one eyebrow raised as though he didn't believe me.

"She was Maori, a bit fat and she had false teeth. She said she had just finished her shift and this was her bus. I am sorry but I had nowhere to sleep and she thought I would be safe here until this morning."

"This bus was driven by a male driver on the last shift. I know because it was me. I parked this bus here at 10pm. I know of no female driver that fits your description."

He walked to the front to see if he could find the note but there was nothing. I told him a little about my situation and he sympathetically asked where I was going.

"I don't know," I replied, silently begging him for help with my sad eyes.

"Listen, I have to leave in five minutes and you have to get off the bus."

"Where is your bus going, sir?" I asked with increasing desperation.

"I am heading to Ellerslie."

It occurred to me that I had dreamed about Ellerslie. It was the area where my mother's cousin, Pao's daughter Rosa, lived with her husband and young children. Rosa was one of the first people my mother sponsored to move to New Zealand. She would do anything my mother asked, even if she knew it was wrong. I was certain there was no way she could refuse if my mother came for me. My brain told me this was the last place in the world I should go, and yet something, some niggling, nagging, gnawing little voice, was insisting that was precisely what I should do.

"Can I catch a ride on your bus to Ellerslie? I have money for my fare," I heard myself asking.

The driver agreed and told me not to worry about paying for my fare. With a relief, I put my head against the window and stared outside as the bus ambled on, occasionally stopping to pick up passengers. When it was closer to my stop, I gathered my things, rose to my feet and pressed the red button. The bus lurched to a halt and I walked to the front, thanking the driver sincerely for his kindness.

"No problem. You take care now," he called cheerily, closing the door and driving off into the distance.

I looked at the time. It was 6.50. The sun was rising and hunger pangs were pounding. I hadn't eaten anything the day before, and so hungrily headed towards the convenience shop across from the bus stop. Extracting my life savings from my pocket, I purchased two pies and a soda. It didn't leave me much money but I would have fainted without the sustenance. After this banquet, my funds were down to $16.

Against my better judgement, I headed to Rosa's place. The line of broken, faded white mailboxes were full of junk mail and fronted by rubbish bags, some broken with rubbish strewn around. An awful smell heralded odious times ahead. Even though it was early, Rosa's door was wide open, and when she spotted me I was excitedly welcomed in. As Rosa hugged me, I glimpsed over her shoulders and spotted Pao himself sitting in a chair quietly waiting for me to come to greet him. I pulled away from Rosa and gave Pao a frantic embrace, sobbing on his shoulders.

"I am so glad to see you, Pao," I cried.

"What's the matter, Sieni? Sit down and tell me what's happened," he offered, patting the chair next to his.

It was obvious they had no idea I'd run away. I told them the whole sorry tale. Rosa was, of course, concerned my mother would be worried sick about me.

"If you left yesterday, where did you just come from?" she questioned.

With tears still pouring, I explained everything – and I mean everything.

Pao wiped a tear from his eye. "Sieni, go in the bathroom and wash your face. Rosa, get up and make something to eat for the poor girl."

I was shocked when I saw my face in the mirror. It was all red and puffy, no doubt from all the crying in the last two days mixed with the bruises from my beating. It was no wonder the bus driver didn't accept any money from me; I looked a pitiful mess. I heard Pao repeatedly telling Rosa that he was disgusted that my mother would allow this to happen. By the time I returned to the living area, he already had a plan for me.

"Rosa is going to call your mother to tell her that you are okay and you are here with me. She will also tell her that you will be staying here from now on. You don't need to go back to them."

Pao assured me that if I didn't want to go back home, as long as he was there nobody would touch me again. "Now, eat while we make the phone call," he instructed me kindly.

Rosa didn't have a phone, so she used the public phone booth across the road to make the call. While she was out,

Pao's youngest daughter, Lite, came in through the back door. It was Saturday morning and Lite had been at a sleepover in her friend's apartment next door. She was the same age as my sister Agnes, and back in Samoa we'd grown up as neighbours and cousins.

We were thrilled to see each other, but Lite couldn't help asking, "What happened to your face? It looks like it got stung by a whole nest of bees."

When Pao explained the situation to her, along with his solution, Lite jumped up and down with excitement. "That's fantastic," she cheered. "You are going to stay here with us."

Pao was in New Zealand at my mother's request to conduct the *Fa'a Samoa* for Agnes's impending wedding in a few months. Tavita's family wanted the full Samoan ceremony and celebration. For such an occasion, Pao was the best *matai* in our family. Not only was he widely regarded as the smartest chief, but he was also treated as an elder brother to my mother and her siblings.

"How did you get to sleep in the bus?" Lite asked.

"A Maori woman let me in. She was a bus driver. Well, she claimed she was and she was wearing a uniform. She woke me while I was sleeping on the bench and told me how dangerous it was. Then she put me in the bus to sleep. Strangely, the driver who arrived the next morning said there was no such driver."

Lite and Pao paused and glanced at each other. "That was your grandmother," Pao stated firmly. "She came to you in the form of another not to frighten you and to keep you safe." Once more, he shook his head in dismay at my mother's callous actions.

"I had a feeling it was her as well," I agreed. "I also believe it was Tina who led me here, because she knew you were here and would help me. I would not have thought of Rosa on my own because I know she is close to my mother and my sister."

"There is no doubt," Pao nodded thoughtfully. "I had a powerful dream about Mele last night. I have never dreamed of her before."

Rosa returned from her call looking a little uncertain. "Your mother will be here this afternoon when her husband gets home from work. Meanwhile, go and get some sleep, Sieni. Use Pao's room. Just put his things on his suitcase on the floor."

The physical, emotional and psychological exhaustion took over any concerns about seeing my mother. I collapsed on the bed and was out cold. It was after 2pm when Lite woke me. Mother's car had just arrived. Through the kitchen window, Rosa saw my stepfather, my mother and, worst of all, Agnes walking down the stairs.

"Lite," Rosa hissed, "stay in the room with Sieni and don't come out until I say."

Silently obeying, Lite joined me. We sat on the bed facing each other, not saying a word, straining to hear every word being spoken. At first there was laughter and happy chatter as the family greeted each other. Pao invited them to sit. In spite of all this joviality, I imagined Agnes getting irritated. I wasn't wrong.

"So where is that fucking bitch?"

In Samoan custom, this was a tremendously disrespectful thing to say in front of elders. Luckily for her, Pao had not understood what she said. Instead of responding, he started by thanking them for coming so promptly and quickly moved on to discuss my predicament. Everyone had to listen without interruption as he spoke; that was the protocol.

"Amilaina, I know our children can bring us grief and make us angry, but I am very upset with what is happening to this girl. She said little, but the state she was in when she came here told me all I needed to know. The thought of her sleeping at bus stops brought tears to my eyes, and I don't cry easily. Here is what I suggest. Leave Sieni here with Rosa while you try to heal your issues with her. When everyone is calm and happy again she can come back to you if she wants to."

Sticking with protocol, mother was next in right of reply, during which time Agnes was audibly mumbling and griping impatiently.

"Thank you, Pao, my big brother and the person I respect the most. Thank you for taking Sieni in. Just to clarify why Sieni got a hiding, I trusted that she went off to work. Instead, she was looking for a husband. We had to remove her from her job because she was moving on other women's husbands and boyfriends. It was very embarrassing for Agnes because she works there too. Pao, this is not the first time she has done this. Thank you for your concern, but I plan to deport her back to Samoa."

The words were coming from my mother's mouth, but Agnes may as well have had her hand up mum's back moving her mouth like a ventriloquist's dummy. It was all lies but told with such sincerity and conviction they almost had me believing them. How could I possibly defend myself? Fortunately I didn't need to. Pao had not earned his reputation without good cause.

"Amilaina, you are obviously still mad at her. You may have every right to be. As your big brother, I advise you to please leave Sieni here. There is nothing in Samoa for her. Everyone came to New Zealand for a better life. You are her mother and you are here. Who are you sending her home to? Leave her with Rosa and Lite. I am here as well for a while so I will talk to her about the issues you have raised. I don't want to hear that this girl was found dead at a bus station because I failed to act," he told her earnestly.

Mother eventually agreed, but I knew this would not satisfy Agnes. Sure enough, the bedroom door pushed open. Agnes strode across to me, and without warning slapped my face with all her might. She raised her hand ready to strike me again, but she had already awoken a terrible fury in me. I sprang up from the bed and punched Agnes square in the face as hard as I could, then another and another. She hadn't expected me to retaliate. Her feeble attempts to cover her face were no match for my wrath. I grabbed fists full of her hair, wrenching her backwards to drag her to the floor so I could spit at her with contempt, telling her what a horrible degrading bitch she was. Poor Lite jumped in and pleaded with me to stop. The commotion was so loud that everyone in the living area came running in. Pao was furious.

"All of you get out of my house," he screamed. "I am very, very disappointed in you, Amilaina. All of this is your fault. You are their mother and your children are fighting like mongrel dogs. Go back home; I don't want to see any of you."

My mother was crying and begging for Pao's forgiveness. Rosa brought Agnes and I in the sitting room and ordered us to sit down. Lite sat next to me on the floor mat and gently stroked my back to calm my shakes. Pao wiped his tears of confusion and anger, calmed himself then fell back in his chair exhausted.

"Let me tell you all a story, especially you Amilaina. I witnessed first-hand this girl taking care of your mother as a young child for years before she died. She wiped her bottom, fed her, tended to your mother's every need while you were here making a life for yourself and your other children. My wife Kaisala and I used to comment what a special girl Sieni was. Our hearts went out to her when we saw the other children playing and living normal lives while she was caring for her grandmother without complaint. Now she is here and she deserves to be treated far, far better than this. This morning, I took what she told me with a pinch of salt, but now I have seen with my own eyes what is really going on. It is vile and contemptible. You should be deeply, deeply ashamed, Amilaina."

Mother apologised profusely; my stepfather sat silent throughout the whole drama and Agnes just sat there looking stunned with bloodstains on her nose. I felt sick in my stomach, hating my mother and my sister. Quietly, I requested permission to be excused to leave the room before I threw up. Pao nodded his permission.

Alone on the bed, I cried again. I was becoming weary of my emotional outbursts; they were draining the life out of me. At least this time I wasn't feeling sorry for myself; it was Pao's words that had touched me deeply. I never knew he thought that way about me. Like my Uncle Migao, he saw from a distance my dedication and sacrifice for Tina. I'd always thought I was alone and that no one really cared.

Mother and her tribe eventually said their goodbyes to Pao, Rosa and Lite. Everything was settled, and I was happy to begin another chapter of my life with another new family. Finally, I was with people who liked me and appeared to be concerned about my welfare. My faith in human decency was restored.

Chapter 22

Things Started To Look Up

Rosa and her family were poor in material wealth but rich in love and laughter. There was another mouth to feed but they managed. With no car for transport, Rosa's husband and Lite had to rise before dawn each day to catch many buses to work.

"As long as everyone is healthy and happy, who cares if we only have bread and water?" Pao would say.

My mother and her husband visited Pao frequently with food or money, not because I was there, but rather because it was customary to show respect in this fashion for an important visiting dignitary of the family. I often hid in the room when they dropped by. Not once did mother ask about me or my well-being. I didn't care if I ever saw her again. My new family liked me for who I was, and that was what was more important to me.

To help Rosa's family out I desperately wanted to work, and so began searching the job ads in newspapers. Circling those that might accept me, I called from the red public phone booth, using what little money I had left. I had limited English, no qualifications and little work experience; most just hung up before I even finished. I began to realise the jobs I wanted were not offered to a school dropout with poor English. I also learned that factory and menial work placements were usually filled the day before the advertisement was even printed. Never one to be thwarted, I began cold calling. Extracting my passport with an approval stamp of my permanent residency in it from my little plastic bag, I walked into local factories, stores and companies to beseech them to give me a chance, explaining I was a quick learner and capable of working hard. Many said no, but I didn't give up. Finally, I came upon a shoe factory. I gave my now well-rehearsed speech to the receptionist. As usual, the office woman shot back, "Sorry! No work at the moment."

"Can I see the boss, the person who makes the final decision please?" I heard myself asking with confidence, as if my Auntie Tilie was sitting right there demanding me to do so. As it happened, the owner was standing within earshot and quickly intervened.

"I'm sure we need someone like her in the packing area." He paused as I looked up hopefully. "She can start next week," he stated, throwing me a smile and a nod of approval.

I was the happiest girl in New Zealand! I thanked him profusely, and was so grateful I felt like dropping myself to the ground to kiss his feet. I had a job! It might only have been a job packing shoes, but I honestly wouldn't have cared if it was a job cleaning toilets. It was a job and I would be able to support myself.

In completing the employment form, I decided to use my middle name Jane, the name my Auntie Tilie preferred to call me. I felt her influence helped me that day to get work. This was a fresh start and I wanted to erase the name my mother chose for me at birth. Doing that I knew I could achieve anything on my own, and I was damn well going to prove to everyone that I was not worthless. What I had learnt from my grandmother and Auntie Tilie became my shield, my guard and my guiding light in battling any obstacles that stood before me. Theirs were the constant and strongest voices within me. Never did they stop reminding me that I was special; I could do anything I wanted and become anything my heart desired.

Rosa and her family were so happy for me they decided to celebrate. When her husband was paid that week, he bought a huge box of Kentucky Fried Chicken and we all chowed down in this rare treat with gusto. With my first pay, I gave Rosa the same amount Lite was paying for her board. I also gave some money to Pao for his necessities, which left me $25 a week for bus fare and lunch. I was over the moon, rich with happiness, and I didn't care if my mother and my sister still loathed the thought of me.

The shoe factory smelt of rubber, leather and dust, but it was an aroma I looked forward to each day. It smelt like victory; I had achieved this myself. Three months after I settled into my new job, I was called in to see the big boss. The supervisor informed me not to worry, advising the owner only summoned people to his office if there was good news. Dutifully, I obeyed.

Entering the high alter of the owner's office, I was relieved to see a warm smile on his face. I was ushered to a chair and the meeting commenced. "So, how do you like it here so far?"

"I am very happy working here, thank you sir," I replied shyly, squirming a little in my seat.

"Your supervisor tells me you are a quick learner and a very fast worker. I knew you were smart and had guts when you came looking for work. Now tell me, what do you really want to do with your life? You are young, not quite seventeen yet. Is working at the shoe factory your dream job?" He paused, waiting for my reply. Although he was kind and welcoming, I felt a bit intimidated and unsure how to reply.

"Truly, sir, I am happy here. Thank you."

"Sure, now you are. But is packing shoes something you want to do for the rest of your life?" he repeated.

I didn't understand what he was getting at, but felt he wanted an honest answer.

"I arrived from Samoa last year and I wanted to go to school to learn English so I can speak it like you do. My mother did not want to send me to school to complete my education. When I was young I wanted to be a doctor or a nurse. I took care of my grandmother; it was then I wished I could help her more – when she was sick and in pain," I admitted honestly.

"Wow! That's amazing! I knew you were special when I saw you. You know you can be whatever you want to be if you have drive and determination – and you have that and more. This is what I suggest. I will give you a ten-dollar bonus a week. It can go towards a course for your dream job. I would like you to work here as many years as you want. Whenever you have saved enough to leave to become a doctor, come and see me and we will part with no hard feelings. I hope the day you become one and I am sick you'll be the one to take care of me."

I couldn't believe my ears! He beamed at me with a smile full of sunshine, stood up, shook my hand and bid me farewell. My heart was pounding. I felt so elated and so special I sprung an embrace on the poor man and planted a kiss on his cheek. I think he almost blushed.

"Thank you, thank you!" I screamed, flying back to my work area as though I had wings. It wasn't just the extra $10 – it was this man's belief in me. The lady I worked with told me that big boss often took young people under his wing in this fashion. He had apparently been brought up by a single mother who had disabilities, and consequently he made a promise to himself that if he ever became rich he would help other young people to make their dreams come true. I began to wonder if fate had intervened, pushing him into the front office on the day I had almost lost hope in finding a job. With not just the financial bonus, but the enormous emotional boost of someone believing in me, somebody noticing me, somebody prepared to give me a chance to make something of my life, I could at last see the jigsaw pieces of my broken life coming together.

When I told my cousins and Pao the news it was as though I'd won the lottery. Pay rises such as this were generally only awarded after many years of devoted, hard toil.

"It is all your blessings, Sieni," Pao cheered. "You are blessed because of your kindness to your grandmother."

I felt free – free *and* content. The next day, Rosa took me to the bank and I opened my own bank account for the very first time. Ten dollars was put in that account every week so I could prove to my big-hearted boss I was following his wise advice. For a few weeks, everything was absolutely roses. In a family such as mine, it was never long before those sublime roses spiked with their prickly thorns.

Two weeks before Agnes's wedding the house was in turmoil. Lite had been detained by immigration for living and working illegally in New Zealand for a year. Someone had reported her. Rosa was told Lite would be deported back to Samoa within two days, and she wasn't allowed home to pack or to say goodbye. There was no arguing with the Department of Immigration, so Pao decided he would return with her for moral support. It all happened so quickly; Lite and Pao would be leaving us. I had so looked forward to coming home each night from work, seeing my uncle Pao's welcoming smile and revelling in Lite's companionship. It would not be the same without them. Rosa was good to me, and I had already made friends with some of the girls in our neighbourhood, but Pao and Lite were special. They were real family to me.

To add further consternation, with Lite gone my mother and Agnes were panicking. They had to find another maid of honour.

Two hundred guests were expected at this wedding, one hundred from each side of the bride and groom's family. My sister wanted five bridesmaids. My sister Ceal was chosen from among her sisters, the rest were close family members and friends. There were also flower girls – my sister Kina was one and our little brother Laurie had been roped in as the ring boy. My jaw hit the floor with a thud when I heard Rosa suggest to my mother that perhaps I should take Lite's place, as I was one of the sisters.

"No!" mother quickly replied. "Hardly anyone even knows she exists!"

Rosa was disgusted and horrified at a mother saying such a thing about her own daughter, but I certainly wasn't surprised. Not only had I become well accustomed to the fact that I was unloved, unwanted and an accident, but the idea of going to Agnes's wedding didn't exactly fill me with joy. I didn't want to go – nor did I expect I would be invited. However, on the eve of the Agnes's big day, mother told Rosa it would be okay for me to attend. Rosa assured me we would leave right away if my sister or my mother became nasty at the wedding towards me.

Early Saturday morning I was the first customer at the Salvo's thrift shop, scavenging for a decent outfit to wear. Lite was a lot bigger than I was, so none of her clothes would do. Thinking it was all a terrible waste of money, I selected a nice dress, a coat and a pair of high heels – the first pair I ever owned.

We all arrived in time for the service at the Catholic church. There were crowds of people, and Agnes looked beautiful in her white gown and veil. Throughout the service, I felt nothing but happiness for her; somewhere inside me I even managed to feel proud of her. I looked over at my mother on the front row in her beautiful dress and caught the sight of a tired woman. She had sewn Agnes's wedding gown, and all of the bridesmaid's and flower girl's dresses. We ignored each other all throughout the day.

After an hour-long sermon, the enormous gathering filed into the reception hall for celebrations to begin. It was a huge Samoan *fia fia* and feast. Tables were covered in white and brightly decorated. The Five Stars band started playing as people arrived. The band Agnes and Tavita had hired was one of the most famous and popular Samoan bands. Everywhere they played packed houses. The father was the manager, and Alofa, the eldest son, was the lead guitarist, main vocalist, songwriter and leader of the group. Alofa's brother expertly played the drums, while the other three guitarists were friends of the boys. That band could really rock the house down. After not wanting to attend, I discovered fate was intervening again.

In my "second-hand Rose" dress smelling of mothballs, ripped pantihose and bare feet, I boogied down on the dance floor. I'd always loved to dance, and just because the heel broke off one of my first-ever high-heeled shoes, I wasn't going to let that stop me! My antics caught Alofa's attention – actually, they caught everyone's attention. I was happy and was having a whale of a time, and I guess my uninhibited display was alluring to the bandleader.

When I stopped for breath he asked me for my phone number. Panting, I told him I didn't have one. He wasn't about to let a little detail like that get in the way of his amorous advances, so he gave me his number instead. In the Samoan community, the Five Stars were an extremely famous and successful act, but I'd never really listened to their music before, and outside of dancing like a maniac to their music, I wasn't really paying them much attention at the wedding reception either. The truth was, as I was starting to be content and had self-assurance, I planted a seed in my head that I wanted to marry a European man. I somehow believed they would be kinder if they found out my shame. Growing up in Samoa, we were told we would be mocked and beaten by our

Samoan husbands if we weren't virgins or good enough. I had enough of people beating the shit out of me. Therefore, I was not interested or attracted anymore to my own kind. I politely accepted Alofa's little piece of paper, put it in my coat pocket and carried on enjoying myself.

All too soon, our lift arrived. We left early, while everyone else was still having a ball. On my way out, Alofa threw me a big smile, reminding me to call him. I smiled back politely, slipped his piece of paper in with my passport when I arrived home and thought no more about it.

An uneventful week slid by after the wedding. Alofa had completely left my mind and work continued as normal at the shoe factory. Within seven days of the wedding, mother visited Rosa, asking if I would move in with Agnes and Tavita to help pay the rent in their new flat! I was weary beyond the telling of it, yet deep in my soul I still yearned to be loved by my mother. I wanted to believe she harboured even the tiniest shred of compassion for me somewhere in her heart. Craving that faint chance of recognition, I conceded.

Thanking Rosa sincerely, and telling her the four months I stayed with her were my happiest since my arrival in New Zealand, I packed up and left. Full of nauseating dread, I piled into the backseat of my mother and her husband's car, having a pretty good idea of what awaited me from my mother's tone.

"If you run away again, I will call the police to lock you up. Remember, you are still under age and I am your legal guardian." With that utterance, I knew I was well and truly fucked over once again. There was no Pao to fight for me this time.

Chapter 23

A Bad Move

Agnes and Tavita's apartment was on the fifth floor in Freeman's Bay. It was a nice area close to the city. Theirs and other surrounding buildings were up market and fairly new – even the paint smelled fresh. It was a small place but I had my own bedroom and a nice view of passing traffic and the nearby shops. Agnes was still working at Nestle and Tavita was still driving buses. At my shoe packing job I had been promoted to stock taking duties and ensuring orders were filled and signed off by my foreman. By the time I was seventeen, I shared the responsibility for any mistakes made from the packing room with a lady who had been working there for nearly ten years. My work experience at Auntie Tilie's estate had come in handy. I was routinely complimented for being methodical, fast and exact. Auntie had taught me well.

Despite my promotion, my income plummeted. Once again my pay packet was demanded by my mother and I was expected to comply. She gave Agnes my board, and I was supposed to be satisfied with $20 a week to cover my fare and lunch. My bank account was frozen. My life was being lived entirely for my sister and my mother, as though it didn't occur to either of them that I had feelings. I had to ask their permission to do anything, and everything I did or didn't do was immediately reported to my mother. Agnes was still gunning for me, although after our last encounter she was a little more circumspect about it these days.

Despite this, by Christmas time everyone was cheerfully morphing into a festive mood. Lights and decorations filled the city streets and Christmas trees could be seen in most people's homes. Companies threw parties for their employees, and mine was no different. The company subsidised half of the cost and the employees were happy to pay the balance. It was a well-catered event with a thumping great disco, and I couldn't wait to attend. One of the Pacific Islanders at work named Hurricane offered to pay for my ticket if I went with him. He was gay, but we got along well as just friends, knowing that he was only interested in guys and I now only fancied *Palagi* men. He agreed to accompany me to ask my sister for her permission. Dressed smartly, Hurricane caught a bus to my residence to request my hand in companionship at the firm's end of year celebration.

Arriving before Agnes and her husband returned home, we had to wait patiently for the charade to play out. We had no dining table or chairs; I invited Hurricane to sit on the floor in the living area. To pass the time I showed him my precious photo album. It contained pictures of my beloved grandparents, including a rare and precious shot of the three of us together. I was standing behind them with a big happy grin on my face as a seven year old. This photo was a real treasure, as no one in the village owned a camera back then. Someone my mother was kind to visited my grandparents on his return to Samoa with a camera to take some pictures for my mother. Because I was in that photo, it somehow got given to my Uncle Migao and I liberated it from him. In that album, I also had photographs of me in my school uniform, a picture of me as a *taupou* of our culture group squeezing out the Samoan kava, and some marching photographs of me when I was at my village primary school. There was also a rare picture of Auntie Tilie and me taken by Bentzen at their estate when I stayed with them. This album was my most treasured possession and completely irreplaceable. I had been carrying these precious photos in my handbag everywhere until I could afford an album to keep them safe. Whenever I felt alone, I would draw out this album from underneath my bed and remember all the warm, wonderful, wide-eyed moments of wonder I'd shared with my loving grandparents. The images and memories never failed to make me smile. After that I was able to sleep, believing life was not always bad.

Hurricane and I were having a good laugh at some of my memories, giggling like little kids, when the door opened and in walked Tavita. It was just after 4pm. Not having been primed for the occasion, my brother-in-law looked surprised. Hurricane and I stood up politely and I explained the situation.

"This is a good friend from work. I have asked him to come with me to ask you and Agnes for permission to go to our work's Christmas do tonight."

"Agnes and a cousin of yours from Samoa are in the car downstairs with your mother," he told me. "We've come to pick you up to join us at your mother's house. But wait here, I will go and ask them for you."

Although I really should have known better, excited and confident I returned my album under my bed and waited for a positive response. Only once I had permission would I start to get ready.

Moments later I heard returning footsteps. With a smile I opened the front door. Agnes and cousin Au were at the top of the stairs, but before I could say hello they both dragged me by the hair down the cold concrete flight of steps as my body bounced and flopped from side to side like a heavy garbage bag ready to be thrown away. The pain was so excruciating, but I didn't want to scream. I refused to give them the pleasure that I was in agony. When they dragged me into the car, mother was in the front seat, grabbing me and pinching me hard. I felt like jumping on her to savagely bite her face off. Agnes briefly returned to the apartment to toss my stunned friend Hurricane out on the street and then joined us in the vehicle with a sneer of contempt on her face.

I was so busy trying to protect myself I didn't notice what she was carrying. I simply couldn't fathom why they were doing this. They could have just said no. Instead, this was Agnes's long-awaited moment of revenge. Au, who was a large woman and much older than us, gave her the opportunity she'd been waiting for. With these two working in tandem, I was doomed to be defeated. The familiar cruel and spiteful words flew around the car while Tavita drove us back to mother's after the poor, well-dressed and completely befuddled Hurricane had been sent on his way. I was pushed, punched, pulled and walloped simultaneously by three big fat females all for wanting to go to my Christmas party.

Once at mother's I was directed into the dining area so my siblings watching television were not disturbed. I was then pushed down on one of the red chairs.

"What gives you the right to bring a boy home and sleep with him at Agnes's place?" mother growled at me.

Stunned by this ridiculous accusation, I impotently offered, "I didn't sleep with him! We were in the living room looking at my photos fully clothed. We were just waiting for Agnes and Tavita to get home. Ask Tavita!" I demanded, trying to protect my face from yet more blows.

"She is a fucking liar! Tavita fucken caught them in bed," Agnes spat. "You are nothing but a fucken slut bitch," she added, slapping the side of my face again.

The three of them kept pounding on me until they'd exhausted themselves. At that point, I was left alone in the dining area, bruised and bleeding – and hating all of them. Warm blood and thick snot from crying seeped from my nose. I just let it drop on the floor. In the next room, I could hear Agnes ranting as though she was demented. Lifting my head, I could see my stepfather outside burning rubbish through the big window. He didn't seem to care about the chaos inside. I rather suspect if he'd come in and discovered my mauled deceased remains on the floor he would calmly ask, "So what shall we do with her body then?"

Humiliated and in great pain, I felt utterly alone. From the deepest part of my soul, I prayed for some sort of lighting to strike me and carry me somewhere far away from this earth. I didn't care if I died in the process. Moments later Agnes walked past me with that evil grimace on her face. To my horror, I realised my grey photo album was in her hand. She marched triumphantly out the back door, turned to make sure I could see what she was doing and threw it into the fire. I could literally feel the searing heat of the flames as though they were burning me. Every happy memory I'd possessed was erased in a damnable fiery fate. I envisaged the pictures of my grandparent's smiling faces curling, blistering, burning and finally crumbling into ashes. I despised my sister and the ground she walked on with an intensity that eclipsed anything that had come before. I wished for her a slow and agonising death. She and mother knew how precious those photos were to me – not just for me, but for the entire family.

As Agnes returned in glorious triumph from her heinous victory grinning like a psychopath, murderous intent boiled within me. I could hear my Auntie Tilie telling me not to put up with this any longer. It was time to get away, far away, and never return to these monsters.

Chapter 24

Taking Control

S eething and still bleeding while the rest of the family was distracted watching TV, I opened the back door and slipped quietly away. I had no money or possessions, just the clothes on my back. When Agnes had taken my precious photo album, she also pilfered my handbag containing an envelope with four week's pay. The whole lot was given to my horrible mother. I was broke, beaten, homeless and once more alone.

There was no point in seeking refuge in the home of any family from my mother's side. Thinking through my limited options, I realised if my life's experiences had taught me anything, they had taught me there was always another way of looking at almost any situation. When I had first arrived in New Zealand it was with my Schwalger stepmother. She had a married brother resident in New Zealand. Although I didn't know them well, I did know they lived only a few streets away from my mother's place. My stepmother had introduced me to them during my prized church visit tour. I was devoid of pride, penniless and completely ignorant to the fact that in a civilised country there was help for abused girls in my situation.

To my utter relief, Paulo and his wife, Sea, welcomed me with open arms. They were incensed at the sight of my swollen face and cut lip. Sea wanted to call the police on my behalf on the spot. The last thing I had the emotional or physical strength for was a police investigation, and bearing witness against those who probably wouldn't hesitate to silence me permanently should I threaten life as they knew it didn't seem a particularly prudent or fruitful course of action. I pleaded with Sea just to be gracious enough to permit me to stay for a while until I sorted myself out. From what I could assess, Sea appeared to be wearing the pants in the family. She was intelligent, outwardly a beauty and inwardly glowing with a heart of gold.

"Don't you worry about a thing. You stay here with us. I'll tell you this – your family better not dare come near this house. I will have all their arses thrown in jail," she threatened.

These virtual strangers who were not even related by blood but rather loosely by marriage, didn't give a second thought about reshaping their lives to accommodate me. Their five-year-old daughter was moved to share a bunk bed with her seven-year-old brother, leaving the little girl's small room free for me. In contrast to the cruel examples of humanity I had all too frequently encountered in my life, these selfless people practiced random acts of kindness for no reward whatsoever.

I wish to state unequivocally and for the record, those random acts of kindness saved my soul from turning completely black with despair. Indeed, they may have saved my physical being as well. For the rest of my days, I will forever think of Paulo and Sea with the deepest affection, immeasurable gratitude and what I count as the highest praise of all. Much as I loved and admired my Tina and Auntie Tilie, if I seek to emulate another in my life, it will always be these good, kind, loving people. They were as much the antithesis of the vile ones in my clan as it was possible to be.

Sea and Paulo were hard workers, devoted to their young children and very family orientated. Paulo was a charming character and an excellent father, but it was Sea with whom I bonded. She was a well-educated and very understanding woman. Every night I still count my blessings that she came into my life. She helped me, guided me and advised me in ways I'd not imagined possible before. She also readily agreed I was more than justified to escape the toxic environment of my own family.

Living with Sea and Paulo also helped me save money. They only asked for $50 from my pay packet to help with food. I resumed my regular savings of $10 per pay packet as I'd promised my wily and kindly boss, and that left me with $60 to spend on having a life. Sea was most adamant I was going to have a life!

"If you're old enough to earn your own money and pay your board, you are old enough to have some fun," Sea cheerfully chided. "Tonight we are going to a Samoan social. Let's see what you have to wear."

Having been clothes shopping – real clothes shopping – for the first time ever, I excitedly ran to my room to fetch my newly procured ensembles to ask Sea's opinion. Together we selected a pair of tailored pants with a smart top, complimented by new shiny black high heels (hoping I would not break them this time). I returned moments later resplendent in my new outfit. Sea beamed at me as if I was her own daughter.

"The Five Stars will play badly tonight. They won't be able to keep their eyes off you," she laughed.

"What?" I mumbled.

"The Five Stars. You *have* heard of them?"

The blood drained from my face. "I'm afraid I can't go," I stuttered.

"Why ever not?"

"I met Alofa, the band's leader, at my sister's wedding. He gave me his number to call him. I never did."

Sea burst out laughing. "Do you know how many girls follow him around? The Five Stars are big news. In Samoa they're better known than King Maleitoa or the Samoan prime minister!" She paused, astutely assessing my nervous state. "You know," she mused cheekily, "I have always wanted to meet him. This could be my chance."

Sea laughed again, clapping her hands together in feigned girlish excitement, which was too infectious to ignore. I heard myself laughing in unison with her.

"I'll see what I can do for you," I shot back teasingly.

Hours later we were dressed for the night, drenched in perfume (or aftershave, respectively) and the three of us headed to the hall. Sea had succeeded in raising my excitement level, but not entirely in calming my apprehension. Butterflies were merrily cavorting in my stomach. Without realising it, I was wiping sweaty palms on my new pants as we parked in the overcrowded car park. There was already a large line of people waiting to get in, and the sound of the band thumping away was clearly audible from outside. I glanced at Sea. She gave me a friendly wink and squeezed my hand.

"Come on," she chided me. "We're going to have a blast."

Taking a deep breath, we handed our tickets to the woman at the door and walked in. The hall was packed, the dance floor full and the whole area was buzzing. The Five Stars certainly knew how to work a crowd. The stage was directly to our left as we entered. I tried to hide behind Sea, hoping Alofa would not recognise me.

"Don't worry," she smiled at me. "He's singing with his eyes closed."

I spent the first half hour sitting down behind anyone who could disguise my presence, until Paulo pulled me onto the floor to dance. Try as I might to keep my eyes focused on my dance partner, they annoyingly disobeyed me to glance in Alofa's direction. The moment his eyes struck mine, that dazzling smile of his all but blinded me. There was no one else in the room after that. My dream of finding a *Palagi* boy went out the window.

Alofa was pleased to see me again. It wasn't long before he unceremoniously dumped the harem he'd been dating. I couldn't believe he even remembered me from one fleeting encounter. From that moment I was his and he was mine. He nicknamed me his Samoan girl in a gesture designed to give me reassurance I was the only one for him.

With pride, Sea and Paulo invited Alofa to come to see me anytime. Equally, I had the freedom to visit him whenever I chose. Life was looking up. I had a good home, a steady income, was respected at work, had a sought-after man who adored me, and most importantly I was in control for the first time – really in control of my own destiny. All of this fuelled my already burning desire to strive for the heavens.

To really succeed I first needed to perfect my English. In the first instance, I practiced by carrying a dictionary in my handbag. I would read newspapers, find words I did not understand and learn their meaning. Each time I learned a new word I wrote it down in a notebook, which I would study regularly. Although my spoken English was polished by listening to and speaking with my work colleagues, my reading and writing skills improved at a far greater speed. Encouraging me with my efforts, Alofa and I constantly wrote love letters to one another, even though we saw each other almost every day. When I made mistakes in my writing he would correct me, and I was grateful for it. Having been educated in New Zealand since he was very young, my beau had a far greater mastery of the language than I did.

From the time I spent caring for my beloved Tina following her accident until her death, I had dreamed of becoming a doctor.

When I really looked into it, speaking and writing English was nothing compared to the seven years at university and many thousands of dollars in fees it would take to make this dream a reality. Initially winded by the harsh facts, I thought my dream seemed impossible. I reminded myself, "Shoot for the moon. Even if you miss, you'll land among the stars."

The stars in this case weren't that stellar, but I was able to start in baby steps by studying nursing. Maintaining my job at the shoe factory during the week, I started attended a nursing course on Saturdays. After passing two modules I was assigned volunteer work, mostly all the dirty jobs at the small private hospitals that nobody else would do. Having performed far more grisly and gruesome tasks back in Samoa, I was far more willing to stride in where others feared to tread. Very little was capable of deterring me, and I knew the work would look great on my resume as I was studying for exams. It never occurred to me that my very first medical assignment might actually lead to paid employment. Perhaps due to my preparedness to take on anything and my diligent work ethic, one of the small private hospitals offered me a part-time position. This presented a dilemma.

My relationship with Alofa was becoming serious. From the first night we spent together, I could feel myself becoming enveloped by this wonderful guy. Sex was no longer something to be loathed and terrified of. Alofa was kind, which gave me some self-esteem. I could speak to him and share things with him. So, when I was faced with a dilemma it was only natural I would discuss it with him. The quandary came about because I had to consider if I could afford to leave my steady income to accept part-time employment, versus being wiser to wait until I had my nursing certificate and then I could secure full-time employment.

Alofa reasoned it would be too much for me to do both jobs, coupled with the fact that we would never have any time to spend together. Part of me felt I would be disloyal and undeserving of my faithful and benevolent employer if I told him I was leaving him to wash patient's bottoms and make their beds. The job offered to me might have been employment in the medical profession, but it was hardly anything to celebrate. I still needed four higher levels of education to work with doctors in the big hospitals. Thus far I had achieved only one. That one piece of paper entitled me to work at nursing in retirement homes – not exactly where I wanted to be. Sure it was a first step, but I still had a long way to go.

If I wasn't working I would be with Alofa and his band. They regularly played at Samoan socials, weddings, twenty-first birthday celebrations and many other Samoan events. Life was good. Alofa treated me well and his entire family accepted me. I was happy – unfortunately my sister and my mother weren't. They couldn't just let me be.

Two months after I ran away they turned up at Paulo and Sea's house. They had no idea my new family didn't like how they treated me. Still, my mother wanted to give her side of the story, hoping it would turn these people against me and they would toss me out. My mother didn't want me back. She and my sister didn't want anyone to like me or, worst of all, to give me shelter. They would rather I was homeless and sleeping in cardboard boxes so people could point and laugh at me.

As my mother was politely speaking to Paulo and Sea, I could see Agnes hovering near the car like a predator waiting for mother's leftover kill. Her poor husband Tavita was like a puppet waiting in the driver's seat. After a long talkfest, Paulo thanked my mother for her kind advice to kick me out on the street as I would be a very bad example to their children; I was a liar and a slut. Equally polite, Paulo suggested it might be a good idea for my mother to leave and never bother them again! She was flummoxed and aghast. Mother was used to people falling at her feet, hanging on her every word, treating her with sympathy and showering her with affection. Not this time!

Agnes wasn't accepting defeat so easily. She came storming through the back door where I was standing, attempting to drag me outside, breaking Paulo's glass door in the process. Rushing to the sound of the commotion, Paulo viewed the vindictive destruction of his property with equal disgust and fury.

"Get out of here before I call the police," he bellowed. "And don't ever show your face near my property again!"

Sea was shocked and was unable to speak. Finally she muttered, "What kind of mother is that woman? A real mother does not go around broadcasting how bad her children are to strangers. A good mother defends her children, no matter what crime they did. Did you ever tell your father what is happening to you?"

"Yes, I wrote a few letters, but I never received a reply."

I was very grateful to Paulo and his wife for standing by me. I also felt protected by Alofa, as he vowed to hurt anyone who dared harm me again.

I was barely eighteen and Alofa twenty two when we officially became boyfriend and girlfriend. With his hectic schedule and my own commitments, it was challenging to snatch any quality time together, but he did give me stability - and more importantly, he didn't beat me up even when we had disagreements. Eventually I moved in with him at his parent's house. Downstairs was the boy's domain with four spartan, messy bedrooms and smelly linen. The living area, where they practiced, was full of band equipment. The parents and the sisters lived upstairs. It wasn't exactly a love nest but we were together.

Perhaps I should have been more accepting, especially after everything I'd been through. Yet despite everything, or maybe because of it, I had big dreams. Strangely, the more I thought of what my mother had reduced me to, as an unwanted daughter, the more I strove to prove my worth. I fantasised about her one day regretting treating me so cruelly. I dreamt of her begging me for mercy and forgiveness when she became old and helpless. I had to achieve and succeed no matter what I did; even when I failed, I had to keep trying.

After a year I became frustrated with my nursing, although I had passed two more certificates. I was becoming bored. My heart and mind ached for new challenges, ached to achieve, ached to create a niche for myself in this world that I could call my own.

Simply for a change of scene, I applied for an office job and, to my amazement, was hired. Despite zero clerical experience, the bosses liked my determined personality, my big smile to greet the walk-in customers and mostly my glowing reference from the shoe factory. I was jumping out of the boring and into outright drudgery. I was bored witless in my new job and now recklessly restless.

In 1979, without discussing it with Alofa, I replied to an ad I saw in the paper for qualified nurses in a hospital outside of New Zealand. Although Alofa loved me, his band and his family came first. Because I was made to grow up so fast, I became very independent as well. I told myself a long time ago there was no one else to rely on but myself. My determination to become somebody and show people I was worth loving made me restless. If New Zealand had been the land of milk and honey to Samoans, the streets in Australia were paved with gold to me. The nurse's job was in Sydney, Australia – a vast glittering capital across the waters and famous throughout the world. Although I didn't possess all the qualifications they were after, I took a little creative license with my application and was accepted. Alofa, thinking he might lose me forever, started discussing marriage and our future together. He even talked about quitting the music business to become a minister, and discussed the idea of us going to theological college together. We had never talked about that before.

"We can go to Malua Theological College in Samoa and then return to New Zealand to serve. It will be more money for us and our children after I graduate," he excitedly explained to me.

Although he thought his idea was a fantastic proposition, it didn't sound enticing to me. I imagined myself becoming fat by such an indulgent and indolent lifestyle. The thought of being unproductive and servile repulsed me. It may be a dream lifestyle for some, but I was driven and proactive, wanting to make money from the fruit of my own hard work and ideas to be successful. Besides, I used to sneer at anyone getting paid for serving God. I told Alofa in no uncertain terms how I felt and left it at that.

In our last few nights together on our bed, with his guitar in his hands and deep in thought, he wrote a song for me, "Lau teine Samoa" (My Samoan girl), declaring his true love for me. Alofa initially wrote the first two lyrics, "*Sau lau teine Samoa. O Jane Schwalger lo na igoa*" on the first two lines, but changed it for commercial reason. It became one of his biggest selling hits.

Sydney Australia was big and shiny, fast and frightening. It was daunting to be in an enormous new country not knowing a single soul. I didn't know if I could hold down my job – after all, I didn't have all the qualifications they'd demanded. Even without the precise pieces of paper required, I was put on a one-month trial. Determined, I told the matron I had travelled all the way to Australia with high hopes she would give me a chance because I was the best nurse there was and I would not disappoint her faith in me.

The money was excellent, the people were friendly and for the first time in my life I was completely free from my past. It felt exhilarating. No one knew me here. I could call myself Sally May

Righteous and none would know the difference. No one knew I'd been raped or came from a dysfunctional, abusive family. No one knew I'd lived on a haunted estate with a maniacal aunt whom I both admired and adored, even if she sometimes terrified me. No one knew any of those things. I felt free – free at last – except for one thing.

Alofa begged me to come back. His commitments to his band made it impossible for him to visit me as we initially planned. I was missing him too. Wisely or foolishly, rightly or wrongly, I placed love before a career. After three months, I returned to Auckland to be with him. By that time, Alofa's band had secured a recording contract. Sometimes we would be at the recording studio from 10pm to 6am trying to cut tracks. Once again we'd become inseparable. It was not surprising that a few short months after I returned his parents summoned us to talk about marriage.

"You're living together now, so why wait?" Alofa's mother reasoned.

I admit I'd been happy in a de facto relationship with Alofa. Alofa's father was one of the most important *matais* of his family and a very proud man. When I left Samoa, I vowed I was never going to be involved in the custom ever again. I grew up watching my grandparents sacrifice everything for it. I had frequently nearly starved because of it. My beloved Puka had been brutally murdered before my eyes because of it. I feared if I married Alofa, our children would not enjoy much of a future – we would forever be struggling.

Alofa adored his mother and feared his father. I knew he would do anything for them. On top of that, it weighed heavily on my mind that I didn't have any family to be part of my wedding. Alofa's parents would stop at nothing to hold a traditional grandiose wedding for their first-born son in the full Samoan custom. In that tradition, it was unthinkable for the girl's family not to come to the grand event. I asked for more time to think about our situation, reasoning we were still young.

Not too long after that discussion, I discovered I was pregnant!

If I wasn't ready to be married, I surely wasn't ready to have a baby. After long, agonising hours, days and weeks of soul searching, I made the excruciating decision to have an abortion. I was scared to discuss this with Alofa. He loved children. He wouldn't approve in anyway with my plan to get rid of his baby. So I also decided not to tell him about the pregnancy.

The procedure would cost $500. By the time I saved the money I was ten weeks along and suffering badly from morning sickness, which aroused suspicion. I maintained my ruse with a string of excuses. My appointment at the hospital was in the morning. I told Alofa it was just for a check-up, to look into why I'd been so ill every morning. I doubt he entirely believed me, but he grudgingly accepted my explanation. I arrived and started filling in forms, feeling desolate and alone. Glancing around at the other girls waiting, I saw some were with their mothers, others with their boyfriends. I was right back to where I was used to being – alone – alone but committed. There was not one doubt in my mind this was the right thing to do. Soon it was my turn.

A nurse prepped me and instructed me on the procedure. "Once we start, there will be no turning back. If you want to change your mind let us know now," she told me sympathetically.

I assured her my decision was final.

I was not going under general anaesthetic; I would be able to feel and see everything. Inside the room, there were two nurses. After I put my white gown on and lie on the bed, an examination was carried out before the nurse inserted a metal object into my vagina and began removing things from my body. Lying like a piece of dead white meat, I felt a suction sensation. It was a horrendous feeling but I dared not make a sound, not wanting to convey my humiliation or distract the nurse from what she was doing. There were feelings of guilt and disgrace, but these too I managed to push to one side. I felt as though my very soul had departed.

As the nurses continued to work on removing my baby from my womb, my mind drifted back to my mother. Did she ever think of getting rid of me while I was in her tummy? My soul re-entered my body when one of the nurses announced it was all done. Then I asked something I should never have asked, which snapped me back to reality of the situation with a vengeance.

"What sex was the baby?"

"It was a girl."

I tried to reach out to see it, but the nurse was already walking away carrying the dead foetus in a white bucket. I was paralysed with grief. A wave of shame and regret surged over me. As they cleaned me up, I sobbed pathetically, not caring who heard me. Knowing my wailing would have disturbed other mothers, I was hastily whisked into another room as I mourned the death of the baby girl I felt I had just murdered. I stared at the ceiling, realising the enormity of my actions. Admonishing myself, I wondered how I was any better than my mother. At least she gave me life, and with life there was a chance of a future. Every year I thought of my daughter with ache in my heart. For many years I prayed for forgiveness.

Chapter 25

Finding Myself

Alofa's band was becoming very successful. They had now been officially recognised as one of the best-known and most popular bands in the Polynesian community. They were planning a tour of Hawaii and Samoa. Thinking it made perfect sense under the circumstances, he encouraged me to apply for a job in the airlines. He reasoned we might more easily be able to travel together this way. It seemed like a reasonable idea. I sent in my application and carried on life as normal.

While waiting for a response from Polynesian Airlines, I saw an advertisement in the paper looking for someone who liked a challenge to help a small family operation that had just started up. Small was an understatement! When I went to the interview, I discovered this was a four-person operation. Father and son co-owned it, worked on machines and did the packing. The daughter was the office girl and her boyfriend was the salesman. The son's girlfriend also lent a hand when her children were at school. The production area was no bigger than a double garage. There was PVC material everywhere, a few second-hand machines and very little room to move around. As raw as it was, I saw a challenge and a chance to thrive. I wanted a job that was more hands on and productive. It was better than watching people suffering or waiting to die in hospitals and nursing homes. Sitting bored to death behind a desk filling forms day after day and answering the telephones was not the answer either. I was not made to do that sort of work.

At my new job, I was assigned to help make the products: wallets, shower curtains, basically anything that could be made out of PVC. The salesman travelled nationwide to find clients. I did not view this work as being a mere factory hand. Rather, I looked at the big picture, believing I was part of the team breathing life into this new venture. Together we might make it grow and thrive. I found that notion quite thrilling and my brain functioned well when I was being challenged.

The father had sold his executive home after his wife passed away to fund his son's dream. I was the only salaried staff – the rest of the family were helping out until it became a success. They had wanted a male employee, but I hit them with my charming smile and enthusiasm and was granted a month's trial. They made it clear that speed and quality were essential. This put me in my element. I worked well under the pressure and deadlines, so well in fact they soon gave me a permanent position and a raise. Frequently I would stay behind with the family, working to get an order out, not expecting any overtime pay.

Nine months after starting this position I received a reply from Polynesian Airlines. They requested I fly to Samoa for an interview. The Five Star Band had just returned from their Hawaiian tour and planned to leave for Samoa in a month's time. It was good timing. I could attend to my interview, wait until Alofa arrived with the band and then we could return to New Zealand together. The small family business gave me my second glowing reference and assured me they would welcome me back if things didn't work out. A few years later that little family start up became a very successful business, employing a lot of people, and the father became husband to one of my village cousins I had introduced him to. She lived a very good life when she married him.

It was my first trip back to Samoa since leaving. Dad was happy to accommodate me and pleased how things had been developing in my life. My interview also went well. I had good references from my last employers, three certificates of nursing, I spoke both English and Samoan well and I was outgoing and looked good for the job. My chances of securing the position were high.

By the time Alofa arrived, I had spiralled out of control. Finally free of any restrictions, I was clubbing and partying like a mad thing, something I had never done before. Returning to Samoa triumphant and transformed was a heady rush. I was also enjoying the company and attention of other men. In fact I was already embroiled in a steamy affair with a young, handsome, half-caste pilot named Norman. I discovered he was married when his wife and all her Samoan relatives threatened to beat me up in the nightclub's toilet. That was the end of Norman and me.

I did return to New Zealand, and Alofa and I agreed we would separate for a year to sort our own lives out. After that, if we found what we were looking for and it didn't involve the other, we would wish each other love and happiness and go on our way. If we still had feelings for each other then we would get married. Alofa was my first true love and we had been together for nearly two and a half years. With all the best will in the world, I would have made a lousy wife and mother at that point in my life. I was both selfish and selfless enough to know it. I recognised if I was forced into a situation where I once again felt trapped, I may have turned into something unthinkable – my mother.

After Alofa and I broke up, I became somehow different. My brief fling with Norman woke up something in me – I was entitled to be happy and no one was going to stop me. I was seduced by the chaos and the unpredictability of a wild life; I became hooked. I started dating businessmen, men with money, power and drive. It mattered little to me if they were married, had children or were in any kind of relationship. I was engaged in a hedonistic fantasy of pleasure and plenty, and I believed I loved every minute of it. I believed I deserved it! It was not uncommon for me to date two men in one week. Cheating on one when he was cheating another charged me with a sense of power, it made me feel alive. I felt so unworthy of my family's love, I tried to compensate with anyone who could possibly love and want me, even if I hurt others in the process.

I thought I was free and in control of my life. I could make whatever decision I wanted, be with whomever I wanted, live wherever I wanted. Obligations, commitments, attachments – those were all words of my past life. This shiny new life was ripe for exploring, and I'd only just begun – or so I thought. I could not have comprehended that what I was really doing was descending into a self-destructive life.

To an unknowing world I was a pretty girl, full of life, the world was her oyster. Inwardly I was scared beyond imagination. By the time the letter arrived from Polynesian Airlines congratulating me for winning the post, I'd already lost interest in it. I was tending to lose interest in all things and people very quickly these days. It was just an avoidance of commitment, dedication and discipline.

For reasons that completely escape any sense of rhyme or reason, mother and I were speaking again. Agnes and her husband had moved to Australia, and out of the blue my mother paid me a surprise visit. Shock and surprise, she had an ulterior motive. But then again, all my mother's motives were ulterior. She wanted my help. She acted like we were in a loving mother-and-daughter relationship. I became very cautious!

My sister Rowena had been taken by child services, and she once again played down the seriousness of the situation. She plastered all the blame on my twelve-year-old sister who was now in a foster home. The department was taking the matter to court. Mother was worried her husband might end up in jail. It would be unseemly. It would be costly. It would be downright embarrassing. This woman who (when it suited) called herself my mother wanted my help to get Rowena out. I reflected back to how my mother had always stood by her husband no matter how terribly wrong or bad he was. A surge of anger flooded my soul when I remembered how this man had treated me like a pathetic dog, often sending me in a smelly garage to sleep as his punishment to my mother. It would have been a great opportunity for revenge, as the department was also gathering more evidence and looking for witnesses to support the strength of their case. I giggled within myself at the thought of my stepfather been chained up and thrown in a cell.

I looked at my mother and saw her sad eyes, which clearly told me that her husband was everything to her. Nothing else mattered, not her children or even her own self. At that moment, I felt like swearing and cursing at her for daring to stand in front of me asking to save him. Inexplicably, the thought of her wanting and needing my help replaced my rage into excitement, like a game. Here was my chance to show her what a smart daughter I had turned out to be without her help. I wanted to prove to her what I was really made of and that she was so stupid to ever think I did not deserve her love. My sister's predicament was overtaken by my sick need for acceptance. I took the phone number and name of the caseworker, promised I would contact the lady and advise mother of the outcome.

I must have had a few wits still left about me, as before I made an appointment with the case worker, I did conduct a little due diligence, phoning around to gather information about my sister's case. I was told that her father had given her a severe beating. According to the lady I spoke with, "It was a cowardly and vicious case of child abuse."

The subsequent meeting was extremely intense. Conflicted and appalled, I could plainly see the lady from welfare was protecting my little sister's interests, while my mother was taking her husband's side. I never saw my sister's face, but according to the social worker the injuries were horrendous. It seemed I was listening to someone else speaking as I assured the social worker I would take control of the situation, inform my parents that this was not acceptable under any circumstances and guaranteed it would never happen again. I also pointed out that as this was a first offence they should allow Rowena to go back home to the people who really loved her, instead of living with strangers. I promised I would be the first one to call them if I saw any more violence in the home.

One lie after another tripped from my lips: our home was loving, peaceful and nothing like this ever happened before, perhaps the folks had been under tremendous stress at the time. We would stick together as a family and make this right. I had no idea I was such a convincing and accomplished liar. Rowena was allowed to go back home to her parents – no court case. My stepfather was again free to do whatever he wanted. Mother was ecstatic. I can never forgive myself for being a party to that.

"You should be a lawyer," mother cheered. "I saw how you fought with your mouth and you didn't stop."

The smirk of victory plastered on her face made me want to vomit. I felt I had been duped and used yet again. What the hell was wrong with me?

"Well I guess if you had allowed me to finish my education, perhaps I would have been a lawyer," I scowled at her. "Maybe if I was treated with loving care, I could have even been something more." I continued to snarl while fighting back all the horrible memories I had tried to erase. It was all I could do to restrain myself from spitting on her.

In spite of everything, I was still seeking what every child needs from every parent – love, approval and recognition. That was my Achilles heel; due to this primal urge, my mother was able to manipulate me with only a smile and pitiful eyes, her voice pathetically lowered as though she was begging in supplication. What a complete idiot I was!

Rowena was sent to Australia after that episode. Agnes and her husband were going to take care of her. To this day my heart aches when I recall my sister's fate. She is blind in one eye from being hit in the face by her father many years later. Rowena was a beautiful girl with big brown eyes and a fun loving spirit. Today she can't look at people or bear to have them look at her. That was the loving home she was released into. I hated myself.

Chapter 26

Settled Yet Unsettled

My next boyfriend was Anthony. For a nice change of pace, he was a single. I met him at one of the better-known nightclubs in Auckland during my twenty-first birthday celebrations, for which I was joined by my sister Ceal and her boyfriend. Twenty-one, being a milestone age, demanded a big celebration. The nightclub I'd chosen had phones on every table. The idea was if you liked the look of someone you just dialled that table number and the conversation could proceed without the other knowing who they were talking to. The caller could see and gauge the reaction of the called. It was a good system, loads of fun and a prime breeding ground for flirting. As was my way, I had not attended such an occasion unescorted. My male companion for the moment was a very sexy rugby player, someone I considered suitable to show off to family and friends.

A few tables away from ours I spotted a very tall, handsome, blond-haired man with rather pale skin talking to a male friend. He had a kindly, trusting face. As had become commonplace in my two-timing, devil-may-care outlook on life, I made a call while my boyfriend was away buying drinks. I only did it as a tease; well, I think it was only meant to be a tease. I was so mixed up that I'm not sure. The reason is immaterial. The fact is, that call ended my liaison with mister rugby guy and began my relationship with Anthony.

Anthony was English. He had been living in New Zealand just over a year when I met him. His German mother and English father met after the Second World War in Germany. His father had been a soldier fighting for the Allies. From my perspective, they were an excruciatingly normal family. For our first date, he wanted to take me to the movies. There was nothing original or exciting about that – it was oh-so-normal, a definite change of pace for me.

To my embarrassment, he collected me in a crappy old Volkswagon. It had trouble starting and spewed out clouds of smoke. After gliding around in Mercedes and Jaguars, what was I doing in an unroadworthy wreck? I was attracted to men prepared to jump out aeroplanes for me without parachutes, after lavishing me with expensive gifts of course. Perhaps I was intrigued by this simple English man. Deep down he reminded me of what a person's true self should be. Anthony was a passive, gentle, genuine guy and I could be myself around him. If I was going to be honest with myself, my deepest need, buried in the subterranean caverns of my psyche, was to be kept safe and secure.

Despite his lack of financial wealth and our different attitudes to life, our relationship blossomed. I discovered he was very articulate, an intellectual who loved reading and art. Within six months, we had moved in together. I must have been smitten; our love nest was a flea-infested, one-bedroom apartment. In no time at all I discovered I was pregnant.

Neither of us expected to have a baby so soon, but there was no way I was going to abort another child. The stunned look on Anthony's face as I told him the happy news left no doubt he was not ready to be a father.

"You don't have to stay. I can take care of the baby by myself," I told him.

Anthony felt he was not financially secure enough to take this all on, but he wasn't going to leave me and assured me we were in this together. We decided to move into more suitable accommodation and then excitedly awaited the birth of our child.

In the first few weeks of my pregnancy I felt something was terribly wrong. I was confused, unable to settle my swirling thoughts. I was riddled with anxiety and consumed by guilt about bringing a new life into the world. I didn't believe I deserved to be given another child; I feared I would not be a good mother. On top of all this doubt, I suffered severely with morning sickness, so badly I was in hospital more frequently than I was at home. I could keep no food down for days at a time. Strong smells, loud noises or bright lights would send me into spasms of retching. My only relief was huddling into a ball with a sheet over me to block out light while I puked out yellow bile. With deep concern, Anthony attended to me, taking me to hospital whenever necessary. There I would be put on a drip to rehydrate and nourish my child and me until I was able to hold down solid food again. The doctors and nurses told me it was normal for new mothers to go through this, some worse than others. Instinctively I knew there was something more going on.

With the support and the constant care I received from Anthony, I gave birth to my beautiful baby girl. We named her Zelma. I was twenty-two years old and Anthony was twenty-seven. It was the happiest day of my life and I vowed to strive to live it well. Anthony had a good job at a printing firm as a graphic artist. He was a good provider and we gradually turned our little nest into our own little world. Whenever we were short of money, Anthony's mother sent cash from England to help us out. None of my family would have been so giving.

I should have been settled and happy. A few weeks after we took our daughter home my issues reappeared, this time with far greater intensity. I was convinced I had gone completely mad; I have no words to describe how awful it was. I felt the world would be better off without me, Anthony was too good for me, and my baby better cared for by another mother. Every second of living now felt so dreadful that the only solution was to die! I went into the bathroom, shut the door, and swallowed a bottle of toilet cleaner. It was all I could find. I am sure if I had a loaded gun I would have blown my head off.

The bleach burnt my throat and stomach badly. I gagged and retched some out. Sanity briefly returned with the shock and I realised what I had done. It took all my will to struggle to the house next door, hoping the neighbour could help me. I had wanted to instantly end my painful life, not suffer the physical aftermath of my actions.

An ambulance was called. I was taken to hospital and my baby was cared for by the kind lady next door while she waited for Anthony to return home. After my stomach was pumped by the nurses, I was sent home many hours later. I didn't want to be released. I was scared; I had lost the part of me that was me and I knew it was only a matter of time before I succeeded in ending my life.

I was terrified of hurting my daughter like my mother did to me. That, and other dark thoughts to end my life, became uncontrollable. I imagined death would have been the kindest thing – for me and for everyone around me. Hell would have been a better place to be. The one small mercy was that my daughter was never in danger of me harming her. Perhaps she saved me many times. My love for her was so potent, so powerful that I was able to fight through the pervading darkness. It was a tremendous struggle, exhausting trying to live another day for my daughter. I wanted to live for her, but I wanted to die for me.

It was during that darkest time of my life that good old mum turned up to inform me that Pao had passed away from a heart attack. She wanted to know if I would give money to help with the funeral. She was flying out to Samoa with Rosa in a few days. I remember telling her that I had been very unwell. Her reaction? Nothing! She was more concerned about her trip.

Although I cried over Pao's sudden death and remembered his kindness, I also cried about my uncaring mother. I was still craving her acceptance and, unbelievably, her love.

I tried to end my suffering with an overdose of Paracetamol after that. It was my fourth attempt. At that point, the hospital staff deduced I needed help. I was committed to the psychiatric ward.

Chapter 27

Mental Breakdown

I was placed in ward ten in the care of a psychiatrist team in Auckland Hospital. I had been diagnosed with severe postnatal depression, a common illness many women suffer after childbirth. In my case, it was a combination of my traumatic prior life blended in with postnatal depression. That made it more extreme and dangerous for both Zelma and I.

It took a while for me to realise I was in a ward for the mentally ill. Initially I presumed it was to have a nice rest and be pampered. It soon became clear most of the patients there had attempted to end their lives. My room was next to an anorexic young girl who was nothing more than skin stretched taut over bones. Next to her was another young lady. She was very pretty with frizzy long blonde hair and wore heavy makeup. She looked like a Barbie doll, but I called her Miss Pretty.

In the large communal area there was a pool table in one corner and nice comfortable chairs randomly scattered around. There was a TV area I never entered and three group session rooms. We could move around freely and were encouraged to socialise. All the interview rooms had large two-way mirrors so we could be observed when interviewed. Depending on our needs, we had group or one-on-one therapy sessions.

When first admitted, I was given medication that rendered me docile. I did not explore or have much interest in what was occurring around the ward. There were large windows that afforded views of the outside world, but I never went near them for fear of being recognised by someone on the outside. Mostly I just hid in my tiny room.

After breakfast, the patients would gather in the therapy room and our doctor encouraged us to talk openly about our problems. With tissue boxes ready in the centre, six or more of us would sit in a circle and share how we were feeling. For first three days I slept – I felt like I wanted to sleep forever. The meds no doubt calmed my tortured mind, allowing me to get some much-needed rest. They also helped put a lid on my waking terrors so I could begin the slow process of recovery. My therapist insisted I start with group sessions, reasoning it was crucial for my healing and the path home to my baby. Anthony was granted a week off work. The poor man was having a hard time dealing with a seven-month-old infant. When I wasn't drugged witless I was missing my baby terribly, praying desperately I would be healed so I could go home to her.

During my first group session I sat next to Miss Pretty. As a newcomer to the group, I was asked to introduce myself before explaining what I could about my problems. Faced with this task, I froze. I wasn't ready to tell complete strangers how fucked my head was. My therapist smiled at me, encouraging me to try. All eyes were on me as though pleased another crazy had not succeeded in killing herself.

"Would you like me to come back to you later, Jane?" the psychologist asked.

"Yes, please," I told her, a flood of relief tingling through me.

The session started with the doctor saying her piece; then, one by one, we would tell our stories and explain how we were feeling. The sessions always began with a man named Leon. He was twenty-five years old. He sat next to the doctor and insisted on speaking first. Leon was tall and slim built, the evidence of self-inflicted injuries easily visible all over his arms and face. He would begin by happily talking about his dog Muffy, before rolling on the floor in a foetal position and descending into a morose recollection of what happened to his pet when he was a young boy. Leon was very badly damaged. His face would change to a grimace. He would cringe and moan as if someone was torturing him. I was to learn he had been at the hospital for over three months, and although one-on-one therapy may have suited him better, he didn't feel safe unless there were others in the room. His father had sexually abused him from the age of seven until his early teens. His loyal dog was killed in front of him when the hound tried to attack his father as he sexually abused his son. His mother knew about the abuse but was too scared to take any action to help her boy. She committed suicide when Leon was sixteen. That was when Leon escaped and lived on the street, ending up a drug addict and a male prostitute to support his habit.

Leon's tale resonated so deeply with me it was frightening. The pain Leon experienced in witnessing the murder of his faithful friend seemed even more profound than I'd suffered when Puka was slaughtered. His story was the first time I had heard anything about this sort of abuse, men having sex with little boys. I'd thought my abuse was bad, but Leon's horrid life showed me there was yet worse than I'd ever imagined. Leon and I became friends through our shared pain. Other patients were scared of him and kept their distance, but even with my own suffering and turmoil, my heart bled for Leon and I embraced him as my dearest friend.

Another character who was hard to ignore was Miss Pretty. When it was her turn, she just burst out sobbing, wiping her tears on the hem of her expensive dress. With a sigh, the doctor stood up and gave her the box of tissues. I couldn't understand what she was so upset about to the point she didn't want to live. She kept saying that the pain was so unbearable she would rather die. When it was my turn to speak, I was already exhausted by the Barbie doll's routine.

"My name is Jane. I arrived three days ago. Thank you," I began nervously.

Everyone looked to me wanting to hear more, but I was fragile and emotionally bereft. I needed to be alone. The pills continued to make me feel sleepy, and my disorder stuck me mute. Nothing further would be confessed by me in public that day. As soon as the session ended, I rushed to my room and slept.

Later that day I was summoned by my appointed psychiatrist. She informed me that my medication went hand in hand with psychological therapy. Both were required for my recovery and I needed to participate if I wanted to go home. She went on to explain that because of my problems my baby was not safe to be around me until I was deemed "cured." I wanted more than anything to be healed, but I was still confused about the group session. To my mind, it was just a bunch of sad nutters regurgitating their pathetic stories. It was laughable in my view.

Desperate to be out, I attended a second time. The usual suspects were there with the same old stories, and Miss Pretty was still balling her eyes out. One man whispered, "Here she goes again." I was glad not to be sitting next to her.

When it was my turn, I was still incapable of explaining how I was really feeling. All I wanted to do was rush back to my room or throttle the blonde beauty. I was, however, fascinated with the anorexic girl. She had locked herself in her room and refused to talk to anyone. Doctors were constantly filing in and out of her quarters for one-on-one therapy as she rebuffed all options to comply any other way. She claimed she was seeing ghosts in the ward and some dead relatives were visiting her at night. I was probably the only person there who believed her, but I said nothing.

I was dreading the third session. I knew everyone was tired of my silence. I truly did not want to listen to other people's problems; I had plenty of my own and needed a quick fix, not waffle. Before I entered the session room that morning I was already anxious and prepared to request one-on-one counselling with the doctor. My first priority was to make sure I was sitting far away from Crying Barbie. The group started differently that day. Each person was to speak about someone in their lives who had inspired them. That little exercise had most of the patients in tears. When it was Barbie's turn, she tried her best to speak without blubbing. She told us all that her mother was her best friend and her dad died a few years ago. She added she was an only child and fortunate to have been brought up by loving parents. They were her inspiration. Then she started crying again. She could not make sense of why her fiancé would leave her for an older woman. She wailed that women like this cradle snatcher (according to her) should suffer for the torture they inflicted on others.

Finally, we all heard the reason for her pathetic upset. Her fiancé dumped her and she wanted him back. That was it! That was her entire problem. She had a privileged, loving upbringing and she was dumped by a man who ran off with someone else – like that had never happened to anyone before! My blood was boiling! Rage overtook me. For a generally sympathetic person I was shocked at my reaction. I stood up while this poor girl was still weeping over her broken heart and ripped into her.

"How dare you? For the last few days I sat here putting up with your sobbing, and it was all over a guy? Have you been abandoned and neglected by your mother? Have you been repeatedly raped by a family member who was supposed to protect you? Have you been beaten by your family for nothing? Have you been pushed unloved and discarded from pillar to post? Have you been homeless and slept at bus stations? Have you ever experienced what real fear and suffering was like? You are young, beautiful and have a nice family with parents who loved you, and you are crying over a fucking man? Do you know what your problem is? You're spoiled! You're not used to people saying no to you."

Her mouth fell open. Hers wasn't the only one!

After my tirade, I was spent and needed to get out of there to calm down. "Sorry Doc, I have to go," I excused myself.

As I left the session, one of the psychologists behind the double-sided mirror ushered me to another room. My outburst was the catalyst for them to get things rolling. They had gathered what they needed from my emotional diatribe and now the healing could begin. From that day I was put in a different program. I had taken the first step on a thousand-mile journey to recovery. I never saw the Barbie doll again. I was told she checked out the very next day. An older woman from the group session joked I may have actually cured her with shock therapy and congratulated me for speaking my mind. Apparently, everyone was getting annoyed around Miss Pretty. I hope that I did help her. In a strange way she helped me too. Without her, I don't know when or if I would have broken down my wall.

It was agreed I would be released after three weeks and referred to a local psychologist to continue my treatment. Although my doctor thought it was a good idea to continue my medication to help put a lid on things, I wanted to have a clear head and the energy to take care of my daughter. Moreover, I was scared of the consequences of becoming addicted to pills again. Armed with a better understanding of my condition, the doctors provided strategies for me to battle the power of my dark side. I came to understand the elusive light at the end of the tunnel wasn't a myth – the tunnel was.

When it was finally time for me to return home, I said goodbye to Leon and gave him a drawing of himself that Anthony had sketched during a visit. I told him whenever he felt angry, sad or scared he should look at his picture and see what a handsome and good man he was. Six months after my discharge I called the ward to see how Leon was doing. I was going to ask for his contact details so I could invite him around for a meal. He was dead. Finally he had succeeded in ending his massive pain. Although I wept for my friend, I was determined that was never going to be me.

Chapter 28

The Possession

Whilst therapy had helped me enormously, I was struggling when I first returned home. Leon's death set me off again, hating the world I was in. I continued to visit my therapist and was prone to irrational anger outbursts, mostly for no good reason. They overwhelmed me when I felt betrayed, unloved, unwanted and used. Poor Anthony was usually the brunt of my savage tongue and my misdirected anger. The poor man lived in terror of what mood I was going to be in when he came home from work. Although he stood by me, he was drifting away. In hindsight, I think if not for Zelma, Anthony would have left me right there and then – and I wouldn't have blamed him. He didn't sign up for this.

I had way too much empty time for my mind to become tangled in. Money was tight. To solve both issues, I decided to return to the workforce. During this period of my life, Agnes, her husband and their two little girls moved back to New Zealand. To keep the peace, everyone pretended nothing had happened between us. Inwardly, I would never forget that in my darkest times none of my family even visited me.

By 1984 Anthony and I saved enough money for a deposit and purchased our first home. It was a 1950s house with high ceilings, bay windows and huge rooms. It was a lovely property bursting with character, and the thought of decorating it excited me. Thoughts of long-ago ghosts were the farthest thing from my mind; those thoughts came hurtling back when I heard people speaking in different languages around the fireplace. I would wake Anthony in the middle of the night asking if he could hear what I was listening to.

"No. Now go back to sleep," he snapped angrily at me for waking him.

The nocturnal supernatural visitations began again. After two months of life in our new ghost-infested home I found I was pregnant with our second child. Anthony managed to convince me that what I was hearing was merely a result of my hormones running rampage. I had to concede that my whole system went into meltdown whenever I was pregnant. Morning sickness kicked in – this time worse than my pregnancy with Zelma. It suited me to accept Anthony's rational, scientific explanation, but try as I might, it just didn't ring true. Not only was I hearing disturbing noises at night, during the day I saw unearthly visages around my home. Some were identical to those seen at Auntie Tilie's estate and some were different. None of these apparitions looked at me but they were clearly present.

On one occasion as I came from the kitchen a woman walked past me then disappeared. I did not see her face. My constant morning sickness left me so weak I had no strength left to try and make sense of it. Having experienced it all before, I just decided to let it be. At night I was exhausted beyond reason and desperately needed sound sleep; the voices persistently denied me any respite. In desperation, I frequently disturbed Anthony from his slumber and repeatedly he told me I was imagining things.

Anthony was an intellectual atheist. If he couldn't see it, it didn't exist. He did not believe in God, demons, ghosts or the afterlife. Frustrated by these disturbances, he would rush into our living room, turn the lights on and wave his arms around dramatically to challenge any spirits to show themselves. No spirits appeared to face Anthony. I learned to keep what I saw and heard to myself. Having a baby to care for, apparitions to contend with, severe morning sickness to manage and finances that were stretched to the limit, without consulting the father of the child, I considered it would be best for all concerned if I aborted the new pregnancy.

My doctor sat considering my request for a time before announcing he'd conduct a scan before making a decision. As I'd aborted my first pregnancy, special precautions were needed if I went through with the procedure again. Wiping the ultra sound paddle over my belly again and again, he listened through his stethoscope with a puzzled look on his face.

"You are over three month's pregnant, almost four," he said with surprise. "This baby is too big to abort."

I complained, "I thought you said I was only two months."

"Perhaps I miscalculated. Early on in pregnancy it can be hard to nail down."

I left his office feeling both relieved and depleted. Two weeks later I was admitted to hospital again for dehydration from the morning sickness. My room in the maternity ward was opposite the nurse's office and had four empty beds at the time of my admission.

The first night I slept well, nourished by the drip in my arm and comforted by professionals caring for me. When I awoke the following morning I was surprised to see a Samoan woman in her late sixties enter the room carrying flowers. These weren't the kind of flowers she would have purchased from the store, but rather they appeared to have been picked from a back garden. She looked around as though confused, studied me for a moment and asked if I was the only one in this room.

"Yes. Why?" I answered.

"I'm here to visit a patient that came in yesterday. This is her room," she insisted.

"Maybe she's gone home already," I offered nonchalantly. "Why don't you ask at the nurse's station next door?"

She left and a few seconds later returned, handing me her flowers. "She's probably gone home, as you said. Since you don't have any flowers, you can have these. By the way, where is your baby?"

It didn't even occur to me to ask, "What baby?" Did she know I was pregnant? Did she mean Zelma? I simply answered like an automaton, "I still have five months to go. I'm here because I suffer badly from morning sickness and can't eat."

"You should go home to Samoa," she told me firmly. "There you will get the right help."

I turned to look at the flowers she'd arranged in a vase before turning back to the old lady to ask her which village she came from. She was already gone, no sign of her anywhere. I buzzed the nurse.

"Yes?" she blustered, agitated at the interruption. "What is it?"

"Did you see a Samoan lady just leave this room?"

"No. What did she look like?"

"An old lady, she came to visit a relative that was supposed to be in this room. Didn't she come to your office to enquire?"

"No, no one's been here and I've been at the front desk the whole time."

The entire situation was odd, but I was more than accustomed to odd. Trying to exercise some of Anthony's rational, scientific thinking, I told myself she must have had the wrong room and out of the kindness of her heart she just gave me the flowers. Maybe she was in a hurry. The flowers were real enough!

Her suggestion of going to Samoa played on my mind. It made sense. Over there plenty of people could care for my daughter and me. My dad lived in Apia, closer to Motootua Hospital and he had cars. We could stay until I was due to have the baby. Anthony would be free to work instead of having to take so many days off to look after his ailing and troubled wife, and he wouldn't have to face sleepless nights. It was an excellent idea. I called Anthony to pick me up and take me to the travel agent. Even though a bit rushed, Anthony agreed the plan made good sense and wasted no time agreeing to my request. Zelma and I were on a flight at 7pm that evening.

The whole flight over and the taxi ride from the airport to my Auntie Sia's home was a complete blur. It was as though I was in the driving seat but someone else was pushing peddles and turning the wheel for me. I had planned to go to my dad's, yet I was inexplicably compelled to return to my village family.

"*Talofa* (good day), I'm here," I awoke the family, yelling cheerily from the taxi at two in the morning.

Auntie Sia didn't like the look of me. She told me later it was as though I was unaware I was travelling with my child. My grandfather Tama was frail with age but still looked fit and healthy. He was delighted to see me. He, Sia, her husband and other members of the family all stayed awake and sat in vigil around me until morning. Unknown to me, I briefly stirred with the morning light, mentioned I was pregnant and crashed out again as garbled nonsense spewed from my mouth. I was told I demanded to be fed a freshly caught fish, specifically cooked on charcoal. Obediently, Auntie Sia ordered the boys to cook a fish for me and she rushed off to get the healer. She also sent for Auntie Vaitogi and other women of the family to help out. Auntie Sia was terrified, convinced I was possessed. By the time she returned with the *taulasea*, people were already clustered outside her home.

Ruta, the healer, invited me to come close to her so she could pamper me. It was normal practise for the *taulasea* to hide from possessing spirits the real reason for their attendance.

"Come here so I can massage your tummy," Ruta politely urged. "So, how far along are you?"

"Over three months."

Ruta felt my stomach then informed me I was only ten weeks along. She then moved towards my head and nestled it on her folded legs. "I'm going to put some drops into your nose to help with the morning sickness," she announced as though she was speaking for someone other than me to hear.

This was her trick to get the real work of exorcism moving. That was the last thing I knew until I woke up an hour later in Kaisala's house (Pao's widow). Inside was Ruta, Auntie Sia, Auntie Vaitogi and Pao's sister Aloema. The rest of the neighbourhood was watching from outside. I didn't remember anything that had happened thirty minutes before that time.

"Where's Zelma?" I asked urgently.

Ruta smiled. This was the first time I'd shown any awareness of my daughter since I'd arrived. According to Ruta, I had been possessed in New Zealand by five spirits. They had apparently banded together to protect me from evil spirits that had been lurking to attack me from Ottilie's farm. She explained my family spirits had come to bring me back to Samoa where I could get help; they did not want me to lose my baby. The driving spirit was Tina. Ruta told me my grandmother had followed me to New Zealand and had been with me ever since as my guardian angel. This wily old healer went on to explain that Tina's voice had spoken to her, using me as a conduit. I was a vessel whose vocal chords and lips were utilised, even though it was Tina's voice speaking. She told the healer about me sleeping at the bus terminal, how she had visited me in the mental ward and that it was Tina who appeared as the old Samoan woman with flowers to tell me to go home to Samoa for treatment.

I suppose I could have burbled all those details in drug-induced sleep or under some form of hypnosis, but to my knowledge no one in the village was aware of any of these incidents. The other four spirits, so Ruta said, were Pao and other family members. The entire clan who had born witness to Ruta's healing assured me those different voices had ushered from me when unconscious. My Auntie Sia still speaks about this event as one of the most terrifying things she ever witnessed. According to her account, I wasn't only speaking with a voice other than my own, but my face was distorting and using mannerisms as though other faces were emerging from within.

I was still weak and confused but deeply grateful; I did feel remarkably improved in every sense. Even the morning sickness had vanished. I was craving mountains of food like any normal pregnant woman would do. I could now smell my food, the breeze and people without feeling sick. Ruta assured me that I would never suffer like that again.

"Your grandmother will continue to watch over you from a distance. She can't leave you," Ruta explained. "But the others are now where they are supposed to be. You will not hear from any of them again."

I smiled, my head flopping back in relief.

"There's one more thing," she added solemnly. "Your grandmother ordered you must return to your home quickly."

"But I must see Auntie Tilie . . . and my father."

"No child, you must not!" Ruta announced firmly. "Ottilie's place is not safe for you. It is full of vengeful, tormented spirits. The very blood that flows in your veins makes you a target."

I didn't need convincing of that point! Tama also strongly added his voice of objection to the suggestion that I visit my auntie. With no car and no phone in the village, it seemed my most prudent course of action was to take the healer's advice – for my baby's sake.

While I was alone with my cousin Kaki, he told me in greater detail what had happened when I was possessed. My grandfather apparently told these tormented spirits to leave me alone.

"You should come after me. My granddaughter had nothing to do with any of the things you suffered," Tama addressed them as if he could clearly see them.

Saying my goodbyes to the family, I told Tama I would send for him after the birth of my baby. He asked me to send him a white suit instead. I didn't get what he meant until a few months later.

My daughter and I were on the plane to go back home a few days after my exorcism. Anthony had to concede I looked much healthier, rationalising it all as some kind of placebo effect. I set up a consultation with my doctor straight away who re-examined me. Ruta was right; I was just over two months pregnant. My doctor was puzzled. Clearly, this child did not want to be aborted.

Chapter 29

Another Blow

From the day Ruta worked on me, I never heard disturbing noises or saw apparitions again. My horrible morning sickness did not return either. My psychological problems were still an issue, but I was getting better. I was glad to be referred to see a psychiatrist who also believed in God. I needed to make sense of why things happened the way it did.

"I believe you! Even Jesus himself exorcised spirits from people," she exclaimed.

My pregnancy seemed normal; I was now fit and healthy and ate well. I did not smoke, drink alcohol or take drugs of any kind, aside from those given in ward ten.

Two months before I was due to give birth, my beloved Tama passed. Granted he was old and he'd believed his time was up long before this moment, but having just seen him in Samoa he'd seemed quite healthy. More than healthy, he had been the driving force in assisting Ruta to negotiate with the spirits to leave me in peace. I was informed that as soon as I left Samoa, Tama started exhibiting very unusual behaviour and was calling out names nobody had heard before. When I received the call to tell me he'd passed, I sat on my kitchen floor and wept like a baby. Did my grandfather really make the ultimate sacrifice for me – the payment for my release did not end there.

My water broke at 7am on 17 May 1986. I was taken to the hospital with contractions coming every five minutes. By 2pm I was in the delivery room. At 8pm I was still trying to push my baby out. I wasn't the first person in history to endure a long and painful labour, but I had reached the end of my strength.

"The baby is stuck in the birth canal," I heard the doctor tell Anthony. "We will have to use forceps. The mother is losing a lot of blood."

Anthony gave his consent for the forceps procedure. Slipping in and out of consciousness, I could feel abrading as sharp metal instruments were forced into me. Local anaesthetic was administered; I was still fully aware of everything going on. Eventually my baby was wrenched from my womb and nurses started to work on him. After a brisk massage, my son screamed his lungs out to the world. I cried. Anthony cried. The baby cried. A new soul had started its journey on this earth. We called our son 'Daniel'.

I required a five-bag blood transfusion before I was stable enough to meet my son and have him placed to my breast. It was then I saw the marks on his face. The left side of his skull was badly bruised, as though he had been in a fight.

"What happened to my baby?" I gasped.

"Oh, don't worry. That's normal for a forceps delivery," the doctor told me calmly. Maybe it was. What did I know?

We were taken to our room; my baby was placed in the fibreglass bassinet close to my bed and we both fell into an exhausted sleep. The next morning Anthony and Zelma visited. As far as I knew everything was normal, so I perfectly normally asked my perfectly normal partner to keep an eye on our perfectly normal son while I went to have a shower – normally. While I was refreshing in the shower, my son was rushed to the intensive care unit. He had stopped breathing while his father held him. Anthony had noticed he was very still for a long time and was beginning to turn a bluish purple. The nurse was called and she resuscitated him, but he stopped breathing again almost immediately.

The intensive care staff was puzzled by his respiratory failure. They placed him in an incubator with wires and tubes connected to his tiny purple body. Every time he stopped breathing, the machine would beep and the nurse would oxygenate him.

After five days visiting my son in the ICU, I was told to go home without him. Daniel's MRI scan results had come back. There were concerns and we were advised to leave him in intensive care a while longer. Concerns! The left side of his brain was haemorrhaging! Daniel remained in hospital for two months until the doctors were satisfied the bleeding had subsided. From that time on Daniel was a sickly baby. His colour was always purplish and he was missing all his milestones. Granted, Zelma was very advanced in reaching the milestones of first smile, first word and first step, but Daniel wasn't even close to catching up. I raised the subject with Anthony.

"He's just a bit slow," my partner assured me. "I read somewhere that boys are slower developers than girls."

Had the situation been less serious I might have made a sexist joke about his observation. If my partner saw no cause for alarm, I pushed my concerns away. His mother offered to pay our fares and expenses to visit England for Christmas. Needing a break, we gratefully accepted. Anthony's mother had been a nurse, which gave me a comfort concerning Daniel's care – at first. She didn't need to spend much time with Daniel before reinforcing my suspicions that there was something seriously wrong with my son. His head was floppy and his discolouration was not right. I promised her I would have him further examined the moment we returned to New Zealand.

We were hardly back on Kiwi soil when the third piece of bad news since my exorcism was delivered. Auntie Tilie had died; she suffered greatly before the end. My dad and some other family members eventually succeeded in taking her to hospital, but it was far from easy to get her out of her house. They had been shocked to find that although she could barely walk, she was discovered upstairs in the room where Alan's corpse was kept. She smelt like rotting meat and was hallucinating, babbling weird, utter nonsense. Mase and one of the family members raced for a priest to assist in moving Auntie Tilie's body out of the house. No matter how hard four strong men tried, they could not lift her from the bed. Whatever was stopping her from leaving wanted her to die horribly there. According to my dad, my two brothers and other family members who were present, an overpowering sense of evil filled the place. Dad told me later that the time he spent in Auntie's home that day strengthened his faith more than any of his time in the church. For the first time he believed he had actually witnessed the power of God against evil.

Initially, when the men had attempted to lift just one of Auntie's arms to clean her, it was like lifting a lead block. After many hours of prayer and consecration, the men stood as one and commanded these other worldly things to allow them to take Auntie to the hospital. Eventually they prevailed. Once free of the undead malevolence, two people could easily lift Auntie from her bed. I wept sincere tears of grief for my Auntie Tilie, but underneath my grief lay a comforting layer of relief and happiness. At last her trials were over and she was at peace. Guilt washed over me for not keeping in contact with my Auntie as I had promised. Since I had arrived in New Zealand, I had been trying to stay alive and had little time to think about anybody else.

By the time Daniel turned one he was still not crawling or making sounds apart from a feeble cry. That tiny little cry was the only sign we had a baby in our house. To accommodate our expanding family, we sold the house we were living in and purchased a more modern three-bedroom home in a better area. Anthony and I were struggling in both our relationship and our finances, but we shared a common desire for our children to grow up in a safe neighbourhood. I worked nights in a fancy restaurant as a hostess to help pay the bills, and with Anthony working days it didn't give us much of an opportunity to connect as a couple. There was, however, one thing we agreed on. Anthony had to concede both his mother's and my concerns might be warranted after all. Daniel was doing little apart from lying motionless on the floor. It was time to pluck up the courage to take him to a paediatrician.

After a very short assessment, the doctor referred Daniel to a place called Wilson Home for a more comprehensive examination. He would have to stay there for five days. I could not ask for a better place to leave our son, as this place boasted a reputation of competence and professionalism. I visited every day, and on the fifth day Anthony and I were summoned to hear their findings. A neurologist, an occupational therapist, a speech therapist and a few other specialists had taken part in the process. I think my heart stopped beating as I waited with trepidation to hear the findings.

As the results were read out, the words "brain damage" and "profoundly disabled" floated in the air as though being spoken in another realm of reality. Any remnant of hope in my soul was pummelled into despair. While the neurologist explained about Daniel's disability, I was already paralysed inside. My lungs became so heavy I could hardly breathe. I had to be excused and left the room. It felt like someone just stabbed my heart and was slowly twisting the knife. A lady came outside to console me, but I'd already dissolved into a soggy pile of tears.

"What am I going to do with a son who might never walk or talk?" I wept inconsolably. "He is going to be depending on me for the rest of his life. I don't think I can do this. I am barely able to cope with my own issues."

"Calm down and listen," the lady said soothingly. "You don't have to make a decision right now. You can leave him here while you consider your options. There are places where Daniel will be well taken care of. Come back inside and perhaps we can discuss what is best for him."

I was a complete mess, feeling even my own child hated me so much that he decided to be born disabled to punish me. I was crippled by a huge burden of guilt and self-loathing. Anthony wasn't processing the news much better. We decided to see our son to say goodbye, both feeling confused, heartbroken and incapable of discussing the matter with each other. We walked into a big room with a few cots, a little kitchen and a play area full of colourful toys. It had been my son's home for nearly a week. Daniel was lying in his cot on his tummy. When he heard my voice, his head flopped back and forth like a turtle as he tried desperately to turn to see me. What happened next energised me in a way I thought impossible. He gave me the most angelic smile, as if he was trying to tell me, "Everything is going to be okay, mummy." Tears streamed down my face as I rushed over to pick up my boy and hug him against my chest, flooding him with all the love in my heart. His smile was haunting and spiritual. His eyes were warm and inviting. As his smile brought tears to my eyes it brought warmth to my soul.

With absolute clarity I knew I was not going to abandon my son. I whispered to him, "I will love and take care of you for the rest of my life."

Turning to the duty nurse, I asked, "Can you please get my son's things? We are taking him home."

I was a twenty-five year old mother with psychological problems and two young children, one with profound disabilities. My faith in God was unrelentingly tested. When I was in horrible situations, when I was beaten or raped, when life was not treating me kindly, I never once asked God, "Why me?" Maybe I had been angry with him in the deeper recesses of my mind, just fleetingly, but it had never occurred to me before to think I was being punished by God. For what? What had I done wrong? But that day I questioned if God did exist. How could he let me suffer again and again? What had little Daniel ever done to deserve this? I resolved to believe that He hated me.

I thought how unfair it was that all my siblings and others I knew had easy lives. Some of them did not even like their children, yet none of them had a child with a disability – not that I would wish such a crushing thing on anyone. If my son was supposed to die, why did God not take him? Were we wrong to revive him? At least Daniel would have been back in heaven with him. Having a disabled child puts a strain on the healthiest of relationships – and my relationship with Anthony was far from that. My world was crumbling around me. I'd been betrayed by so many people, but now I was facing the biggest betrayal of all. I felt utterly betrayed by God.

I had to seek comfort and help from my Christian psychiatrist. Through my therapy treatment, she shared something with me that gave me hope and a new perspective – every time I looked at Daniel, I thanked him for being his mother.

"Look back at the trail of your life and remember who you have helped and showed true human compassion to. It is not a test or a curse. It is your calling and your purpose which you will be well blessed for both here and in the afterlife. Out of all your extended family members, you were chosen by God to take care of one of his very special angels, because he knew you were strong and could do it. Think about it, why a loving and a very smart God would punish you, while all you did throughout your whole life was selflessly helping others. You should be glad and thank him because he put his trust in you. Not many people would be given that opportunity," she enthusiastically stated.

Chapter 30

Raising My Disabled Son

I would be lying if I said I didn't spent many days and nights feeling wronged, but eventually I shook myself out of self-pity and resigned to move forward with fighting determination. Without a clue how I was going to achieve it, I decided I could prove the doctors wrong. I was going to make my son as normal as he could possibly be. The first priority was getting him to walk. Daniel's diagnosis of "profound intellectual disability with cerebral palsy" meant he would require physiotherapy, occupational therapy, speech therapy and massaging in the bath. Wilson Home took care of the professional therapies five days a week, after which I would take him home to work with him some more. My poor boy had enough by then, but his crazy mother was determined to make him better. Nothing else mattered. I was so dedicated trying to make my son whole I was neglecting Zelma and forcing a wedge into the shaky relationship I held onto with Anthony. In spite of our efforts, by age three Daniel was still not walking or talking. I refused to give up.

In an effort to save our relationship, Anthony and I finally got married. I knew Anthony was a good, stable man, and hoped with patience and love we could all survive this turbulent life together. Anthony continued to be a good provider and I continued to put my heart and soul into Daniel. My daily morning routine consisted of preparing the children, dropping Zelma off at primary school and rushing through traffic to take Daniel to Wilson Home. I remained at Wilson Home to help out with Daniel's treatment until 2pm, at which time I would buckle him in the car and rush back for Zelma. We would always be late. By the time we arrived home, cooked dinner, bathed and massaged Daniel, Anthony had returned to take over the kids. At 6pm I was out the door to start my night job. After four to five hours sleep we were ready to do it all over again.

We did squeeze in some social activities, weekend parties and barbeques with friends, but those times were filled with resentment, accusations and fights. Usually these were initiated by an anger outburst from me. Because Anthony feared my moods, he was also scared to come near me; it made me feel more unloved and unwanted. My past was still haunting me. Even when I scored some modelling jobs trying to boost my low self esteem, I still thought of myself as a pathetic human being. More anger filled me and was starting to affect my relationship with my daughter.

My fierce dedication to Daniel became the focus of my existence. I had no comprehension of the fact that my delusional notion of my son becoming normal one day was serving as a temporary distraction from my severe emotional problems. At least some of my dedicated efforts bore fruit. By age four, Daniel was walking. It was nothing short of a minor miracle. Even the slightest improvement was cause for celebration. His big sister was trying in her own way to maintain some normalcy in her own young life. She was eight before I was informed by one of Zelma's teachers that she was still unable to read. How could this be? Anthony was at home with the children at night. He was a voracious reader and yet his own daughter was illiterate. Instead of talking about what we could do to help our daughter, resentment surged through me and I blamed poor Anthony for everything. It was unthinkable to have two children who would be disadvantaged in life. I was determined to get help for Zelma. Today my daughter is an avid reader and a very beautiful, intelligent young lady. She is also a nutritionist and a health coach. Zelma is now studying to be a yoga teacher and I am very proud of her!

At age five, Daniel had to be enrolled in a local special school. I knew he would never progress to my satisfaction in such a place, but private therapists were not cheap. As determined as ever, I signed myself up to a quick correspondence course and I found a job as a financial advisor/insurance agent for a finance company. The work suited me perfectly, as I could set my own hours to adequately facilitate family commitments. Within two months my name was among the top three achievers. The money was good and rolling in fast. Unfortunately, the more money I was bringing in for the company, the more expectation they placed on me. It took the wind right out of my motivation. After two long years I resigned, taking my experience with me to my next job.

Anthony and I were extremely unhappy most of the time but neither of us wanted to separate – or I didn't. Aside from latent affection we held for one another, remnants of which occasionally flickered in moments of closeness, we had two children together. Prepared to try almost anything to salvage something from the wreckage of our relationship, in January 1994 I suggested we could move to England. Anthony's mother lived in Penzance, Cornwall, a very quaint and charming area in the UK. I fooled myself into believing a breath of fresh air would make a world of difference to everything. I also reasoned that as my family members were not offering any kind of support, at least with the move Anthony's family would be close by and helpful. I was grasping at straws to hold onto a marriage that was very obviously already broken. I was more scared of being alone than anything else, to be a single mother of two children, one of them needing help for the rest of his life.

Anthony decided he would move first to look for a job and a place for us to live. I would sell our house and furniture as soon as he was ready. We both agreed it would have been monumental folly to uproot the children from their school and treatment before there was something established back "in the old country" to go to. After a brief discussion with his mother, Anthony was on the plane the following month.

Before he left, I had been working as a real estate agent for a well-known company in our area. Once again working on commission, I was able to dictate my own hours to fit in with my children's schedules. Again, I excelled in my new job and consequently was able to save enough money to see us through after Anthony departed. The expertise I'd acquired in loans and insurance from my previous position helped me enormously to secure high sales in real estate. Most of my competitors merely listed and sold houses. I was able to go the extra mile, giving advice on the best banks to secure a mortgage from, often taking clients to the banks personally if their case was complicated; I earned a reputation as the "go-to" girl. I was also able to assist many Samoans, Maoris and Pacific Islanders who had bad credit ratings secure a mortgage. As I charged no fee for the extra service I provided, I soon became so busy that special and quality times with my children were affected.

When Anthony left, I realised the importance of a husband and wife partnership, especially caring for a special needs child. Naively, I had assumed I could continue as normal while my husband was sorting out a new life for us in the UK. Seven months into that arrangement I was desperate to be reunited with Anthony. He told me he still hadn't found a suitable job, but with my insistence the children and I were soon on a plane, determined to resettle our lives on the other side of the planet.

On our way to London we stayed in Los Angeles for a week. I had long dreamed of taking the children to Disneyland. It was not only a wonderful distraction for us all but also a fairy tale palace of pure fantasy and magic. There was no one in history capable of transforming almost any dire situation into a world of wonder, delight and joy like Mister Walt Disney. I wanted my children to experience the things I had never experienced as a child. To see their eyes sparkle, the happy smiles on their faces, made it feel as though any problem in the world must be a million miles away.

During our last day in Los Angeles, I saw a homeless man rummaging through a dumpster for something to eat. I put my children in the room, took out some money and rushed back outside to give it to him.

"I was homeless once," I told him. "I understand."

The man gazed at me with such amazed gratitude I thought he was going to kiss my feet.

"What did you do that for, mum?" Zelma asked me when I returned.

"If you can help someone like that, never hesitate. One day it could happen to you. This life is about give and take," I explained to my daughter.

She stared up at me with her big innocent eyes. Zelma had never known what it was like to live in a hut, go hungry, to be beaten, raped or abandoned. To my daughter, having a mother and a father, a roof over her head and food always on the table was entirely normal. To Zelma, life was unfair if Daniel received more attention than she did or I was late to collect her from school. How could such a child have any concept of homelessness, abandonment, heartbreak, betrayal and despair? I prayed to God that she would never experience any of those things.

Anthony met us at Heathrow Airport, from where we had an eight-hour train ride to Cornwall. His family welcomed us with excitement, and I could only pray again that this fresh start was going to be what we needed to perhaps save our relationship. It was not meant to be. I came to the realisation that our marriage was already doomed shortly after we arrived. After twelve years together, it was time to call it quits.

Sonia, a Swiss girlfriend of mine from New Zealand, had also been going through marital problems at this time. To facilitate a fresh perspective on her own problems, she decided to return home to Switzerland. As the UK was a small distance away, she suggested I join her. Grateful for the distraction, I flew to be with Sonia as soon as I was able, leaving Anthony to care for Zelma and Daniel in England for a month.

I had never been separated from my children before, it was hard but I needed the time to clear my head while I pondered my next step. Thankfully, Sonia was a master of distraction. To take my mind of my problems she organised to take me on a tour of Europe, introducing me to all the beauty in other people's lives. I don't believe it occurred to me before then that while many are suffering in this world there are many also cheerfully enjoying their lives. Life was not to be endured but enjoyed. It was a celebration of existence, and up until my European tour I'd been completely missing that point. A month later I returned to the UK refreshed and renewed. I said my farewells to Anthony and packed up my life and my children to return to New Zealand. Anthony left me all the responsibilities to care for Zelma and Daniel and to meet all their needs, including all decisions about their future path. He even told me that he would understand if I ever decided to give Daniel up.

Chapter 31

The Offer of a Lifetime

When I returned to real estate sales in New Zealand, I scored the listing of a magnificent property in a very exclusive area near a marina. The house and décor were breathtaking. It had been superbly designed with balconies on every corner and stunning vistas of the Harbour Bridge and bay. My commission, if I sold this property, would have been over $12,000. That sort of money would make a huge difference to us, so I was extremely focused on the sale. Not in a million years could I have imagined the fringe benefit that accompanied this listing. It was the catalyst to meeting Rod.

Rod was in his late sixties and lived opposite the palace I was trying to sell. During the weekends, when the property was open for inspection, I would take Zelma and Daniel with me. Zelma waited in the car, looking after her little brother, while I showed people around for the open hour. I did this every weekend. Seeing me struggle to balance my load, Rod offered to take care of my children while I worked. From the outset he came across as a very kind and gentle man. When my listing finally sold and I quit my job, Rod and I had become good friends. He admired my work ethic and how I cared for my children, especially the way I dealt with Daniel. Our relationship was purely platonic, more like a father and daughter who enjoyed each other's company.

"I've never seen such a beautiful young mother with so much potential and personality carrying her eight year old around with high heels on," Rod joked to me.

I didn't think anything of it. It was nice to have a father figure around. He was someone I could spend time with, speak to, be confident around and it seemed he wanted nothing from me in return except my friendship.

Out of the big pay packet I received from the property sale, I decided to make a return trip to Samoa with my children. I wanted to see my surviving family, but there was a secondary purpose to my visit. I had a promise to fulfil. Ever since I heard of Auntie Tilie's passing, despite everything else going on in my life, it had been gnawing at me. I knew no one else would have attended to her final wish. I doubted anyone else was even aware what it was. I needed to verify with my own eyes whether or not this most precious and sacred of requests had been honoured. If not, it fell to me to make sure the situation was rectified. Finally, I had the money at my disposal to guarantee I could address the matter if needed.

My dad and step-mum collected us at the airport. We had a great deal to catch up on, so raising Auntie Tilie's final requests had to be put on temporary hold. It was a delicate subject requiring just the right moment to broach. I knew that out of all Auntie's many nephews and nieces, my dad had received the bulk of her estate: a large chunk of cash, car, artwork and furniture. He had always been favoured by Auntie, who looked upon him as more of a son. He was always there when she was sick and kind to her right up until the end. Dad was always the nephew who made sure she was cared for during her many hospital internments. Many nieces and nephews didn't receive a cent from her estate, only the ones who kept in touch and assured her of their loyalties right to the bitter end.

Long before her illness, she had sold the property on condition that the new owner would not take possession until after her death. Other members of the family tried to convince her to leave six acres where the house and the graves stood to pass down the family line. They reasoned they wanted to visit Grandpa Wilhelm and tidy up his tomb. None of them realised it was the last thing Auntie would have wanted her family to do. In Samoan tradition, passed family members were considered as important as if they were alive. Relatives took pride in decorating tombs, washing them and keeping them tidy as marks of respect and love. In stark contrast to this custom, when the new owner of Auntie's plantation asked what she wanted him to do with the grave, her response was immediate: "Burn it!"

To this day, my dad and some of his family still complain about Auntie selling the plantation. They believe it was one of Auntie's last cruel and controlling tactics. But I know the good intentions behind her decision. I had always known what she wanted to happen to the estate after her death. She was adamant that none of her family would suffer like she did. She knew the tormented spirits that tortured whoever entered the place would live on should family continue to reside in that cursed place. She wanted the curse to end with her. Future events proved new owners did not end the curse. The house had many more victims in the following decades.

Somewhere in her psyche, the great Auntie Ottilie had deemed she deserved to suffer for her crimes, those her father had committed before her and the blight the tortured spirits had continued to commit thereafter. But with her it would end – so she thought. At the very least she would guarantee that no member of our clan would ever face the hellish undead. There was just one detail that remained.

Alan's tiny bones were buried with Auntie just as she had wished. Finally they could both be at peace and leave the cursed place. For my part, I never intended to set foot in it again. I returned to New Zealand happy and proud my dad fulfilled Auntie's fervent wish. He deserved everything he inherited from Auntie's estate.

***

Although Rod lived in one of the richest suburbs of Auckland, his house was probably the least impressive one. Even the car he drove was ten years old, and he dressed like a pensioner who struggled to buy groceries. It never occurred to me he was an eccentric and lonely old millionaire. All I knew was he'd been kind enough to help me out with my children when I was trying to make the biggest sale of my life. I wanted to express my gratitude for his kindness and so invited him to join me and the children to celebrate. The tab was on me. I was indebted to him, as without his intervention I would really have struggled to seal the deal.

When Rod asked me out of the blue to marry him after that I nearly fell off my chair! "You will never have to worry about money again," he told me, trying to give me a reason to accept. "You and your kids will be set for life. Marry me, and if you decided to leave after one year, I will sign a contract giving you half of my estate. Or if you like, I can give you a cash cheque of $10 million as a wedding gift the day of our union."

I was stunned speechless! I stared at poor Rod in abject astonishment. I couldn't conceive what $10 million looked like. I just gawped at him in disbelief, lost for words. I couldn't think straight, never mind speak.

His eyes continued to plead with me, begging for a response. It was an offer half the women on earth would have killed for.

Surely it was a no brainer. Surely I would say yes. How could I say anything other than yes? Finally I recovered my powers of speech.

"I'm sorry Rod, I can't do it. I love you like a father and truly value your friendship. I don't want to hurt you. I know I will hurt you. I have a mountain of problems. Sometimes I am not a very nice person."

It was Rod's turn to be speechless, hurt, and rejected. I felt awful but I felt it was the honest thing to do. I felt very empty and miserable within myself money was not what I wished for although I didn't have any. I craved for inner fulfilment and happiness. When I was growing up in my poor village family, I'd thought my Auntie Tilie was a goddess because she was rich. However when I lived with her, I soon learned my Auntie would have given away all her wealth to be happy. She believed her money was more of a curse than a blessing.

After much persuasion I convinced him we could continue to be friends, although he assured me he wasn't going to give up. Not long after his proposal, in a never-ending attempt to seduce me with his wealth, he announced he had purchased a bigger, more modern house for me and my children for over $200,000! It had a swimming pool for the kids and spectacular views. Without my knowledge, he also went to the bank and paid the big mortgage off the house I owned with Anthony. Instantly, I had more money than I ever dreamed of in my entire life. Even when we had absolutely no money I had never asked anyone for help. I would rather starve than humiliate myself that way.

As if one miracle perpetuated another, miraculously the people who had abandoned me, abused me, turned their back on me during my times of need – they all suddenly wanted to be my best friend. My mother turned up unexpectedly looking for shelter. For six months, I let her stay. My sister Agnes was having an affair and needed a place to stay – again I helped. Again and again, I tried to push away all the anger and hurt they had caused me until I'd had a gut full. I needed to get away from them to start a new life with my children – away from other people's problems and selfishness. I decided to move to Australia.

When I told Rod I was leaving the country he was sad, but had come to realise I was not attracted by material things. I was searching for something more meaningful – myself. I added that I wouldn't take a cent from the property he bought for me. I would sign it over to him. I thanked him from the bottom of my heart for helping my children and me.

I had enough money to start over because Rod had paid off my own mortgage. Otherwise it would have been an impossible plan. Wilson Home took care of Daniel, and Zelma stayed with a friend of mine during the day while she went to school. Agnes offered to pick Zelma up in the evening on her way home from work while I made a flying reconnaissance mission to Australia to set up my new life.

With a few personal belongings stuffed in a sports bag, my travelling documents and $20,000 Australian dollars in cash, I boarded a flight to Brisbane. Nestling into my seat aboard my fight to freedom, I could hear my Auntie Tilie and grandmother cheering. They had told me I could do anything and I was going to prove them right.

Chapter 32

Our New Home

I had two short weeks to organise things. It wasn't much time to find a home near a school and a special school, to buy a car and furnish our new abode. Zelma was eleven, Daniel was nearly nine and I was thirty-three years old. My mission was daunting – but not impossible.

The shuttle bus from Brisbane International Airport took me to the city. There I found a motel for $50 a night and paid for the whole two weeks in advance. Knowing I had to be prudent with my money, I hired the cheapest car I could find, which frequently needed push starting in the mornings. My first two days of reconnaissance yielded nothing. In immense frustration, I purchased the daily newspaper and took it to the dining area of my motel to peruse over breakfast. It was then I saw him. Across the dining room, a handsome man sat eating his meal alone. He kept smiling at me. There was something intriguing and warm about his smile.

"Wake up Jane!" I shouted to myself. "Remember your children. You have twelve more days to sort things out before you go back to get them!"

I shook off my attraction to the sexy man flirting with me, instructed the waitress to charge my meal to my room and left. Taking the paper with me, I returned to my room. I wasn't two steps inside when the phone rang. The receptionist told me there was a man downstairs who wanted to see me.

"What now?" I muttered to myself, returning downstairs.

"Hi. My name is Boyd. I saw you at breakfast. I am sorry to be so forward, but if you are on your own, I would like to take you out tonight," he offered charmingly.

"I'm sorry, but I don't have much time," I replied dismissively. "I just arrived from New Zealand and need to sort out a hundred things before going back to collect my children." I thought that would cool him down, but just in case I hadn't made my point I quickly added, "Do you know some nice suburbs with special schools?"

"Yes, I know Brisbane very well. I can definitely help you," he shot back without a moment's hesitation.

We agreed he would pick me up at seven to take me out for dinner. We could talk about special schools and the better suburbs then. Boyd explained he was a technician and had just stopped off at the hotel for breakfast after fixing one machine before he attended to another. I watched him leave for work, ran back to my room, dropped myself on my bed and realised my heart was pounding like a love-struck teenager.

Some hours later I called my children as I did every day, telling them how much I had missed and loved them. After speaking with my daughter, Agnes came to the phone. After a few words, she asked to borrow $10,000. She was thinking of moving to Australia with us and needed the money to pay off her debts. She didn't want to leave her husband and daughters burdened after she left them behind to start life anew.

The conversation shocked me. I was on my own with two children. No one helped me. No one changed my son's nappy or offered to give me a break. She was at my house for her own benefit and now she was asking me for a tidy sum of money. I needed every cent to take care of my children. I told her we would talk when I returned to New Zealand.

After that conversation, I was so looking forward to see Boyd again. I was grateful he had asked to take me out and happy I agreed. I needed not to think of what my sister had asked of me. Soaking in the bathtub, I thought only happy thoughts about my evening ahead. It was not quite 7pm when Boyd picked me up. I had such a wonderful time with him; I forgot I had met him a few hours ago.

Boyd was not only handsome, he was charming, very intelligent and he was something none of my former beaus had been – he was fun. He made me feel alive . . . again. I found him extremely sexy and was delighted to discover he really knew how to treat a woman. From the instant we connected there was chemistry. Fate had been moving us around like chess pieces on a giant celestial chessboard. I could have skipped breakfast that morning. His previous job could have run over time. We never would have met. I might not have looked up from my newspaper. He might have been seated at a different table where he wouldn't see me.

During our conversation over dinner we also discovered at one point in time we had both been in Japan in the same hotel at the same time. This occurred when I transited through Japan for two days with my children before we continued back to New Zealand from England. Boyd had stopped over for a rest en route to England on business. Like two ships, we had crossed in the night, oblivious to the existence of the other. Perhaps those karmic chess players deemed my wounds too raw from leaving Anthony to connect with Boyd in the Orient and hence orchestrated a second-chance encounter.

Our date was wonderful. We both knew we wanted to see each other again. We had so much in common. We had both travelled extensively. We were both hopeless dreamers and risk takers – probably not a great combination for a stable home, but certainly life would seldom be boring. Boyd had once lived in Southern Africa running a music business for fifteen years. There he met his first wife and had two children about Zelma's age, a boy and a girl. They divorced when the children were very young. South Africa became unsafe and Boyd decided to sell up and move back home to Australia. Although he was originally from England, his family moved to Australia when Boyd was eighteen months old.

Telling each other our life stories, it seemed as though we'd been searching for each other our entire lives. Neither of us had an easy run, we had both collected baggage on our journey. Perhaps it was necessary to have those life experiences to be ready to move forward together. I was thirty-three and Boyd was thirty-seven when we met. He immediately took two weeks off work to drive me around, show me the best areas to settle in, select a suitable vehicle and purchase the furniture for my new home. I don't believe I would ever have accomplished so much in such a short space of time without Boyd's help.

I was in love with this man already. It was exhilarating and scary at the same time but the real test was yet to come. I had two children and Daniel had severe disabilities. Although he was mobile, my son still could not communicate, wore nappies and he needed help with everything. My children were my life. As much as I was having fun with Boyd, Zelma and Daniel were my first and foremost priority. No one would ever hurt my children. I would *not* – not *ever* – become my mother! With the same expanse and clarity of the glorious sub-tropical sky above us in Brisbane, I made this aspect crystal clear to Boyd. It seemed nothing I could say would dissuade him.

My new beau kept a watchful eye on my new home in Australia while I returned to New Zealand to collect my children.

I said goodbye to everyone in Auckland and signed the house I had been living in over to Rod. I was truly humbled by Rod's generosity. He had been mana from heaven – a gift I could never have dreamed of in my wildest imagination. If he hadn't entered my life, no matter how transiently, precisely when he did, I never would have met the one true love of my life.

Before I could escape, I loaned Agnes $5,000. I told myself it was to help my nieces, whom I adored, before she abandoned them.

Even though there were times it deserted me, it was that level of optimism that had kept me alive. As we left Auckland, Rod gave me a card in the departure lounge of the airport and asked me not to open it until I arrived in Australia. I slipped it into my bag, hugged him, thanked him for his kindness and friendship, and assured him he would always be welcome in my home.

As the plane taxied onto the runway, took its position for takeoff and the captain moved the throttle to full for takeoff, I breathed a huge sigh of relief. I was really this time leaving the past behind, cruising through the heavens to reunite with Boyd. Goodbye cruel past. Hello new life.

Good to his word, Boyd was standing patiently awaiting our arrival at Brisbane airport, ready to greet me with his huge sexy smile. We embraced warmly and I introduced him to my children. A week later Zelma and Daniel had settled into their new schools and it was time to think of new ways to support myself and my children. After the sale of our house, I had $70,000 AUD left. This gave me a little time to breathe, but I couldn't live off it forever. I needed work and I needed something I could schedule around my commitments to Zelma and Daniel.

Agnes and her new man were arriving in a month's time, so I had purposely rented a house with an extra room and en suite for them, which made our rental commitment more than I had anticipated. I wasn't comfortable with the situation at all. I was loyal to my ex-brother-in-law and felt awful for my nieces; they were a little bit older than my own daughter. I felt my sister had dumped another selfish act on me, but again my heart was too soft to refuse her. Agnes was still my sister and no matter what took place in the past, I didn't want anything bad to have happened to her. I feared if Tavita found out about the affair, he would lose it all together and perhaps do something unthinkable. I didn't want their children to end up without parents.

Going through my papers, contemplating my next move, I noticed Rod's sealed card slip out. In all the excitement I had quite forgotten about it. I picked it up and looked at it. The pretty envelope twinkled back at me, begging to be read. I took it to the privacy of my bedroom, sat on my bed and opened it. A small piece of paper fluttered out from inside. I picked it up and read it over and over and over again. I could not believe what I was seeing. The innocuous piece of paper was a cheque; I had to keep recounting the zeros. I thought I was hallucinating. It was made out for one million dollars in Australian currency. I thought I was going to faint. The card read:

My dearest Jane,

I hope this money will help you and your children settle nicely in your new country. If things don't work out, please come back, I will be waiting.

Lots of love,
Rod.

In the quiet privacy of my bedroom, I bawled my eyes out. Somewhere amongst my tears I recalled the saying, "When God closes one door, he opens a window." It was too much to believe. Was this for real? I wiped my tears away, composed myself, drove to my bank and deposited the cheque of many zeros to see if it would bounce before I made any firm plans.

Rod passed away four years later from a heart attack. He was due to make his second trip to visit us in Australia. Rod was truly a prince among men. I will never be able to thank him sufficiently.

Chapter 33

My First Business

With a million dollars at my disposal, I decided to buy my own business and make the money work. Having my own business allowed my work schedule to fit around my children. I needed to be challenged, to learn something new, to improve myself.

At our local shopping centre I spied a "for sale: sign in the window of a beauty salon. I asked to speak with the tall pretty English owner about the business and have a quick look around. The shop was well-worn and a bit dated. There was a small client list and not much equipment to speak of. It seemed perfect. To my way of thinking, it was a bargain. "I can make this work," I naively told myself. "It just needs ME!"

The very next day I signed the sale contract and handed over $20,000. When I called the insurance company for public liability, the man informed me I was not allowed to touch a single client until I became a qualified beauty therapist. I was not even a nail technician. If I worked on someone and it went bad I could lose everything. Well done, Jane; that was great planning!

I was in a blind. The salon outgoings were more than it brought in. It had been running at a loss for some time. No wonder the lady who sold it had been operating without staff. Never having run a business before, I had charged in headlong believing I could walk on water; due diligence never crossed my mind. Granted, I had wanted to test my abilities, but not like this. I enquired about becoming a beauty therapist. It was going to take four years to qualify! Oh my goodness, I did not have time to take courses and still work. I wanted to be self-employed so I could be home for my kids when they needed me. This was not a good outcome for the $20,000 I invested.

Luckily, when you have a million, less $20,000, in the bank there are always solutions. I hired two beauty therapists and a nail technician; at least the business could operate while I figured out what to do. The salon needed to pick up so it wasn't running at a loss, hopefully not just covering expenses but turning a profit. Boyd's previous business expertise and marketing skills were dusted off. We devised a campaign to blanket the local area, offering free treatments or big discounts to get people through the doors and establish repeat business. Once through the doors, it was up to us girls to give great service and keep them coming back.

My role was manager, standing behind the counter taking phone calls, making bookings and greeting client – everything I could to free the girls to do their job. In the long term that was never going to work for me. I needed to be hands on; I had no choice but take a beautician course. It was around this time that Agnes and her man moved out and Boyd moved in. It seemed logical as he spent all his time here anyway. It was a big step and neither made the decision lightly. I felt I'd made one good decision. Everything with Boyd was developing perfectly. He was bored with his contract technician business and happy to step up to help with both my children and my salon.

Six months later we bought a beautiful new home. Boyd designed our swimming pool with a waterfall, which was brilliant for Daniel's therapy, and as he had been a swimming coach, Boyd was also able to teach my son to swim. We were both really happy for the first time in a long time – moreover, we were very much in love.

After some furious study I was qualified as a beautician. Now I put all my heart, body and soul into the business. It seemed whenever I applied myself beautiful roses grew from my labours. I became adept at my craft and was fast gaining a reputation as one of the fastest waxers ever. I could rip unsightly hair out with blinding speed and accuracy. Clients travelled from near and far for treatment. The salon was making good money and our family life was hectic but happy. I was the most content woman on the planet, and seeing Boyd treat my children like his own made me love him even more. He would change my nine-year-old son's diapers without a complaint. Luckily for me, he had also been an ambulance driver during the Rhodesian civil war and had worked in the UK with profoundly disabled children. Dealing with Daniel's issues was nothing new to him. Boyd was my gift from God.

We were married on 14 March 1998, three years after we first met. We have rarely had a day apart since. We loved our happy, if dysfunctional, life together and were thrilled when, after five years of running my own business, we discovered I was pregnant. Boyd wondered if he was too old for the task, but the thought of bringing a new life created from our love was potent and profound. The business had served us well until then, but with a new baby on the way, it was time to sell up and move on. We were both restless gypsies and happy to pursue any hair-brained scheme we had dreamed up.

When I first met Boyd his surname was Roebuck. After we married and our son Dayne was born, our surname was still Roebuck. Boyd was a wonderful father and loved his own children so much he had remarried their mother (before I met him) to bring them to Australia for a safer and brighter future. Southern Africa was a dangerous place. Home invasions were commonplace, and Boyd himself had narrowly escaped with his life more than once. Instead of his ex-wife, Beverley, being grateful, Boyd became the reason for all her problems. She would place extortionate demands on him, using access to his children as leverage in her negotiating tactics. Of course, she was hardly the first disgruntled ex-wife in history to deploy those tactics, but as with everything in this narrative ...

Without going into convoluted details of another family feud, when a woman's magazine published an innocent puff piece about my romantic love affair with my wonderful husband, Beverley used every round of ammunition in the arsenal to cut her two-time ex-husband down to size. Not long after Boyd had tragically and suddenly lost his beloved mother to a brain tumour, Beverley succeeded in driving a wedge between Boyd and his father. When other members of the family made it their business to dig their noses where they didn't belong, the situation became worse. So serious was the fracas that Boyd changed his surname legally from his father's surname of Roebuck to his mother's maiden name of Wyatt, which is now our family name and we are very proud of it. Throughout my life whilst dealing with my many trials, I learned what 'Real Families' really meant ... they stick together no matter what. After all blood is supposed to be thicker than water!

Chapter 34

The Last Straw

After I moved to Australia and Agnes followed, my mother also changed her country of residence. Most of her children were in Australia and she had no money left. After she settled in Brisbane she had a nasty fight with Agnes. I wasn't privy to it, but heard each side of the story. They were both trying to find allies, and it was this fact alone that finally drove my big sister to try and make peace with me. Agnes tried to blame the dark heinous past onto our mother, claiming everything she had done, every nasty little thing she'd ever said to me was under our mother's instructions and influence. She also announced that our mother had told members of her family to shut their doors in my face if I came seeking their help. My name wasn't even in my mother's will, Agnes informed me.

I was stirred to anger once again and stormed off to confront my mother. On the way to mum's I remembered feeling so wretched in the mental hospital the same time my mother was calmly writing a will that did not include me; even in death she planned to cut me off.

As I travelled from my place to hers, accusations rebounded in my mind. How could you? Do you know how despicable Agnes is? Do you have any concept of how I have suffered because of the two of you? Now this, denying my existence even in death?

When I arrived at her place the aroma of cooking fish and onion was oddly comforting, and my mother stood before me all welcoming smiles –until I said I was there to discover some truth.

"Why did you leave me behind in Samoa when you went to New Zealand with your other daughters? Why did you hide me from your husband and my other siblings? Why did you treat me so badly and allow others to violently abuse and torture me? Why do you hate me so much?"

I would like to say that my mother said she was sorry, that she explained things I had never known, but she didn't. What she did was lie and justify her actions, never once apologising or showing remorse. I listened to her empty words, the wounded child that longed for her to say, "I love you and I am sorry." Instead, I felt like a cockroach crushed beneath her foot.

With tears streaming once more, I exclaimed, "I wish my step-mum was my biological mother."

I left with my heart pounding and a whirlwind's roar filling my ears, the hurt so deep I thought I would die from the pain of it before I reached my car.

I couldn't drive fast enough. After a while I slowed down and peace filled me: I was going home to my husband, my children, to the family I had created for myself, the only people who truly love me unconditionally. I didn't need anyone else's love. In that moment, I decided I would never refer to her again as my mother.

I never saw her again until she was dying back home in Samoa. In those final days when there was nothing left to gain or lose, she finally acknowledged me. "Sieni, my child. *O lena lava ete aulelei. Ete aulelei i lau fanau uma* – you are the prettiest of all my children."

As I left to return to Australia, I remembered my mother as she had been before she became wizened to the point of death. Always larger than life, she was also among the most beautiful of Samoa's women. I wondered if it was her looks that betrayed her. Too often women whose beauty defines them never learn to compromise, to accommodate. The terrible things they do are overshadowed by their beauty, and lack of consequence turns them into monsters.

On that last day in American Samoa, my mother said, "I love you, Sieni." I would like to write that they were the most important words I had ever heard, but I cannot. By then they held no meaning.

Me (NZ 1979)

Me with my baby girl (NZ 1984)

Taken with my son Daniel in England (Dec 1986)

With Zelma and Daniel (NZ 1988)

Anthony and I's wedding photo with our children (1988)

My modelling picture (NZ 1990)

Boyd and I courting (Australia 1995)

Boyd and I's wedding picture (Australia 1998)

Me and my son Daniel (Australia 2000)

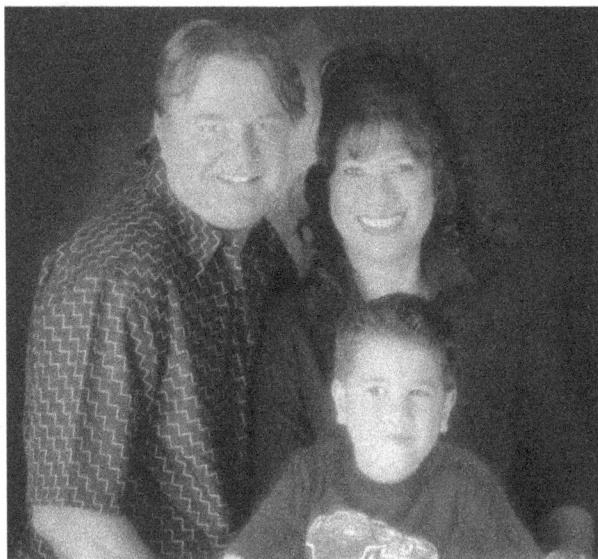

Boyd, me and our son Dayne (Australia 2005)

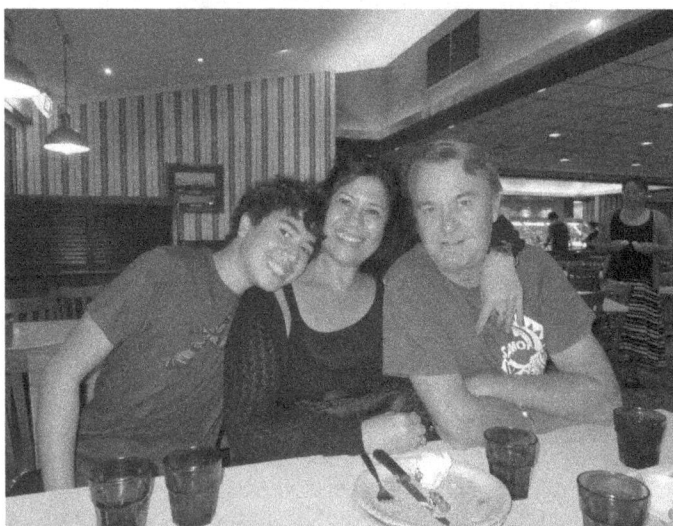

Celebrating Dayne's 13th birthday (2013)

Epilogue

From the people who should have loved and cared for me, I have been demeaned with every insult that could be hurled at me. I've been called a whore, an unwanted bastard child, a hopeless dreamer, a mental case and they're just the highlights. After all I had been through I could have justified being many of those things and more. I could have been sitting under a bridge somewhere shooting up drugs. I could have ended up squatting in a corner of a mental institution babbling to myself while dribbling and pissing my pants. It would have been easier for some if I was dead, long buried and now forgotten. I endured and prevailed because a human being can draw on unknown strengths when it comes to survival.

Now, as I come to the completion of my story, I have shed the last of my tears for the past. I shed them in gratitude for that little girl who lived through it all and had the strength left to tell her story. I am strong and proud now that when I look back, I may have been abandoned but I have also seen the world and experienced the magic of living life to the fullest. I have been homeless, but I have also stayed in the finest hotels. I have been witness to the evil of malevolent ghosts, but I have also been to Kensington Palace. I have been abused, but I have also stood on the Swiss Alps and rolled around in the snow. Perhaps most importantly, I may have been unloved, but I have discovered I can be loved and love others deeply. Looking back at my life,

I now know God has never left my side. He was always there, guiding, guarding and carrying me whenever I couldn't get up. I can't change the past or other people, but I can change myself and the present for a better future.

The only thing necessary for evil to triumph is for good people to do nothing. The great 19th century philosopher Ralph Waldo Emerson once said, "If one life breathes easier because you have lived, this is to have succeeded." Many people, myself included, said nothing when I was a child suffering unspeakable and unbearable abuse. Many people continue to say nothing to embedded cultural extremes that can cause devastation even as they can manifest joy.

Now that my story is out in the open, it is my intention to return to Samoa as a landowner. I have forgiven all those who wronged me; I have to if I wish to live free of the past. I no longer hold any ill will toward my mother or anyone else who hurt or caused me harm. My sister Agnes was also a victim of child abuse and a violent upbringing. Evil begets evil, and she has been trying to heal. I know there is a good heart in Agnes. Even when she caused me physical harm and emotional distress, I believe it was her shield against her own pain. While this neither makes her actions excusable or acceptable, it does make them understandable. For me to move forward with love, light and hope, the past belongs in the past. In finally speaking about it all, I hope to have exorcised it all.

When I finally completed this manuscript in the beginning of 2014, Auntie Tilie's old estate was deserted. Surrounded by poor islanders from impoverished villagers and yet rich with mangoes, bananas an abundance of other nourishing fruits, no one dared set foot inside the wretched property. It was unguarded and available for looting. Any other place would have been picked clean long ago, but this property was left alone. Those in the surrounding villages all learnt of the dark and deadly secrets that to this day besiege the legacy that's been left. Many modern-thinking people may find it difficult, or even impossible, to believe the truth of the supernatural elements to this story. Even so, there are far too many witnesses, both living and dead, who have attested to the validity of it all for it to be denied. At our recent family reunion, my dad re-confirmed his terrifying experiences and the ghosts he saw at auntie Tilie's estate while we all listened in horror. My dad is seventy-seven years old, very sane and a man of great faith.

From darkness there shall be light.

In Memorium

In loving memory of the two most extraordinary women who did the best they could to help and shape me to be the person I am today.

To my beloved grandmother, Melekihna (Tina) Ta'ateo Fasia
1906–74
You brought rays of sunshine into my life.
You taught me compassion, unconditional love, loyalty, sacrifice, perseverance and strength.

To my late auntie, Ottilie Olida Cucie Bentzen
1901–87
My life had depth and colour because of you.
You taught me courage, resilient, motivation, gratitude, patience, faith and hope.

"If we are fortunate, God gives us what we need not what we want."

He must have loved me so much that he gave me the two of you to be my guardian angels both on earth and in heaven.

In remembrance of my late grandfather, Ta'ateo Fasia (Tama), and my late uncle, Borge Bentzen, whom I always appreciated for making me a special girl in your lives.

Family Tree

SCHWALGER

Wilhelm married Silafaga and had five children:

1. Fritz
2. August
3. Ottilie (only girl) my great auntie, who married Bentzen
4. Hanz
5. Martin, who married Mama and had six children; my father Karl was one of the sons.

TA'ATEO (Fasia, chief name)

Ta'ateo married Melekihna. They had eight children:

1. Salaki (Auntie) married Aukuso; they adopted me in name only.
2. Fai (uncle)
3. Vaitogi (auntie)
4. Amilaina (my mother); had a love affair with Karl, and I was born.
5. Sia (auntie)
6. Migao (uncle)
7. Siaega (uncle)
8. Faalua (uncle)

Review Requested:

If you loved this book, would you please provide
a review at Amazon.com?

Printed in the USA
CPSIA information can be obtained
at www.ICGtesting.com
LVHW070255210923
758819LV00001B/33